S0-BSH-429

F6

ica

HQ 535 .L38 1974
LeMasters, E. E.
Parents in modern America

THE DORSEY SERIES IN SOCIOLOGY

EDITOR ROBIN M. WILLIAMS, JR. *Cornell University*

Parents in modern America

by

E. E. LeMASTERS
School of Social Work
The University of Wisconsin

 1974
Revised Edition

THE DORSEY PRESS   *Homewood, Illinois 60430*
Irwin-Dorsey International   *London, England WC2H 9NJ*
Irwin-Dorsey Limited   *Georgetown, Ontario L7G 4B3*

HQ
535
.L38
1974

© THE DORSEY PRESS, 1970 and 1974

All rights reserved. No part of this publication may be
reproduced, stored in a retrieval system, or transmitted,
in any form or by any means, electronic, mechanical,
photocopying, recording, or otherwise, without the prior
written permission of the publisher.

Revised Edition
First Printing, January 1974
Second Printing, June 1974
Third Printing, March 1975

ISBN 0-256-01524-4
Library of Congress Catalog Card No. 73–87264
Printed in the United States of America

For my wife, Billie,
and our two sons,
Bill and Gary

The relationship between parents and children is no less difficult, no less fraught with drama, than that between lovers. The growing child, developing into an independent individual, surprises and annoys its parents. What once was a charming plaything becomes an adversary.

ANDRÉ MAUROIS
Lelia: The Life of George Sand

Preface

In this revised edition the focus is still on parents—not children. In essence, the author attempts to find out what happens to fathers and mothers in the child-rearing process, not what happens to the children. Judging by the response to the first edition there seems to have been a need for this approach.

The book is sociological rather than psychological or psychiatric. The analysis is centered on the features of American society that parents have to cope with in rearing their sons and daughters. Hopefully, the various chapters look at the so-called "normal parent" (if there are any), not the sick or incompetent parent.

It is recognized that the book is controversial. The writer makes no apology for this—people have been arguing about parenthood for a long time and this is hardly the time to end the debate.

One serious omission in the first edition was the failure to thank Robin M. Williams, Jr., the Consulting Editor in Sociology and Anthropology for The Dorsey Press, for his critical reading of the original manuscript. Numerous improvements were made both in the first edition and this revised edition as the result of his suggestions. Any defects which remain are strictly the responsibility of the author.

Madison, Wisconsin   E. E. LeMasters
December 1973

Contents

parenthood. The complexity of human behavior. Some examples of inadequate science and its impact on parents: *Parents and schizophrenia. Parents and homosexuality in their children.* Positive contributions of modern science to parents.

chapter
one

Parents in
modern America

In his autobiography, Norbert Wiener, one of the true geniuses of our time, confesses his humility in his attempts to cope with the baffling complexities of parenthood. He writes: "Thus, like all families, we had our problems to consider and our decisions to make. I am neither certain of the correctness of the policies I have adopted nor ashamed of any mistakes I might have made. One has only one life to live, *and there is not time enough in which to master the art of being a parent.*"[1]

In writing this book the author was inspired (or motivated) by hundreds of interviews with parents who echoed the feelings of Norbert Wiener—a man who could design a computer modeled on the human brain but who found parenthood a mystery and a confusion.

Many of the parents we talked with—perhaps a majority—were quite competent in their jobs and in the other areas of their lives, yet they felt insecure and inadequate as parents.

Talking with these fathers and mothers the writer found himself haunted by the question: *why* do these people find parenthood so difficult? How can a man run a corporation and fail miserably as a father?[2]

---

[1] Norbert Wiener, *I Am a Mathematician* (New York: Doubleday & Co., 1956), p. 224 (italics not in original). Wiener, a child prodigy, is often given credit for being the brain behind the development of the modern computer.

[2] All of the case illustrations used in this book refer to actual parents, but certain details may have been altered to protect their identity.

1

How can a woman be regarded as a superior teacher in a suburban school system and be told by her daughter that she is a poor mother?

Max Lerner, in an interesting book, has written: "It is evident that in no other culture has there been so pervasive a cultural anxiety about the rearing of children."[3] The writer shares this feeling, and this book may be regarded as one sociologist's attempt to account for this cultural complex.

In this first chapter we wish to explore some of the features of our society that seem to pose problems for parents. In subsequent chapters most of these variables will be analyzed in depth—here we only wish to sketch them in.

The reader should remember that this book does not attempt to deal with the *personal* or *individual* problems that any given father or mother might have—on the contrary, we are concerned with the problems that *most* American parents seem to have. In other words, it is a sociological, not a psychiatric, study.

In reviewing the literature on parents, it seemed to us that the vast majority of the material was concerned with children—not with parents. We were impressed by an observation of Brim that most family writers seemed to think that parents operated in a social and cultural vacuum because so little was said about the social situations confronting fathers and mothers.[4]

It also seemed to us that the American father was virtually ignored by most of the writers.

In this book, then, we wish to look long and hard at the social system —or systems—in which American parents operate; we want to analyze the problems that plague *most* of these fathers and mothers—not just the inadequate ones; we want to talk with fathers as well as mothers, to lower- and upper-class parents, as well as middle-class ones.

Not much will be said about children—the libraries are full of books about them.

We will begin, in this first chapter, by noting some of the features of our society that constitute the social framework in which American fathers and mothers must function.

---

[3] Max Lerner, *America as a Civilization* (New York: Simon & Schuster, 1957), p. 562. We cite this book often in this study because we regard it as one of the better attempts to delineate American civilization. For another analysis, see Robin M. Williams, Jr., *American Society*, 3d ed. (New York: Alfred A. Knopf, 1970).

[4] For a discussion of the failure of parent specialists to consider the social conditions under which parents function, see Orville G. Brim, Jr., "Causes of Parent Behavior," *Education for Child Rearing* (New York: Russell Sage Foundation, 1959), chap. 3. This is the definitive analysis of parent education in the United States and is cited often in this book. One sociologist who made a consistent effort to understand the social forces affecting parents was the late James H. S. Bossard of the University of Pennsylvania; see his *The Sociology of Childhood* (New York: Harper & Bros., 1948), also other volumes he wrote over a period of years.

Sociological factors that affect parents

In his classic 1940 paper, "The Sociology of Parent-Youth Conflict,"[5] Kingsley Davis discussed 11 variables that he believed to be related to the problems that American parents have. These are as follows:

1. *The rate of social change.* It seems obvious that parents in a relatively static society would have less difficulty than those in one in which social change is rapid and deep—as in the United States. In a slowly changing society parents would be closer to their children—the generation gap would be minimized. In such a society parents need only to produce children like themselves. The models do not change so often or so drastically as they do in modern America.

2. *The decelerating rate of socialization of the parent in contrast to that of the child.* Davis is referring to the fact that the learning curve of the parent is almost the exact opposite of that of the child: during adolescence, for example, when the boy or girl is in the process of discovering sex, the parent may be well past the peak of his or her interest in sex. In terms of learning theory, the child reaches a peak of psychological and social change at a time when the average parent is learning and changing less and less.

If the child is learning about the same things that the parent learned earlier, no great problems may arise; but in societies such as the United States, social change is so rapid, and so deep, that the new generation does not learn the same things the parents learned. One exasperated mother put it this way: "How in the hell am I supposed to help my kids with their homework when even *adding* and *subtraction* have changed?"

It will be seen in later chapters that rapid and deep social change poses serious problems for American parents.

3. *A combination of physiological and psychological differences between parent and child.* This is a sort of *gestalt* effect—the parent is not only different physiologically from the child, but also psychologically and culturally.

4. *Adult realism versus youthful idealism.* Davis argues that as parents mature they tend to compromise their ideals—they still teach them to their children but only partially believe in them—or they have become cynical about the practicality of their ideals.

---

[5] Kingsley Davis, "The Sociology of Parent-Youth Conflict," *American Sociological Review* 5 (August 1940): 523–35. Although published in 1940, this paper was being reprinted as late as 1965; see Hyman Rodman, *Marriage, Family, and Society* (New York: Random House, 1965). It is also available in Herman D. Stein and Richard A. Cloward, eds., *Social Perspectives on Behavior* (Glencoe, Ill.: Free Press, 1958). In many ways, this paper was the original impetus behind the present book.

Youths, in contrast, take the ideals seriously and are upset when they find their parents giving only lip service to such ideals as racial equality.

It does not help to tell the child, "Wait until you are as old as I am and then you will understand." This only widens the gap between parents and child.

5. *The nature of parental authority.* Davis cites Simmel to the effect "that authority is bearable for the subordinate because it touches only one aspect of his life."[6] But in a primary group such as the family, parental authority extends over all phases of the child's life. The wise parent, of course, limits his exercise of authority as much as he can—but in the last analysis the father and/or mother is responsible for all phases of the child's life as long as the youngster is not of legal age.

6. *Conflicting norms.* In a rapidly changing, pluralistic society, children can often challenge parents as to what constitutes moral or good behavior. Not only do the two generations hold different norms, but *within* each generation the standards also vary. This greatly complicates the enforcement of discipline.

7. *Competing authorities.* Parents are not the only source of wisdom and propriety in modern society—the schools, mass media, the youth peer groups—all of these tell the child what he should think and how he should behave. Fathers and mothers are always in competition with these forces when they seek to influence their children.

8. *Poor age grading.* We lack a series of clear steps by which boys and girls move from the status of a child to that of an adult. A male college student put it this way to the writer: "The local movie theater decided I was an adult when I was 12 and has been charging me adult prices ever since. The Bureau of Motor Vehicles gave me the nod to drive a car at 16—but if I had been living in Texas I could have driven at 14. The draft board says I mature at 18, but the bars, the marriage license bureau, and the voting authorities say I am not a man until 21. It is very confusing."

9. *Concentration within the small family.* Davis argues that in larger family systems authority and its related feelings are more diffused among several adults than in our intense nuclear system.

Not only are the parent-child feelings very intense in our society, but the smallness and detachment of our family units make them vulnerable to dissolution, thus adding to parent-child tensions.

Riesman[7] argues that the margin for parental error shrinks as the family system becomes smaller—each child becomes more crucial. An only child put this to the writer in these words: "I am all the children my par-

---

[6] Davis (in Stein and Cloward, *Social Perspectives*, p. 40).

[7] David Riesman et al., *The Lonely Crowd* (New Haven, Conn.: Yale University Press, 1961), p. 49.

ents have. If I get into trouble *all* of their children are in trouble. It is not a very comforting thought."

10. *Vertical social mobility.* The adult status of children in our social class system is not finally settled at birth. The child may eventually occupy a social position quite different from that of the parents. This means, essentially, that the parents do not know for what set of roles they are preparing the child. Furthermore, they are often unable to comprehend the social world their child will ultimately have to cope with. An analogy here would be a professional training program in which the faculty did not know whether the graduates would become physicians, dentists, or veterinarians.

11. *Sex tension.* Davis contends that sex "tensions not only make the adolescent capricious, but create a genuine conflict of interest between the two generations."[8]

These, then, are the features of Western society that Davis believed to be sociological factors in creating parent-youth conflict. Since 1940, when Davis was writing, American society has undergone deep and pervasive changes—some of which may have simplified the role of parent, while others made it more difficult. Let us look, first, at the negative impact of recent social change on American parents, and then we will close the chapter with a review of the positive aspects of recent social change as it affects parents.[9]

Negative aspects of recent social change on parents

Higher standards for parents

It is the belief of the writer that parents are being judged by higher standards—by their children, by professionals such as schoolteachers and social workers—and by parents themselves.

There seems to be no way to prove or disprove this empirically. It appears logical, however, to assume that in a society in which other standards are being raised those applied to parents would be elevated also. We refer to school standards enforced on elementary and secondary students, higher living standards, and others.

During the writer's own lifetime it seems quite obvious that parents in the 1920s were not expected to have their children's teeth straightened—only the very wealthy ever did that. But today even blue-collar parents are expected to make sure that the teeth of their offspring are not crooked.

---

[8] Davis (in Stein and Cloward, *Social Perspectives,* p. 43).

[9] See chap. 11 of this book for an extensive analysis of parents and social change.

Illustrations of this sort could be added endlessly—what was good enough for children in 1900 or 1920 is not good enough today—and this means that fathers and mothers are judging themselves more harshly. This may be a crucial factor in explaining why American fathers and mothers feel so inadequate.[10]

The concept of progress

In most human societies, according to social scientists, it is enough if parents produce and rear children as good as the parents are—biologically and socially.[11] But in modern America this is not good enough: the children have to be *superior* to the parents. This may be functional for the society, but it may also help to produce a negative self-image in parents.

The cult of the child

Lerner writes about the "cult of the child" in American society[12]— parents are expendable but children are "precious"—the salt of the earth. To the extent that this is true of our society, it has to have a negative impact on parents as well as all other older persons; it means that any person not a child is a second-class citizen. This may be one of the reasons why people in the United States do not want to become old—they know what that means.

Judgment by professionals

It is one thing for parents to be judged by their peers (other parents), but it is quite a different experience to have your efforts evaluated by professionals. It seems that, increasingly, fathers and mothers in our society have to submit to the judgment of school counselors, social workers, clinical psychologists, speech therapists, psychiatrists, and a host of other experts if anything happens to the child.

This was certainly not the case when our parents and our grandparents were rearing their children. In those days a parent could hold up his

---

[10] We are in the same position as Davis, Lerner, and Williams in that, while we believe American parents to be more uneasy than parents in most other modern societies we are unable to prove the assertion. For the Williams discussion, see "Kinship and the Family in the United States," *American Society*, chap. 4.

[11] Bell points out that in most human societies parents are not expected to rear children who are "different" from the parents; they are only expected to produce images of themselves: see Robert R. Bell, *Marriage and Family Interaction*, rev. ed. (Homewood, Ill.: Dorsey Press, 1967), p. 405.

[12] For a discussion of "the cult of the child," see Lerner, *America as a Civilization*, pp. 560–70.

head if he did what other parents in the community regarded as right and decent, even if his child did get into difficulty. A grandmother of ours—the mother of 15 children—had a rebellious son who ran away from home at the age of 14 and was not seen again for 10 years. As we recall family history, nobody called this woman a bad mother; after all, her other 14 children had not found it necessary to run away from home. It was simply felt in the community that some boys are more restless than others and that these things had to be expected. This was judgment by our grandmother's peers.

A few years ago a friend of ours also had a boy run away—he simply took off at age 16 and was not heard from for 18 months. Meanwhile, the parents had consulted a child-guidance clinic and came away burdened with guilt. They were led to believe that boys do not run away from good parents.

It would be interesting to know how many boys have left home in America since 1800. This was apparently quite common during frontier days, when restless sons would decide to "go West."[13]

It is a fact that the boy who ran away from our grandparents eventually came home and always claimed that he left home not because of anything his parents had ever done but because he wanted to see the world. It is also true that he was very close to his parents once he had returned to his native community.

We live in a world of specialists, some of whom are very helpful to parents. But fathers and mothers are *amateurs* in their parental roles, not professionals.

In a book that has received wide acclaim Toffler makes this statement: "Despite the increasing complexity of the task, parenthood remains the single preserve of the amateur."[14]

Our criminal courts provide that an accused person be judged by a jury of his peers. It seems to us that parents are entitled to the same consideration.

Marital instability

It is often assumed that fathers and mothers operate as a team in their parental role in our society. This may still be true for a majority of American parents, but it is not true of a sizable minority. This is discussed at length in chapter 9, but it needs to be noted here that 20 to 40 percent of American parents see their team broken at some time or other.

---

[13] An interesting description of the process of families "splitting up" as the sons left for the West may be found in Lura Beam, *Maine Hamlet* (New York: Wilfred Funk, 1957).

[14] Alvin Toffler, *Future Shock* (New York: Random House, 1970), pp. 207–8.

Rearing children is difficult in our society with the best of marriages, but one can only imagine what it is like for couples whose marriages are failing or have already broken.[15]

New roles for American mothers

Since grandmother's day American mothers have taken on new community roles and new economic roles—they raise money for Red Cross and about one third of them are employed outside the home.[16] In many ways they have more responsibility than their mothers and grandmothers ever had. Maybe some of them try to do too much, but that is the world they find themselves living in.

America is no longer a rural society

Parents do not operate in a social vacuum—they struggle to rear their offspring in a laboratory that consists of the world they live in. One can hardly imagine that being a father or mother was not easier in the rural America of 1850 or 1900 than it is today in Chicago or Los Angeles or any other major urban center.[17] The contemporary parent has less knowledge of the various facets of the urban scene—and his or her children have more choices to make.

On the farm, children could be kept busy with chores, while in the city they have nothing to do. The long school vacations pose very real problems for urban parents, but on the farm these recesses simply provided more hands to do all the things that have to be done on a farm.

In chapter 11 the impact of urbanization on parents will be discussed at greater length. Here we simply note that the critics of American parents need to remember that the child-rearing "laboratory" is vastly more complex today than it was 50 years ago.

Rise of the mass media

Parents today are only one of several powerful influences on their children—at least this is so once the youngsters are old enough to read the comics, go to movies, listen to the radio, or watch television. Madison

---

[15] For discussion of parents in unusual circumstances, see chap. 9, "Parents without Partners."

[16] The most complete analysis of the employed mother in our society is that by F. Ivan Nye and Lois Wladis Hoffman, *The Employed Mother in America* (Chicago: Rand-McNally & Co., 1963).

[17] In 1970 the Census Bureau found 72 percent of all Americans living in urban communities. The bulk of the nonurban residents were not farming but merely living outside of the city. According to reports by the federal government, only 8 percent of American families were engaged in farming in the early 1970s.

Avenue would like to have us believe that television does not influence children, but parents are skeptical. It is a bit difficult to grasp why advertisers would spend hundreds of millions of dollars on television programs for children if they didn't influence anybody.[18]

Parents and children today both are so immersed in messages from the mass media that they are scarcely aware of it.

It seems clear that neither Hollywood nor the local rock 'n' roll radio station worry about whether they support the values that parents are struggling to promote. The mass media are commercial enterprises, and they promote what sells. If this happens to be sex, as in the movies, or violence, as on television, that is not their concern—parents are supposed to see that their children avoid such movies and such programs. And some parents, of course, are able to do just that. But many others are not so skillful or so fortunate.

We were reminded of this recently when we took time to read an information sticker on a cigarette machine. It read: "Minors are prohibited by state law from purchasing cigarettes from this machine. *Parents will please cooperate.*" Parents should cooperate! In an earlier America, cigarette vending machines were illegal; you had to prove your age to buy cigarettes over the counter.

It is perfectly obvious that the legislators who authorized these machines were primarily interested in only one thing—the easier sale of cigarettes. They were certainly not concerned about helping parents prevent or control smoking among teenagers.

Why not have a beer machine, or a martini dispenser, with the same hypocritical sticker stating "Parents will please cooperate"?

Emergence of the youth peer group

One of the most dramatic developments of modern urban America has been the phenomenal rise to power and influence (also affluence) of the youth peer group.[19] In rural America young people might spend one

---

18 There is considerable controversy about the net effect of such mass media as television on children (see Seymour Feshbach and Robert D. Singer, *Television and Aggression* (San Francisco: Jossey-Bass, Inc., 1970). Some studies indicate that a child spends more hours watching television before he goes to kindergarten than a student spends in the classroom in four years of college (Associated Press News Report, *Wisconsin State Journal*, October 19, 1971).

19 For discussions of teen-age culture in our society see: "The Youth Ghetto" in Toffler, *Future Shock*, pp. 248–51; "The Village Beat Scene: Summer 1960," in Ned Polsky, *Hustlers, Beats, and Others* (Chicago: Aldine Publishing Co., 1967), pp. 150–85; "Becoming a Marihuana User," in Howard S. Becker, *Outsiders* (New York: Free Press, 1963), pp. 41–58; James S. Coleman, *The Adolescent Society* (New York: Free Press, 1961); Grace and Fred Hechinger, *Teen-Age Tyranny* (New York: William Morrow & Co., 1963); also Jessie Bernard, ed., *Teen-Age Culture*, special issue of *Annals*, vol. 338 (November 1961).

evening a week together, but most of their time was absorbed by the work on the farm. Today, however, high school students and other young people may spend several hours *daily* within a subsociety often labeled "teen-age society." These young people have their own mass idols, their own music, their own clothes, their own language—in a very real sense they have created their own world.

Parents find that to buck this youth peer group is not an easy matter. More will be said about this later, but it needs to be remembered that this youth peer group is a new force in American society that parents (as well as university administrators) have to reckon with.[20] It is the writer's belief that only the more skillful parents can challenge the youth peer group with any consistent success.

Parents today have to deal with the experts on child rearing

After World War I, psychiatry, sociology, anthropology, and psychology (the behavioral sciences) became very prominent in the United States.[21] The psychiatric casualties of the war and concern about the causes of war led the more intelligent members of our society to turn to the sciences of man in an effort to understand human behavior.

This development soon raised serious questions about the methods parents were using to rear their children.

Two specific threads in this new behavioral science tended to bother parents: (1) Freudian theory, which revolutionized the concept of what children were like and took the position that what parents did (or did not do) in the first five years of the child's life would shape the person forever; and (2) the conclusion of sociology and anthropology that children were born with few (if any) instincts, that their eventual behavior would essentially reflect the socialization they received (or did not receive) from their family and other social institutions. This extremely plastic view of the child frightened the more intelligent parents and left them apprehensive. Later on, if their child did not turn out well, they were saddled with guilt.

It is the writer's thesis, discussed in chapter 3, that these new behavioral sciences have not, as yet, been of much help to parents. Much of the research has not been good enough to stand up over the years, with the

---

[20] A faculty committee at the University of Wisconsin in 1967 decided that the university should no longer accept the role of *in loco parentis* (substitute parent) in dealing with its students. This may be possible for a university, but fathers and mothers cannot yield responsibility just because the going gets rough.

[21] The development of child-rearing experts is treated in Lerner, *America as a Civilization;* Brim, *Education for Child Rearing;* and also Daniel R. Miller and Guy E. Swanson, *The Changing American Parent* (New York: John Wiley & Sons, 1958).

result that the recommendations to parents on child-rearing methods have changed from one decade to the next.[22] This has resulted in the term *child-rearing expert* becoming almost a national joke in our society.

There were undoubtedly many different factors involved in the developments discussed above, just as there were many different results—both positive and negative. But one result was that traditional parental methods, based on hundreds of years of experience, were discarded (or at least downgraded) before a mature and reliable science of child rearing became available. Thus, a great many of the more progressive parents were caught between the old and the new. To a considerable extent, this situation still prevails.

Poor preparation for parental roles

In a study of young parents,[23] the writer was impressed by the frequency of the comment, "We didn't know what we were getting into." Even though this sample included only couples who had wanted a baby, the actual process of becoming parents had posed problems and stresses they had not anticipated.

It seemed to us that these couples had received very inadequate preparation for the parental role. Most of the husbands felt that they had had no preparation whatsoever for the father role, and even a majority of the wives felt that their preparation for the role of mother had been quite inadequate.

One obvious factor in this feeling of not being prepared for the parental role was the almost complete failure of our high schools and colleges to include this subject in their courses of study.

Another factor, less obvious, was that these parents had grown up in relatively small families and had had very little experience caring for younger brothers and sisters.[24]

---

[22] See, for example, the research of William H. Sewell, "Infant Training and the Personality of the Child," *American Journal of Sociology* 58 (1952): 150–59; also Martha Wolfenstein, "Trends in Infant Care," *American Journal of Orthopsychiatry* 23 (1953): 120–30.

[23] E. E. LeMasters, "Parenthood as Crisis," *Marriage and Family Living* 19 (1957): 325–55. The writer was first made aware of the widespread interest in parental problems by the reception given this paper. Feature stories appeared in such newspapers as the *New York Times* and the *Chicago Tribune;* the paper was summarized for a group of newspapers in Australia; several hundred reprints were requested from all over the world; as late as 1968 (11 years after publication), feature stories were still appearing in mass magazines and metropolitan newspapers based on the findings of this paper.

[24] For a discussion of the parental role played by siblings in the large family, see Salvador Minuchin et al., *Families of the Slums* (New York: Basic Books, 1967), p. 219.

A third factor was the existence in our culture of a very real "romantic complex" about children (especially babies) and parenthood. If you interview parents whose children are 15 to 20 years of age, they will usually admit that the parent role is perhaps the most challenging thing they have ever done in their lives—exciting, thrilling, exhausting, and (at times) heartbreaking. These are not bitter or cynical parents; they are just realistic. They remind the writer of war veterans: they find the experience unforgettable but are not enthused about going back and going through it again.

Young parents lack any of this feeling of what parenthood involves. And when they begin to find out, they often experience a temporary state of shock or disbelief. As one young mother, an honors graduate from a famous women's college, put it to us: "I just couldn't believe that the baby could upset me the way she did. But when she cried so much during the first few weeks and the doctor couldn't find out what was wrong, I thought I would lose my mind."

The complexity of the parent role

In addition to not being prepared for the role of parent, many young fathers and mothers have expressed to the writer their consternation at discovering the role of parent to be more baffling and more frustrating than they had anticipated. This same sentiment is echoed by a number of writers on the family:

In a study of 571 mothers Lopata concluded that "the concern over this role (parenthood) is very high." She also states that the birth of the first child is "the event causing the greatest discontinuity in American middle-class women."[25]

A well-known student of the American family, Virginia Satir, has this to say about the role of parent: "Parenting is probably the most crucial, challenging, and interesting job for each adult engaged in it."[26]

In one of her famous analyses of American society, Margaret Mead observes that parents rear their children with "the sidewise look"—that is, they are not quite sure how they should rear their offspring so they keep a watchful eye on how other parents are bringing up their children.[27] This stance, of course, betrays insecurity and doubt on the part of these fathers and mothers.

---

[25] See Helena Z. Lopata, *Occupation: Housewife* (New York: Oxford University Press, 1971), pp. 200, 205–6.

[26] Virginia Satir, "Marriage as a Human-actualizing Contract," in *The Family in Search of a Future*, ed. Herbert A. Otto (New York: Meredith Books, 1970), p. 58.

[27] See Margaret Mead, *And Keep Your Powder Dry* (New York: William Morrow & Co., 1943), p. 109.

Riesman points out that modern parents are more apprehensive than their ancestors in thinking about child rearing: "Increasingly in doubt as to how to bring up their children, parents turn to other contemporaries for advice."[28]

This concludes the discussion of features of our society that the writer believes pose problems for parents.

In order to balance the picture somewhat, let us look briefly at some of the developments in modern America that have been supportive to fathers and mothers in this crucial role.

Positive features of American society in relationship to parents

Modern medicine

There can be no doubt that the substantial progress made in understanding and controlling childhood diseases has lifted some of the fear and agony from the hearts and shoulders of parents. One has only to remember back a few years when polio stalked the land to appreciate this type of progress.

The dramatic decline in infant mortality since 1920 has alone saved millions of parents from tragedy and despair.

As a branch of modern medicine, child psychiatry has undoubtedly helped some parents; but the writer feels that other parents have actually been damaged by the inadequate scientific base upon which psychiatric diagnoses are made.

Greater affluence in the society

In an urban society parenthood is an expensive business. Since more parents have more money in the 1970s than ever before in our society they should be in a better position to finance their child-rearing efforts.

This is undoubtedly true, yet only a few interviews with affluent parents are needed to uncover some of the hazards of this affluence. One father said to the writer: "It worries me that kids today get almost everything they want just by asking for it. My wife and I have tried not to spoil our children, yet I am afraid they have not learned the value of a dollar. Things come too easy for them these days." This father had grown up in a family of modest means and was concerned that some of the lessons he had learned as a child were being denied his children.

---

[28] Riesman et al., *Lonely Crowd*, p. 47.

Better means of contraception

For a long time most American parents have used some means of limiting the size of their families.[29] This was one of the strategies employed by the various immigrant groups to climb out of the lower income levels.

But until recently a significant margin of error in family planning was almost inevitable because of the contraceptive methods used. The pill has improved family planning, but even more simple and effective means of birth control are promised in the future.

This should mean that the great majority of parents in our society will have their children because they *want* them—certainly one of the prerequisites for successful performance of the role of father or mother.

Miscellaneous positive factors

Most American parents are no longer immigrants reared in a society quite different from the one in which they are trying to rear their children.[30] Most of the fathers and mothers today have another advantage in that they grew up in an urban community; they are not migrants from the farm trying to rear their sons and daughters in the strange world of the city.[31]

There are, however, striking exceptions to the above statement—southern black parents recently moved to the urban jungles of the North and the West; southern rural whites from Appalachia and elsewhere trying to make a new start in Chicago or Detroit or some other city where the jobs are supposed to be; American Indians resettled in Chicago or Denver or some other city; and Puerto Rican parents trying to make the long jump from the island to the mainland. These parents and their problems are very real and very dramatic, but they comprise a relatively small proportion of all American parents.[32]

---

[29] One recent study concludes: "Obviously, the practice of fertility control in the United States has become almost universal among married women" (see Leslie Aldridge Westoff and Charles F. Westoff, *From Now to Zero* [Boston: Little, Brown & Co., 1971], p. 60). The same authors also report a high rate of failure in family planning as late as the 1960s: "As many as one-third of these couples will fail and have a pregnancy within two years" (ibid, p. 69).

[30] See Oscar Handlin, *The Uprooted* (Boston: Little, Brown & Co., 1952).

[31] The writer's father, for example, grew up on a small farm and attended school for only three years; the mother lived in a small rural village until her marriage; later the parents moved to a small city of 12,000 population, where they reared their four children. In contrast, the writer grew up in an urban world and is rearing his children in an urban world.

[32] For a systematic analysis of the problems of minority group parents in our society, see chap. 6.

Most fathers and mothers today have more education than their parents had—and, in a society that places so much stress on formal education, one would like to think that this should be an advantage.

Some general observations

Earlier in the chapter the point was made that modern America lacks consensus-based, clearly articulated age-grading steps, which would define for both young people and their parents the specific point in the maturation cycle occupied by the child at any given time. When such age grading exists, for example, that children enter the first grade at six years of age, the parent and the child both know what the next step in growth consists of and when it will occur. An even better example, mentioned earlier, is the legal age of driving an automobile, a step clearly enunciated in most of the 50 states.

Based on the writer's personal experience as a parent and on interviews with other parents, situations of this nature which have been clearly defined appear to produce relatively little conflict between parents and their children. But in many other areas, such as dating and the hours to be observed in dating, there seems to exist considerable leeway and variation in many local communities. This produces a situation in which parents and young people must bargain and haggle. This in itself may not be undesirable, but it places parents who do not possess great skill in handling their children at a considerable disadvantage. In an ideal social system, even the average person can manage his role assignments—this is the plan for most armed-forces units, for example—but the absence of age grading sets up situations that only the superior parent can manage.

Another observation that might be pertinent at this point is the fragmentation of family functions in our society: other social institutions such as the school have been expanding their responsibilities since World War I, which means that it is not always clear whether parents or teachers (or somebody else) are supposed to do certain things for children.[33] A good example of this may be found in the area of sex education: in some school systems young people are given excellent courses in human reproduction, the part that sex plays in marriage, and other aspects of human sexuality. In such communities the function of parents in sex education might be limited to the inculcation and/or discussion of values. But in other com-

---

[33] The standard reference on the changing functions of the American family is W. F. Ogburn and M. F. Nimkoff, *Technology and the Changing Family* (Boston: Houghton Mifflin Co., 1955). For a more recent analysis, see Robert F. Winch, "The Family in America and Its Functional Matrix," *The Modern Family*, rev. ed. (New York: Holt, Rinehart, & Winston, 1963), Part II.

munities the parent would have to assume the entire responsibility for sex education—or else concede it to the adolescent peer group and the mass media.

Contrast the confused state of sex education in American society with that in Sweden, which has a uniform nationwide compulsory sex-education program for all school children from the first grade through secondary school.[34]

Here, again, superior parents would probably not experience too much difficulty, but less adequate parents would find the situation difficult.

The transfer of functions from the family does not necessarily represent social decline, nor does it foretell the demise of the American family. Childbirth, for example, has been almost entirely shifted from the home to the maternity ward since 1900, with benefits to both family and society. Such transfer of function, however, does produce a more specialized type of family, as Pitts has pointed out.[35] A specialized family system may be desirable and more efficient, but it has to perform its specialty, not just exist.

One of the reasons why many parents feel inadequate in modern America is the pervasive nature of negative news-media stories about fathers and mothers: one seldom reads or hears or sees any items about successful parents—we only know about those that have failed. It is as if the only business news available would be that about firms that have gone bankrupt, whereas, in truth, most of the news about private corporations in our society today tells how successful they have been in the current year.

It is true that a few outstanding newspapers, such as the *Christian Science Monitor*, make a determined effort to report positive news about the American family, but, for the most part, the stories about parents and their children in the mass media are tragic and sad. They may make some parents feel superior, but it hardly encourages most of us to think that we are on a winning team.

Constants and variables in parenthood

In the paper by Davis cited earlier a distinction is made between the constants (or universals) in parenthood and the variables (factors found only in certain societies at specific periods in history). An example of a

---

[34] For a description of the Swedish sex-education program, see Birgitta Linner, *Sex and Society in Sweden* (New York: Pantheon Books, 1967); see also Anne McCreary Juhasz, ed., *Sexual Development and Behavior* (Homewood, Ill.: Dorsey Press, 1973).

[35] See Jesse R. Pitts, "The Structural-Functional Approach" in *Handbook of Marriage and the Family*, ed. Harold T. Christensen (Chicago: Rand-McNally & Co., 1964), pp. 51–124.

constant would be the physiological differences found between the parent and child—the fact that each is at a different stage of physical growth or decline but yet must accommodate himself to the other. This would be true of parenthood in any society, and yet social factors might still be operative to some extent: persons age faster in most so-called primitive societies than in most modern societies, and attitudes toward aging also vary from one culture to another.

An example of a variable would be social change: not only its rate but also its depth would vary from one society to another and from one historical period to another within the same society.

In this book we are primarily concerned with the variables in parenthood: the particular characteristics of our society that seem to affect the role of father and mother.

To some extent parenthood in any society is probably traumatic for both parent and child—at least this seems to be the point of Feuer, who comments: "The conflict of generations is a universal theme in history."[36]

Conclusions and summary

In this first chapter some of the structural features of American society which affect parents were analyzed in a preliminary fashion. Since most of these cultural patterns will be discussed in greater depth in subsequent chapters, no effort was made to examine them systematically.

In the early part of the chapter we drew heavily on the classic 1940 paper by Davis; in the later sections cultural characteristics were noted which were not dealt with by Davis.

In the balance of the book systematic analysis will be attempted on those features of our society that constitute the social setting in which fathers and mothers must function.

---

[36] Lewis S. Feuer, *The Conflict of Generations* (New York: Basic Books, 1969), p. 68.

chapter
two

Folklore
about parenthood

Some years ago Thurman Arnold wrote a very interesting and provocative book called *The Folklore of Capitalism*.[1] In this study Arnold was analyzing folk beliefs or myths about the American economy. His thesis was that capitalism in the United States had changed so drastically in the last century that hardly any of the traditional theories about it were relevant any more—and yet they were constantly being quoted by persons who opposed any change in the government's economic policies.

In later years John Galbraith has taken up where Arnold left off and uses the term *conventional wisdom* to describe beliefs about American society that he regards as erroneous.[2]

The clinical psychologist Albert Ellis has also used this approach in analyzing American attitudes and beliefs about sex.[3]

In a previous book about the American courtship and marriage systems the present writer made extensive use of the concept of folklore.[4]

---

[1] Thurman Arnold, *The Folklore of Capitalism* (New Haven: Yale University Press, 1937).

[2] John Kenneth Galbraith, *The Affluent Society* (Boston: Houghton Mifflin Co., 1958). For another treatment of folklore, see William J. Lederer and Don D. Jackson, *The Mirages of Marriage* (New York: W. W. Norton & Co., 1968).

[3] Albert Ellis, *The Folklore of Sex* (New York: Charles Boni, 1951).

[4] E. E. LeMasters, *Modern Courtship and Marriage* (New York: Macmillan Co., 1957).

The reception of the Arnold and Galbraith books leads one to believe that this type of analysis is interesting and worthwhile.[5]

In this chapter an attempt will be made to analyze folk beliefs about parenthood. In any civilization there is always a large body of folk belief about anything very important. As the term *folklore* or *folk belief* is used here, it means widely held beliefs that are not supported by the facts. Usually, these beliefs tend to romanticize the truth, although in some cases the reverse might be true: reality might not be as bad as the folk belief would imply.

It is the writer's contention that persons living in modern civilizations are apt to think they do not believe in folklore, whereas in actual fact they do. Thus, they are apt to think their behavior is based on sound rational principles when in reality it is not.

The approach will be to state the folk belief and then to subject it and its implications to systematic analysis.

1. *That rearing children is fun.* No one can teach high school or college courses in the family without being impressed by this belief that rearing children is fun. It derives from the notion that "children are cute" (to be analyzed later). Young people are often heard to say: "Oh I just cannot wait to have children." The odd thing is that *parents* do not talk that way. This leads one to the conclusion that this belief reflects folklore and has no substantial basis in reality.

The truth is—as every parent knows—that rearing children is probably the hardest, and most thankless, job in the world. No intelligent father or mother would deny that it is *exciting*, as well as *interesting*, but to call it "fun" is a serious error. The idea of something being fun implies that you can take it or leave it, whereas parents do not have this choice. Fathers and mothers must stay with the child and keep trying, whether it is fun, or whether they are enjoying it or not. Any comparison to bowling or listening to jazz records is strictly coincidental.

We do not mean to deny that a great many parents enjoy their work and that they derive a certain amount of satisfaction from it. But to describe what parents do as fun is to miss the point. It would be like describing the sweat and tears involved in the artist's creation as fun. The life of Thomas Wolfe or that of almost any serious artist will convey the point.[6]

Now that his military service is well in the past, the author of this book can truthfully say that he enjoyed his years in the U.S. Naval Air Corps

[5] For a brief and popular discussion of myths in our society, see Leo Rosten, *The Many Worlds of Leo Rosten* (New York: Harper & Row, 1964), esp. pp. 206–8.

[6] Persons who think it is fun to be a great writer should read the following: Andrew Turnbull, *Thomas Wolfe* (New York: Charles Scribner's Sons, 1967); and Arthur and Barbara Gelb, *O'Neill* (New York: Harper & Bros., 1962).

and that he would not have wanted to miss the experience. But it is also true that on almost any day of those three years he would have accepted his immediate discharge had it been offered. This feeling is very common to the millions of men who served in the armed forces during World War II (or any other war, for that matter). We think the sentiment also describes very accurately the feelings of millions of fathers and mothers.

The truth is somewhat as follows: rearing children is hard work; it is often nerve-racking work; it involves tremendous responsibility; it takes all the ability one has (and more); and once you have begun you cannot quit when you feel like it. It would be helpful to young parents if they could be made to realize all of this before they enlist—or before they are drafted, as the case may be.

In pursuing the analogy between military service and parenthood, the writer has often heard parents refer to married couples who have no children as draft-dodgers. The sentiment is similar to that which veterans of the armed forces have toward able-bodied men who somehow escaped military service in the last war (any last war will do). The veteran feels that military service is a rough experience but that it has to be endured for the sake of the country; his feeling toward men who did not have this experience is ambivalent: in a sense he resents their escaping what he had to go through, but in another sense he recognizes that there may have been valid reasons why they were not in the armed forces.

Parents are also ambivalent toward nonparents: since children represent the future of the society, it is reasonable to expect that all of us would make some contribution to that future, and this, of course, nonparents have not done;[7] but there is also a sense in which parents envy the nonparents—their freedom, their less strenuous way of life, their lack of responsibility for another human being's welfare.

This does not mean, however, that most parents regret having had children any more than it means that veterans regret having served their country. Of course, we do not hear much from the men who were killed or maimed in the wars, and we also do not hear too much from parents who have suffered much the same fate rearing their children.

2. *That children are sweet and cute.* When young people see small children they are apt to remark: "Your children are so cute!" It is true, of course, that small children *are* cute (at times), but this hardly exhausts the subject—or the adjectives parents use to describe their children when they are *not* being cute.

Several years ago the author published the results of a study of young parents entitled "Parenthood as Crisis."[8] In this report it was stated that

---

[7] Nonparents, however, may well have made other valuable contributions to the future of the society. A classic example would be the spinster schoolteacher of an earlier era who devoted her life to helping children get an education.

[8] E. E. LeMasters, "Parenthood as Crisis," *Marriage and Family Living* 19 (1957):

parents in our society have a romantic complex about child rearing and that they tend to suffer from a process of disenchantment after they become parents. When this study was summarized in the *New York Times*, a flood of mail descended on the writer from parents, with the vast bulk of it agreeing with the findings of the study. The response to this dry scientific paper (first published in a professional journal) led the writer to feel that he had struck a responsive chord in the collective bosom of American fathers and mothers.[9]

3. *That children will turn out well if they have "good" parents.* Logically, this should be so, and one would certainly like to believe that it is so. For that matter, it probably is *usually* a correct statement—but not always. Almost everyone knows of at least one nice family with a black sheep in the fold. It seems to be a rare family, indeed, that has not had some tragic experience with at least one child (assuming the family consists of several children).

It would be comforting to think that parents can guarantee happiness and success (the twin gods of our civilization), but the sad truth is that they cannot. Children are so complex, and so different, and our society is so complicated, that fathers and mothers simply do not have the "quality control" one finds in industrial production. Parents with skill and ability, of course, probably have a better batting average than those of us with more modest talents—but even the good parents do not bat a thousand.

Someone has observed that marriage is perhaps the only game of chance at which both players can lose.[10] It might be that rearing children should be added to this list.

It would be fascinating and interesting (and perhaps frightening) to know what the actual success and failure rate is in rearing children in modern America. The writer has seen no respectable research (including his own) which would answer this question, and in a certain sense it cannot be answered because the terms are so hard to define.[11] When has a

---

pp. 325–55. See also Arnold W. Green, "The Middle Class Male Child and Neurosis," *American Sociological Review* 11 (1946): 31–41.

[9] A more recent study of new parents came to different conclusions; see Daniel F. Hobbs, Jr., "Transition to Parenthood: A Replication and an Extension," *Marriage and the Family* 30 (August 1968): 413–17. Although Hobbs refers to his study as a replication of the earlier study by LeMasters, an important difference is that the LeMasters sample was limited to middle-class parents. This does not appear to be true of the Hobbs sample.

[10] Someone else commented to the writer that marriage may also be the only game of chance in which both players *can win*.

[11] In their study of married couples in Detroit, Blood and Wolfe report that only 3 percent of the sample said they would not want any children if they had their life to live over again; see Robert O. Blood, Jr., and Donald M. Wolfe, *Husbands and Wives* (New York: Free Press, 1960), p. 137. It is interesting to note that of the 909 spouses interviewed for this study not one was a male.

parent been successful with any given child? At what age do we judge the product—adolescence, early adulthood, middle age, or the life span? Do we include material success, physical health, mental health, spiritual health, or what?

In an extremely unscientific manner, the writer has surveyed a few families, with very sobering results. Winston Churchill and his wife, for example, appear to have been successful with only two of their children, yet both of these parents were remarkably successful in the other areas of life.[12] Franklin D. Roosevelt and Eleanor Roosevelt, certainly two of the most loved and revered Americans of the modern era, seem to have been only moderately successful in rearing their children—and this appraisal comes from Democrats, not Republicans.[13]

It is true that such families have most unusual family stresses because of the heavy burden carried by the father and mother in discharging their many public responsibilities, but the writer has also studied some families at very modest social levels with somewhat similar results: three families selected at random agreed that only about one half of their children had turned out very well—not in material matters, but as human beings. One wonders whether the parental batting average in modern America would exceed 50 percent. But in baseball, of course, .300 is considered to be an exceptional batting average. The problem in parenthood is that fathers and mothers are not supposed to fail with any child, no matter what the difficulties.

4. *That girls are harder to rear than boys.* It seems to be true that in the past American fathers and mothers have worried more about their daughters than their sons—at least that was the conclusion reached in a study by Komarovsky.[14] Undoubtedly, this concern was based on the fact that girls can get pregnant while boys cannot.

In the 1970s it would appear that parents are facing other problems with their daughters as American women search for social equality and more meaningful lives.[15]

---

12 On the difficulties of child rearing in the Churchill family, see Jack Fishman, *My Darling Clementine* (New York: David McKay Co., 1963). This is the story of Mrs. Winston Churchill and her married life. See also Randolph Churchill, *Twenty-one Years* (Boston: Houghton Mifflin Co., 1965), the story of his childhood; and his *Winston S. Churchill* (New York: Houghton Mifflin Co., 1966). The latter volume details how seldom Winston Churchill saw his upper-upper class parents when he was a child.

13 At various times, almost all of the Roosevelt children seem to have had fairly serious problems when they were growing up; see Joseph P. Lash, *Franklin and Eleanor* (New York: W. W. Norton & Co., 1971).

14 Mirra Komarovsky, "Functional Analysis of Sex Roles," *American Sociological Review* 15 (1950): 508–16.

15 The literature on the contemporary dilemmas of American females is vast. A good statement is to be found in Carol Andreas, *Sex and Caste in America* (Englewood Cliffs, N.J.: Prentice-Hall, 1971).

It is the opinion of the writer that the worry of fathers and mothers has been misplaced: there is abundant evidence that young males in our society get into more trouble than young females do.[16] Juvenile-delinquency studies, adult-crime rates, the incidence of alcoholism—data of this nature tend to support the above conclusion.

5. *That today's parents are not as good as those of yesterday.* It is impossible to prove or disprove this sort of belief, of course, but it does seem to be prevalent. The truth is, as shown elsewhere in this study,[17] that standards applied to parents today have been raised, and it is also true that the laboratory in which parents have to operate (the modern world) has become infinitely more complex. All this tends to create the impression that parents as a group have deteriorated since the good old days of the 18th or 19th century. This sort of argument is usually clinched (at least to the satisfaction of the critic) by reference to the family of John Adams or Jefferson. Actually, nobody knows what most parents were like in the old days, but if we can compare them to what doctors and other practitioners of the era were like, it seems possible that they were not supermen or superwomen, but just plain fathers and mothers sweating out every child.

There is always a tendency to romanticize the past, and this seems to have done a very real disservice to modern parents.[18]

6. *That child rearing today is easier because of modern medicine, modern appliances, child psychology, and so on.* According to this belief, modern mothers have an easy time of it because of the weekly diaper service and the automatic dishwasher. Actually, the truth is probably just the opposite: that mothers today are in much more of a rat race than their grandmothers ever dreamed of. Middle-class mothers, in particular, have become poorly paid cab drivers, racing from one place to another trying to get all of the children to their various appointments, helping to run the PTA, being a buddy to their husbands—plus holding a full- or part-time job in many instances.[19]

The odd thing is that modern medicine and modern child psychology have really made matters worse in some ways, for we now are more aware of all of the terrible things that can happen to children and are

---

[16] A volume would be needed to document the problems of the American male. For one author's view, see Myron Brenton, *The American Male* (New York: Coward-McCann, 1966).

[17] See chap. 4, "Role Analysis of Parenthood."

[18] A well-known family sociologist, William J. Goode, takes the position that we have no reliable history of the American family; see his paper, "The Sociology of the Family," in *Sociology Today,* ed. Robert K. Merton et al. (New York: Basic Books, 1959), p. 195.

[19] For a popular account of the hectic schedule of many American mothers, see Betty Friedan, *The Feminine Mystique* (New York: W. W. Norton & Co., 1963). This subject is pursued in greater depth in chap. 7, "The American Mother."

expected to recognize them early enough to take the proper preventive action. Example: the writer has crooked teeth. He has never, however, held his father and mother responsible for this. With his own two sons, however, it is expected that he and their mother will take the necessary action to prevent their children from having such teeth. This, of course, will cost a small fortune if an orthodontist has to improve on nature—but in addition to the financial outlay will be the concern about whether "we have done the right thing about Bill's teeth," and so on. The writer's parents never had to shoulder such burdens.[20] And *their* parents had it even easier.

It is true, of course, that there are times when the pediatrician, or the surgeon, or the child psychiatrist can make you glad you are living in the 20th century instead of the 18th. But for every such moment modern parents pay dearly—and not just in terms of money. They pay in terms of awareness, and fear, and responsibility and in ways their ancestors never thought of.

7. *That children today really appreciate all the advantages their parents are able to give them.* Oddly enough, the reverse seems to be true: that children today are less appreciative and not more so. Numerous observers of the American family have come to this conclusion.[21]

College students are very frank about this: they regard what they have received as their *right* and not as something to be thankful for.[22]

In a sense, this same sort of psychology is characteristic of all of us living in the modern world; we take for granted inside toilets, painless dentistry, and religious freedom and simply complain when the system fails to deliver what we have come to consider our birthright. Thus, parents derive very little satisfaction from giving children all the modern advantages: they only feel guilty when they *cannot* deliver the goods.

8. *That the hard work of rearing children is justified by the fact that we are going to make a better world.* This is a comforting thought, and one that most parents need desperately to believe, but there is very little evidence to sustain it. It has more to do with hope than reality.

Actually, a great many schoolteachers and other persons who work with children believe they are getting worse, not better. And, except for material progress, it is hard to see how the modern world is better than the one preceding it.

---

[20] Actually, in all fairness to our parents, they at least preserved the writer's teeth, even though they are crooked, whereas they themselves never saw a dentist in their childhood.

[21] See David Riesman et al., "From Morality to Morale: Changes in the Agents of Character Formation," *The Lonely Crowd*, rev. ed. (New Haven: Yale University Press, 1961), chap. 2. See also Max Lerner, "Children and Parents," *America as a Civilization* (New York: Simon & Schuster, 1957), pp. 560–70.

[22] This statement is based on an unpublished study of college seniors done by the writer at Beloit College, Beloit, Wisc., in 1958.

One can always hope, of course, that this new generation will be braver, wiser, and happier than their parents have been. It is doubtful, however, that this will prove to be true.

9. *The sex education myth: that children will not get into trouble if they have been told the facts of life.* One mother said to the writer: "I do not see how such a thing (premarital pregnancy) could have happened to our daughter. She has known where babies come from since she was six years old."

This indicates how naïve some parents in our society are about the mystic power of sex education, which, at best, usually covers only the physiology of reproduction. Nothing is said about passion or seduction or the role of unconscious factors in heterosexual interaction. It seems to be assumed by such parents that sex is always a cold calculating act—as if Freud had never written a word to the contrary.[23]

The truth is that much (if not most) human sexual behavior is non-rational and only partly subject to continuous intellectual control. If this were not the case, illegitimate pregnancies in our society would be much fewer than they are and Kinsey's data on adultery would be less massive.[24]

A great many human societies, such as the Latin cultures, have always assumed that sex was too powerful for most humans to control, and they therefore arranged that persons for whom sexual relations were taboo were never left alone together.[25] Our society is relatively unique in that we have adopted just the opposite policy—at least for single persons: they are permitted (and even expected) to spend hundreds of hours alone without ever having sex relations until they marry. Research tells us, of course, that considerable proportions of them do have sexual relations before marriage, but only a relatively few ever get pregnant. Or if they get pregnant they marry before the birth of the child.[26]

The writer believes in sex education and thinks it belongs in every school and college curriculum, also in every family. But one should not

---

[23] See Sigmund Freud, *Sexuality and the Psychology of Love* (New York: Collier Books, 1963); almost any page will do.

[24] Kinsey reported a significant amount of adultery by both wives and husbands in his sample—but considerably higher rates for husbands than for wives; see Alfred C. Kinsey et al., *Sexual Behavior and the Human Female* (Philadelphia: W. B. Saunders Co., 1953), pp. 409–45. In this second volume, Kinsey summarizes the data on men from the first volume and compares it with data on women.

[25] For the Italian view of sex as too overpowering for individuals to control, see Luigi Barzini, *The Italians* (New York: Atheneum Press, 1964); also Irving R. Levine, *Main Street, Italy* (New York: Doubleday & Co., 1963).

[26] In the 1940s a study in Indiana concluded that 20 percent of all first births in that state were conceived before marriage; see Harold T. Christensen, *Marriage Analysis* (New York: Ronald Press, 1950), p. 153. A 1970 survey by the Department of Health, Education, and Welfare estimated the premature conceptions at closer to one third of all first births.

expect too much of sexual knowledge: attitudes, values, passion, and a host of factors determine the sexual behavior of any person at any given time with a particular partner. It could well be that the art of seduction has as much to do with premarital sexual relations as sex education does. Certainly the subconscious and unconscious factors analyzed by Freudians have to be taken into account in understanding why people behave the way they do sexually.

10. *There are no bad children—only bad parents.* This, in the opinion of the writer, is one of the most destructive bits of folklore relating to parenthood. As Max Lerner points out, parents have become the bad guys in modern America, while children and teachers and other custodians and child-shapers (such as the television station owners) have become the good guys.[27] And, just as on television, the bad guys always lose.

Actually, Brim has analyzed a rather lengthy list of factors other than parents which affect the destinies of children.[28] These include: genetic factors; siblings; members of the extended family, such as grandparents; schoolteachers; playmates; the youth peer group; and so on. He concludes that parents have been held unduly responsible for shaping the destiny of their offspring.

Lerner takes the position that parental critics tend to be "child worshippers"—the child can do no wrong, all children are potentially perfect (or near perfect), and parents should be able to rear *any* child successfully is they only knew enough and only tried hard enough.[29]

The writer is inclined to the view that some children are doomed almost from the point of birth: try as they will, their parents seem destined to fail in their efforts to solve the various problems that arise during the child-rearing process. In an earlier America this was conceptualized as fate, but in contemporary America there is no such thing as fate; fate is just another word for poor parental role performance. It seems to us that this is folklore or mythology. It is also very unfair to parents who have made valiant efforts to help their children attain a decent and productive life.

These matters will be discussed at some length in the next chapter on "Parents and the Behavioral Sciences."

11. *That two parents are necessary to rear children successfully.* No one would deny that it is nice to have both a father and a mother in the home when children are growing up. But is it absolutely necessary for proper parenting? At least two studies make one doubt the proposition:

---

27 Lerner, *America as a Civilization,* pp. 560–70.

28 See Orville G. Brim, Jr., "The Influence of Parent on Child," *Education for Child Rearing* (New York: Russell Sage Foundation, 1959), chap. 2.

29 This discussion is in the section cited previously.

Kadushin, after a careful search of the empirical studies on the one-parent family, reached this conclusion: "The association between single-parent familyhood and psychosocial pathology is neither strong nor invariable."[30]

In a study of Head Start children, Aldous did not find significant differences in perception of adult male and female roles between the father-present and the father-absent children when race and social class variables were controlled.[31]

It does seem to be well established, however, that the chances of a child being in the so-called poverty group are significantly higher in our society when the father is absent.[32]

12. *That modern behavioral science has been helpful to parents.* The writer considers this to be folklore or mythology. For details see the next chapter. Our basic contention is that psychiatry, sociology, and the related fields have functioned largely to make parents feel more guilty and inadequate. We also argue, with Brim, that the research on which most professionals in the parent-education field have based their programs has been relatively poor.[33]

13. *That love is enough to sustain good parental performance.* Bruno Bettelheim has argued that love is not enough.[34] His main point is that love has to be guided by knowledge and insight and also tempered with self-control on the part of the parent.

It is quite probable, however, that the reverse proposition is true: that no amount of scientific or professional knowledge about child development will do parents (or their children) any good unless it is mixed with love for the child and acceptance of the parental role.

14. *That all married couples should have children.* One of the tragedies of the baby boom in the United States following World War II was the implicit assumption that marriage was incomplete unless accompanied by parenthood. In the 1940s and the 1950s having children became a sort of cultural compulsion in America. One young wife of that era said to the writer: "I feel so conspicuous not being pregnant after two years

---

[30] See Alfred Kadushin, "Single Parent Adoption—An Overview and Some Relevant Research" (Child Welfare League of America, 1968), p. 30.

[31] Joan Aldous, "Children's Perceptions of Adult Role Assignment," *Journal of Marriage and the Family* 34 (1972): 55–65.

[32] These data are analyzed in Alvin L. Schorr, *Poor Kids* (New York: Basic Books, 1966). A useful annotated bibliography on the one-parent family will be found in Benjamin Schlesinger, ed., *The One-Parent Family* (Toronto: University of Toronto Press, 1970).

[33] See Brim, *Education for Child Rearing;* this is a careful review of the research related to parent education, and almost every chapter includes criticism of the research methods employed in parental studies.

[34] See Bruno Bettelheim, *Love Is Not Enough* (Glencoe, Ill.: Free Press, 1950).

of marriage that I am embarassed to go to my bridge club." Couples with only two children during this period felt as if they were sterile.

This appears to have changed somewhat during the 1960s and the early 1970s—couples are now beginning to question the notion that all married people should try parenthood at least once.

Various surveys have shown that the vast majority of young Americans do want children at some time,[35] but this should not confuse persons who are really not the parental type. Some of us would do well to leave child rearing to those who are good at it and seem to enjoy the role. There are other significant contributions that can be made to the world by non-parents. In a very real sense, the need of society today is not for *more* children but for more quality control in the production and rearing of the next generation.[36] This will not be achieved by unplanned parenthood or by childbearing because it is fashionable.

15. *That childless married couples are frustrated and unhappy.* This might seem only natural and logical, yet one has to take it with a grain of salt. Judging from the experience of adoption agencies, which deal with a great many married couples who desire children but do not have any, it seems perfectly evident that these couples are frustrated and unhappy at not being able to be parents.[37] And one of the functions of such organizations is to help meet this need of childless couples. But, at the same time, adoption agencies have learned from long and bitter experience not to accept at face value the notion that childless couples only need children to make their lives happy and complete. Some couples may be seeking a child in a desperate effort to save their marriages; others seek children to fill the void of their unhappy and empty lives; and still others only imagine that they want a child—parenthood might be the last experience in the world which would be good for them, their marriage, or the adoptive child.

Actually, some childless couples seem to be quite happy in their marriages and their personal lives. They have accepted life as they find it, have perhaps wanted children at some point in their marriage or perhaps never planned on having children, but in any event they have evolved a satisfying way of life without adding the role of parent to their other roles. Some of the married women in this group have demanding careers, some have suffered some disability that makes them doubt their ability

[35] On the desire for children among Americans after World War II, see Blood and Wolfe, *Husbands and Wives.* In the 1970s some couples are questioning whether they should have children (see *U.S. News and World Report*, April 12, 1973).

[36] Bell points out that biological parenthood does not guarantee the presence of other qualities required of parents (see Robert R. Bell, *Marriage and Family Interaction*, rev. ed. (Homewood, Ill.: Dorsey Press, 1967), p. 386.

[37] On adoption, see Alfred Kadushin, *Child Welfare Services* (New York: Macmillan Co., 1967), chap. 10.

to care for children, and others simply do not see themselves as being good parents. One such wife said to the writer: "I can understand that for most persons being a father or mother would be one of the most interesting and rewarding experiences of life. But in our family there was so much misery and so much bickering about children that I never had any desire to rear children myself. I simply do not think I would be any good at it. And my husband feels the same way."

It is an interesting fact that in the Chicago studies of married couples which came out of the pioneering work of Ernest Burgess, some of the highest marital compatibility scores were made by childless couples.[38] It is also an interesting fact that a great many married couples *with* children are unhappy and frustrated. Thus, those of us who are parents have to be somewhat careful about feeling sorry for couples who do not have children. They may feel the same way about us.

16. *That children improve a marriage.* There is statistical evidence that children stabilize marriages,[39] but this is not quite the same as improving them. It is obvious, of course, that children deepen and enrich millions of marriages in the United States, but it is less obvious that some married couples have their worst conflicts over their parental role. There are also marriages that are destroyed by children. It is certainly true that most married couples try harder to preserve their marriage because they have children, but this does not prove that the husband-wife relationship itself is made more congenial by the presence of children. It only means that they are willing to endure more frustration to provide a stable family environment for their offspring.

Jessie Bernard, well-known student of the family, has been quoted as follows on the relationship of children to marital adjustment: "Children rarely make for added happiness between husband and wife."[40] In his study of fatherhood, Benson comes to this conclusion: "There is no evidence to suggest that having children improves or enhances a couple's ability to handle marriage problems."[41]

17. *That parents are mature and grown up.* It is usually assumed that

---

[38] In the pioneer study of marital adjustment and its prediction, the conclusion was reached that couples with no children or one child rate their marriages significantly higher than couples with two or more children; see Ernest W. Burgess and Leonard S. Cottrell, Jr., *Predicting Success or Failure in Marriage* (New York: Prentice-Hall, Inc., 1939), pp. 258–59; see also a later study, Ernest W. Burgess and Paul Wallin, *Engagement and Marriage* (Philadelphia: J. B. Lippincott Co., 1953), pp. 712–13.

[39] Winch thinks the data on divorce rates and the presence or absence of children are misleading; see Robert F. Winch, *The Modern Family*, 3d ed. (New York: Holt, Rinehart & Winston, 1971), pp. 254–55.

[40] Associated Press interview, *Milwaukee Journal*, June 18, 1972.

[41] Leonard Benson, *Fatherhood: A Sociological Perspective* (New York: Random House, 1968), p. 114.

fathers and mothers in our society are grown up and mature when they begin having children. As of the 1960s, however, about 11 percent of all teen-age girls in the United States were married and one sixth of them were pregnant when they took the marital vows.[42] It is possible, of course, that some teen-agers are mature and ready for parenthood, but this would seem to be the exception rather than the rule.

18. *That parents are parents because they wanted to be parents.* Well, this would be nice if it were true, but, unfortunately, it is not—at least for a substantial minority of American parents. Even as late as the early 1970s, and even after the mass use of the oral contraceptives, it has been estimated that about one third of all pregnancies in our society are not planned.[43] This does not mean that all of these children are unwanted or unloved—only that the conception came as somewhat of a surprise (or shock) to the expectant father and/or mother.

In the earlier centuries of American life, married couples often believed that they were parents because God had chosen them to be so. Some people, of course, still view the matter in this light. More and more, however, as the society becomes more secular, married couples feel that they are parents because (a) they chose to be, or (b) they failed to take the necessary steps to prevent conception.

The goal of the planned-parenthood movement in the United States is "Every child a wanted child." This might be transposed to read "Every parent a willing parent." While we are far from attaining this goal in the 1970s, it seems to be a desirable one.

19. *That parenthood receives top priority in our society.* This is a choice bit of folklore. Ask any employee if the company gives priority to his role as parent when they need a man in another branch in a different city. As a matter of fact, parenthood in American society has always had to defer to military and industrial needs, to say nothing about other community needs. Millions of fathers and mothers have to sandwich their parental role into niches between their other roles in the society.

The wife of a famous "authority" on the family once said to the writer: "My husband would have made a wonderful father, but he was never home when the children were young. He was always away making speeches on how people should solve their marital problems or rear their children. I took care of the children myself."

20. *That American parents can be studied without interviewing fathers.* This is scientific folklore if you will. In reviewing material for this book, the writer was amazed to discover that most of the empirical stud-

---

[42] See *Parenthood in Adolescence,* Report of a HEW conference held in Washington, D.C., January 22–24, 1970.

[43] See Leslie Aldridge Westoff and Charles F. Westoff, *From Now to Zero* (Boston: Little, Brown & Co., 1971), pp. 68–71.

ies of American parents failed to interview the fathers in the sample.[44] Most of the studies simply state blandly that it was not possible or convenient to interview fathers and then go on to generalize about parents as if fathers were simply carbon copies of mothers. Otto Pollak is almost the only student of parents who rejects this notion.[45] Indeed, books on the American father are almost nonexistent.[46] As a father, and as a family sociologist, the writer does not accept the proposition that only mothers need to be interviewed in studying modern American parents. And in one major study, Crestwood Heights, in which fathers were included in the study, major differences in values and child-rearing methods were discovered to exist between mothers and fathers.[47] More will be said about this later in chapter 8, "The American Father."

The social function of folklore about parenthood

It is a truism in sociology that one of the functional imperatives of any society (or social group) is that of replacement: the production and training of the people who will make tomorrow possible.[48] Along with defense of the group from attack, the replacement function is indispensable.

It follows from the above that every society makes sure that reproduction (parenthood) will take place. Most societies, in addition, try to make sure that persons will only reproduce in some approved fashion—usually through some system of marriage. According to Murdock,[49] random reproduction is approved or permitted in very few human societies.

---

[44] A good example is the widely quoted study The Changing American Parent by Daniel R. Miller and Guy E. Swanson (New York: John Wiley & Sons, 1958). All of the 582 "depth" interviews were with mothers. In the study Husbands and Wives by Blood and Wolfe, all of the 909 interviews were with wife-mothers. In another well-known study, Patterns of Child Rearing, by Robert R. Sears et al. (Evanston, Ill.: Row, Peterson & Co., 1957), 379 mothers were interviewed but not one father. The writer is very skeptical of marital and parent samples that automatically exclude one half of those who might be in the sample (husbands and fathers). It is our belief that the two sexes are not that similar in our society.

[45] Otto Pollak seems to concur with this writer on the exclusion of husbands and fathers from studies and social work treatment programs; see Otto Pollak, Integrating Sociological and Psychoanalytic Concepts (New York: Russell Sage Foundation, 1956), passim. It should be added that Brim, Education for Child Rearing, also includes fathers in his analysis.

[46] A notable exception is Benson's Fatherhood: A Sociological Perspective.

[47] John R. Seeley et al., Crestwood Heights (New York: Basic Books, 1956), esp. chap. 9.

[48] Strictly speaking, we are referring to two separate functions here: that of reproduction or replacement, and that of socialization or training for adult roles (see Kingsley Davis, Human Society [New York: Macmillan Co., 1949]).

[49] George Peter Murdock, Social Structure (New York: Macmillan Co., 1949).

When a societal function is relatively rigorous, as parenthood seems to be in our society, a rich ethos or romantic folklore evolves to assure that the role is not avoided by most adults. This can be seen in relationship to military service: almost nobody in his right mind would agree to bear arms if it were not for the parades, the bands, the speeches about "serving your country," and the culture complex associated with patriotism. In the 1960s all of this was not enough to get young men to go to Vietnam, and the society has experienced a crisis as the result.

The main point here is that parenthood is so surrounded by myth and folklore that most parents do not actually know what they are getting into until they are already fathers and mothers. This creates many problems when the role proves to be more frustrating than they had expected.

Summary and conclusion

In this chapter we have been considering some of the folk beliefs (or myths) which cluster about parenthood in our society. It is not difficult to understand why these beliefs should exist: they tend to sustain parents in what is at best a very difficult and discouraging job; furthermore, they explain (or seek to explain) many of the mysteries that the experts have not been able to explain to the satisfaction of most parents. These beliefs in some instances represent tradition, while in other instances they represent so-called scientific fact.

Given the inadequate state of knowledge about parenthood and child rearing in our society, it is not surprising that otherwise-intelligent fathers and mothers are found harboring folk beliefs and scientific fallacies about parenthood and child rearing. The fact remains, however, that some of these beliefs can be harmful at times and damage the morale of conscientious parents. Some of the case studies in later chapters should illuminate this point.

chapter
three

Parents and the
behavioral sciences

In this chapter an attempt will be made to assess the impact of the behavioral sciences on American parents. The disciplines of sociology, psychology, psychiatry, and anthropology are included in the analysis.

The basic thesis presented is that parents have not really derived much help or encouragement from the behavioral sciences. On the contrary, it seems to the writer, fathers and mothers have been left feeling more confused, more guilty, and more inadequate by the incomplete and often contradictory findings of the above disciplines.

The procedure will be to examine, first, the impact of sociology, psychology, and anthropology on parents, with a separate section on psychiatry after that. Some specific examples of inadequate behavioral science and its impact on parents will also be presented.

The impact of sociology, psychology, and anthropology on modern American parents

In the last several decades, beginning roughly in the 1920s, the social and behavioral sciences have become a major force in America. Literally thousands of sociologists, psychologists, psychiatrists, social workers, educators, child-development specialists, and anthropologists have been studying children and drawing conclusions about their parents. Their findings have appeared in a vast stream of books, magazine articles, professional journals, and newspaper stories.[1] One can hardly read a magazine or newspaper today without seeing at least one article on child rearing and/or parents. This is a relatively new development in human society, and one can hardly doubt that it has had considerable impact on fathers and mothers.

As a behavioral scientist himself, the writer must of necessity believe, as most Americans believe, that this mass of research and observation will eventually be in the best interests of all of us—but, at the same time, it is hard to escape the conclusion that so far its main impact on parents has been to make them feel more confused and inadequate than ever.

In a recent talk the writer had with a pediatrician, the physician was deploring the mass of articles on children's diseases in the news media. "Every time the *Reader's Digest* comes out with a story on some new disease or wonder drug," he said, "my telephone rings for days. Every mother has diagnosed her child as having the disease, or as needing the new drug, and she merely wants me to confirm the diagnosis. I wish they would stop publishing that stuff."

There is some logic to what he says. It is hazardous to release to the public partial bits of research that only a well-trained professional can evaluate properly. In the behavioral sciences, for example, the nature of the sample studied is crucial to professionals reading the material, but very few readers of the public press are able to evaluate sampling design. In questionnaire studies the nature of the questions asked is crucial, but newspaper men are not noted for their sophistication in these matters, and their readers even less so. The same sort of problem could be cited about any research method used in obtaining data about people.

In attempting to assess the impact of behavioral science on modern American parents, the writer has identified several concepts or developments since the 1920s which he feels have had an essentially negative influence on fathers and mothers. These are discussed below.

1. *Overemphasis on environmental factors in behavior.*   John Watson's extreme version of environmentalism in psychology during the 1920s easily led to the conclusion that parents could do anything with any child if the parents were only skillful enough.[2] It is true that professional psychologists soon outgrew such simple theories of personality, but Watson and his followers had considerable influence on the new profession of

---

[1] According to Foote and Cottrell there were 1,031 papers published on the American family during the period 1945–54; see Nelson N. Foote and Leonard S. Cottrell, *Identity and Interpersonal Competence* (Chicago: University of Chicago Press, 1955), pp. 231–90.

[2] This early version of environmentalism is found in J. B. Watson, *Behaviorism* (New York: W. W. Norton & Co., 1925). For a review and critique of this personality theory, see Calvin S. Hall and Gardner Lindzey, *Theories of Personality* (New York: John Wiley & Sons, 1957), chap. 11.

advertising—and mass advertising has influenced *all* Americans in some ways.

Sociologists embraced environmentalism in their theories of social interaction and personality. They discarded any belief in human instincts and evolved essentially a plastic personality model that was largely the product of its social environment.

2. *Underemphasis on man's organic nature.* Sociologists, in particular, tended to ignore the fact that man is an animal and that all of his behavior has some relationship to his organic nature. It is true that the anthropologists were much more careful in this matter, but this aspect of anthropology did not seem to influence sociologists to any great extent.[3]

It is also true that psychologists stayed much closer to organic factors in their research, an example being their interest in intellectual capacity in children and means of measuring it. But outside of IQ tests and other measurements of motor skills, it is hard to see how the knowledge of man's physical nature has entered into modern clinical psychology as it filters down to parents in clinics or guidance centers.[4]

Sociologists have tended to assume a random distribution of organic factors in human populations, and hence they have felt that these variables could be ignored in studying human behavior. Alex Inkeles has stated bluntly that he thinks this proposition needs to be reexamined by sociologists.[5]

---

[3] In a well-known text, the anthropologist Gillin devotes the first 171 pages to man's organic nature and his biological relationships to other mammals and other primates; see John Gillin, *The Ways of Men* (New York: Appleton-Century-Crofts, 1948). In a cursory survey of sociology textbooks, the writer found little coverage of man's organic nature and his relationship to other animals. For example: out of 556 pages of text, Sutherland and Woodward devote 15 pages to man's organic nature; on p. 101 they refer to "the elimination of heredity folklore"; see Robert L. Sutherland, Julian L. Woodward, and Milton A. Maxwell, *Introductory Sociology*, 5th ed. (Philadelphia: J. B. Lippincott Co., 1956). Another well-known text gives two pages out of 642 to man's organic nature; see Leonard Broom and Philip Selznick, *Sociology*, 2d. ed. (Evanston, Ill.: Row, Peterson & Co., 1958). A widely used text by Arnold Green, *Sociology*, 2d ed. (New York: McGraw-Hill Book Co., 1956), devotes 14 pages to man's organic nature out of 557 pages.

[4] It is interesting to note that in the survey of personality theories by Hall and Lindzey, cited above, the index lists only two pages devoted to man's organic nature (p. 569). The terms *organism* and *organismic* are used frequently in the various chapters but refer to gestalt theory: that numerous factors are involved in human behavior, but these references do not spell out man's biological inheritance as the above analysis by Gillin does. For an excellent review of man's organic nature, see Weston LaBarre, *The Human Animal* (Chicago: University of Chicago Press, 1954). A mass of material on the similarity of human behavior to that of other animals has appeared in recent years: see Konrad Lorenz, *On Aggression* (New York: Harcourt, Brace & World, 1963), Robert Ardrey, *The Territorial Imperative* (New York: Atheneum Press, 1966), and others.

[5] For a good (and rare) discussion of this, see Alex Inkeles, "Personality and Social Structure," in *Sociology Today,* ed. Robert K. Merton et al. (New York: Basic Books, 1959), pp. 249–76; see also Dennis H. Wrong, "The Over Socialized Conception of Man in Sociology," *American Sociological Review* 26 (1961): 183–93.

3. *Overemphasis on cultural factors.* Sociologists and anthropologists, in particular, have tended to believe that almost any behavior at the human level can be explained by reference to culture patterns,[6] and yet in complex societies such as the United States there is almost endless variation in behavior within families, within social classes, within the sexes, within subcultures, and so on. It is not enough to explain the uniformities in behavior: the variations have to be accounted for also.

4. *Oversimplified reasoning from the group to the individual.* Parents are not confronted with a statistical aggregate, they are faced with a particular child or a small group of particular children. Any statistician will admit that when the size of any given cell is very small in quantitative research the chances of error being present are very great. Thus, we can generalize about boys when we are analyzing thousands of cases, but any given boy may not be masculine at all—he may actually be more representative of the feminine sample than of the male sample.

It is very tricky reasoning from group behavior to individual behavior, but some writers do not worry about it very much.

5. *Poor sampling.* Kinsey was constantly belabored for his sampling deficiencies in his studies of American sexual behavior, yet there are relatively few studies of parents and their children that will stand close scrutiny of their sampling method or the conclusions that can be drawn from such a sample.[7] Social class bias is usually present, age factors are not held constant, religious affiliation is usually a problem, urban-rural composition is at variance with the general population, and so on. The universe studied may be very limited, but the conclusions drawn are often quite sweeping—especially so when the study is reported in the general press.

6. *The research design itself is poor.* Behavioral science at best is not apt to be too good. Brim, Orlansky, Sewell, and others have found it possible to criticize almost every study of parents and children published during the past several decades in the United States from the point of view of research design.[8] Control groups are not usually employed, sam-

---

[6] For a critique of the "cultural explanation" of human behavior, see Elliott Liebow, *Tally's Corner* (Boston: Little, Brown & Co., 1967), pp. 208–9. In commenting on the shift from genetic or biological explanations of behavior to a cultural theory, Brim writes: "One characteristic after another of the person was transferred, so to speak, from the domain of inheritance to the territory of environment"; see Orville G. Brim, Jr., *Education for Child Rearing* (New York: Russell Sage Foundation, 1959), p. 33.

[7] Vincent notes that Kinsey's data are often questioned on sampling grounds but other studies with even more bias in their sample are quoted without criticism; see Clark Vincent, *Unmarried Mothers* (Glencoe, Ill.: Free Press, 1961), pp. 27–28.

[8] See Brim, *Education for Child Rearing*, various chapters. This is the most complete critique of "scientific research" on child rearing that this writer has found. An earlier work by Orlansky also contains a voluminous review and evaluation of the research material given out to parents in our society in recent decades; see Harold Orlansky, "Infant Care and Personality," *Psychological Bulletin* **46** (January 1949):

ples are inadequate, questions are vague, interviews are brief, hypotheses are not explicitly stated or else they are evolved after the data are collected and tabulated.

These limitations may not do much harm within the profession, and the studies may indeed be worthwhile; but, by the time they reach the general public, the findings have often become the "scientific finding of an eminent research specialist."

7. *American fathers and husbands are usually not studied.* The writer has been appalled in reviewing the studies of American parents to see that only people like Brim and Pollak seem to worry about husbands and/or fathers.[9] Goode, for example, in probably the best empirical study of divorce we have had, did not find it possible (or necessary?) to include any of the divorced men in his sample.[10] Miller and Swanson, Sears, and others, in quite elaborate studies of American "parents" (*sic*) did not find it necessary to interview any fathers.[11]

The failure to include husbands and fathers in such research is disturbing enough, but one seldom finds that the research team has been very upset by the absence of any males in the sample. The two sexes are surely not that homogeneous in America, not even in the 1970s.

8. *Social environment has been equated with parental influence.* It is one thing to assume (or conclude) that personality is the net result of social interaction and exposure to cultural patterns, but it is quite another thing to assume that the social world of the child is the net result of the interaction *with parents*. It is true that in the early years the outside world is mediated by and through the family, but, as Clinard has pointed out, there are forces such as the youth peer group, siblings, and mass media.[12] Parental influence is not even synonymous with *family* influence, let alone *social environment*.

1–48. The sociologist Sewell has done well-designed field research on children which failed to support many Freudian theories about breast feeding and other child-rearing practices; see William H. Sewell, "Infant Training and the Personality of the Child," *American Journal of Sociology* 58 (September 1952): 150–59. Wolfenstein, through an analysis of federal government bulletins on child rearing, has been able to demonstrate that the advice given parents has fluctuated from one decade to the next; see Martha Wolfenstein, "Trends in Infant Care," *American Journal of Orthopsychiatry* 23 (1953): 120–30. In Alvin Toffler's study, *Future Shock* (New York: Random House, 1970), he refers to the great fluctuations in advice given to parents over the last several decades (see pp. 137–39).

[9] For Brim's discussion of the father's role, see Brim, *Education for Child Rearing*, pp. 36–38 and 69–70. For Pollak's analysis of the neglect of fathers in child-guidance clinics, see Otto Pollak, *Social Science and Psychotherapy for Children* (New York: Russell Sage Foundation, 1952).

[10] See William J. Goode, *After Divorce* (New York: Free Press, 1956), p. 21.

[11] For a review of several studies of parents that did not include interviews with any fathers, see chap. 8 of this volume, "The American Father."

[12] See Marshall B. Clinard, *Sociology of Deviant Behavior*, rev. ed. (New York: Rinehart, 1968), p. 133.

The net result of this sort of approach is to saddle fathers and mothers with complete responsibility for the molding or shaping of their children.[13]

9. *The failure to account for accidental combinations of events that affect children and parents.* In interviewing parents, the writer has been impressed with the fact that in some cases an odd combination of events seems to have determined what happened to a child or a parent. These might be conceptualized as "statistical freaks" that normally would not occur but occasionally do. For example, a child will meet a peer-group member at exactly the point in life when his father or mother is unable to give him close supervision, and then it happens that this particular peer is the one that could influence the child at this time in a negative way. A girl on the rebound from her parents could meet a nice boy in college, but to express her revolt becomes friendly with a young man who is able to influence her in almost any direction. It is easy, of course, to argue with the psychiatrists that there must have been some reason why she took up with this particular boy, but the fact is that all of us at some point in life have been so desperate for a relationship that we have accepted anybody who offered himself or herself—and sometimes we have met some very nice people that way. But other persons do not seem to have been so fortunate.

The writer believes that there are such things as statistical accidents that affect children and parents, but apparently most behavioral scientists do not. At least they do not refer to them in their research findings.

Summary

It would easily be possible to expand this discussion almost endlessly —as indeed it has been done by some severe critics of behavioral science in the United States.[14] The writer's purpose has not been to condemn the

---

[13] The anthropologist Gorer has commented: "In American psychoanalytic thinking the child is born faultless, a *tabula rasa,* and any defects which subsequently develop are the fault of uncontrollable circumstances or of the ignorance or malice of its parents who mar what should otherwise be a perfect, or at least a perfectly adjusted, human being"; see Geoffrey Gorer, *The American People,* rev. ed. (New York: W. W. Norton & Co., 1964), p. 70.

[14] A scathing attack on social science was contained in a best seller by William H. Whyte, Jr.: "Scientism is the promise that with the same techniques that have worked in the physical sciences we can eventually create an exact science of man. In one form or another, it has had a long and dismal record of achievement"; see Whyte, *The Organization Man* (New York: Doubleday & Co., Anchor Books, 1957), p. 26. Another attack on social science was published in another best seller, *The Feminine Mystique* by Betty Friedan (New York: W. W. Norton & Co., 1963). For a third attack, see *The Experts* by Seymour Freidin and George Bailey (New York: Macmillan Co., 1968); the dust jacket of this book has the following statement: "A scathing indictment of the opinion makers who flood the press, the networks and the

effort to study human behavior systematically and scientifically, but rather to point out that the general public (in this case, parents) can be hurt if the research is not well designed, well conducted, and accurately reported in the public press. It is hard to argue that this has been the case with studies of parents and children published in the United States since the 1920s.[15]

Psychiatric theory and parenthood

It probably is true that most American parents know very little about Sigmund Freud and his personality theory, but the fact remains that they have been influenced by Freudian theory whether they were aware of the gentle man from Vienna or not. This is true for two reasons: (1) American psychiatry and American social work have been basically Freudian since World War I, and (2) Freudian ideas have been widely disseminated to the general public through the mass media.[16]

It also seems to be true that many of the books that have criticized American parents—such as the best seller by Strecker after World War II[17]—have been written by psychiatrists whose training was essentially Freudian.

For the above reasons it is essential that we take a good look at Freudian theory *from the parents' point of view.* This is not an evaluation of Freudian theory as it applies to marriage or psychotherapy: we are looking at it from the point of view of fathers and mothers. How adequately does it explain behavior, both that of the child and that of the parent? How helpful has it been to parents? How destructive? Has it been practical for most American parents?

These are difficult questions, and the writer has no illusions about his ability to answer them adequately. But they are important questions that need to be asked, and perhaps a beginning can be made here.

---

policy-makers of our government with their special brand of instantaneous wisdom." It is an interesting fact that these attacks have all sold very well.

[15] This statement is based on Brim, *Education for Child Rearing;* Wolfenstein, "Trends in Infant Care"; and Orlansky, "Infant Care and Personality."

[16] The writer recognizes that not all psychiatrists are followers of Freud. We cite Freudian theory here because we feel it has had the most impact on American parents. Miller and Swanson, for example, report that of 146 articles on psychoanalysis indexed in *The Reader's Guide to Periodical Literature* for the years 1910–35 only 27 were basically negative. They concluded that millions of American parents must have been subjected to psychoanalytic influence during this period; see Daniel R. Miller and Guy E. Swanson, *The Changing American Parent* (New York: John Wiley & Sons, 1958), pp. 185–86. On the history of American social work see, Roy Lubove, *The Professional Altruist* (Cambridge, Mass.: Harvard University Press, 1965).

[17] Edward A. Strecker, M.D., *Their Mothers' Sons* (Philadelphia: J. B. Lippincott Co., 1946); Strecker blames the psychiatric casualties of our military forces in World War II on the American mother.

There may well have been some positive influences from Freudian theory on parents, but it is the writer's belief that the net effect was negative.[18] The next few pages will attempt to support this argument.

1. *It placed too much responsibility on parents.* Freudian theory was part of the broad theory of environmentalism, considered above. Along with Watsonian psychology and the personality theories of American sociologists, it held that the child was essentially the product of parental influence.[19] Freud probably placed greater emphasis on the role of siblings in personality development than did the sociologists and psychologists; but even there parents were the ultimate culprits, because they were supposed to create a family climate in which sibling relationships would be healthy or constructive.

It is the writer's contention that parents are only one set of factors which determine the outcome of the child's life[20] and that Freudian theory was one of the instruments used to enslave the modern parent. It may well be true that Freud himself did not intend that his concepts should be used in this way, but this does not mean that they were *not* used to that end. In the same vein, one can find that the teachings of Christ have been used at various times in the United States to justify the enslavement of the Negro by the white race, yet we can hardly imagine that Christ had this in mind when he was teaching his ethical system.[21]

It is true, of course, that Freud described the child as having "instinctual" drives and needs, and in this sense Freud viewed the human infant as being less passive than did the sociologists, the psychologists, and the cultural anthropologists. But Freud's instincts did not automatically produce any specific behavior—even the sexual instinct in Freudian theory is subject to endless conditioning and modification. Thus, the concept of instinct as used by Freud did not relieve parents of any responsibility because the end product was still undetermined at the point of birth. This

---

[18] For a devastating attack on Freudian theory, see Richard LaPiere, *The Freudian Ethic* (New York: Duell, Sloan & Pearce, 1959). A more detached critique will be found in R. R. Sears, *Survey of Objective Studies of Psychoanalytic Concepts,* Bulletin no. 51 (New York: Social Science Research Council, 1943).

[19] Clarence Darrow, the great criminal lawyer, is credited with developing the theory of environmentalism as a defense for certain types of crime—such as the famous Loeb-Leopold murder trial of the 1920s. But Darrow did not equate the influence of parents with environment—he indicted the entire society in which the child was reared; see Arthur Weinberg, ed., *Attorney for the Damned* (New York: Simon & Schuster, 1957); also Irving Stone, *Clarence Darrow for the Defense* (New York: Doubleday & Co., 1941).

[20] Brim develops this thesis in *Education for Child Rearing,* chap 2.

[21] See Lerone Bennett, Jr., *Black Power USA: The Human Side of Reconstruction 1867–1877* (Chicago: Johnson Publishing Co., 1967).

was a somewhat different use of the concept of instinct than had been customary in biology and earlier psychology.[22]

2. *In Freudian theory parents are responsible for what happens to the child even after it becomes an adult.* In psychoanalysis childhood never really ends: adults only live out in a sort of dreamlike trance what happened to them in the first four or five years of life. They never really outgrow their childhood—they only relive it in different forms. Thus, parents are forever saddled with guilt and responsibility because mistakes made in the first few years are never really outgrown or outlived. They may be modified by expensive and long-term psychotherapy, but their influence is permanent.

As the writer reads the history of parenthood in America, this was not always the case. Parents were expected to do the best they could with children, but at some point children became adults and were responsible for their own destiny. And if they believed in God even miracles could be wrought—without benefit of psychotherapy. There was also the notion that fate had something to do with what happened to people in this world as well as the next.

3. *Freudian theory overemphasized the preschool years as determinants of adult personality.* Some critics of Freud have labeled this "diaper determinism":[23] that nothing happens after the first few years which was not predetermined in the early years of life. Brim, however, cites several studies to the effect that people in modern society *do* change in behavior as they move into adult status—experiences in the nonfamily world (such as military service) have an impact that is not within the realm of parents to control. The peer group in urban society is powerful, as are occupational roles and marital relationships.[24]

It is true that the parent has the child first, but behavior is not always the result of first experiences. Sometimes the *last* event is crucial. By the same logic, one could lean toward the genetic theory of personality because the genes precede what the parents do. Yet most of the behavioral scientists and psychiatrists have been willing to forget genetic factors, and as a rule have emphasized them little in their studies of personality.

4. *Freudian theory made psychosexual development too tentative and too hazardous.* It is hard to believe that the human race would have sur-

---

[22] Hall and Lindzey review Freud's use of the concept of instinct (see *Theories of Personality*, pp. 36–41).

[23] The writer first heard this expression used by the late Howard Becker, sociologist at the University of Wisconsin. We do not know the origin of the phrase.

[24] These influences are summarized in Brim, *Education for Child Rearing*, chap. 2. For an analysis of learning after the years of childhood, see Orville G. Brim, Jr., and Stanton Wheeler, *Socialization after Childhood* (New York: John Wiley & Sons, 1966).

vived this long if reproduction were as tentative as some analysts have made it out to be—that is, that any boy or girl might become homosexual if the right stimuli were supplied (or not supplied) at the right moment. Brim has commented on this to the effect that it may be possible to make a girl out of a male infant but it seems to be a lot easier to make a boy out of him in most societies.[25]

In the Freudian system there seems to be nothing *guaranteed* about the child's psychosexual development—it all depends on what the parents do, how they do it, when they do it, how often they do it—or what they do not do. There is no automatic unfolding of the male or female traits, as earlier generations apparently thought.

Actually, this is probably far too tenuous a picture of human growth and development. It could probably be demonstrated, if the research were adequate, that *most* people would be seriously neurotic or psychotic if their personalities were as malleable as the Freudians and other psychiatrists have described them. In a very real sense, all child rearing is traumatic, not only for the child but also for the parents.[26] But most adults do manage to stay out of mental hospitals and to perform their basic roles in society.

In recent years writers such as Orlansky and Spock have rejected this fragile view of human nature and have pointed out that the human infant is pretty tough and is capable of surviving almost incredible experiences.[27] One rarely finds this point of view in psychiatric agencies that deal with parents.

It seems likely that this fragile theory of human personality resulted from the limited sample observed by analysts and other psychiatrists; they see only those who seem to have been damaged by their experiences, and this sample is seldom matched against one from the general population. It may well be true, for example, that for every adult sex deviate who had certain experiences as a child there is also an adult who had the same set of experiences but did not become a deviate.

There is a revealing example of this sort of research problem in the literature on unmarried mothers. Several years ago Leontine Young pub-

---

25 See Brim, *Education for Child Rearing*, p. 34.

26 Leo Rosten, who has a Ph.D. in social science from the University of Chicago as well as being an editor of *Look* magazine and a writer of Hollywood films, puts this point as follows: "There is the myth that you can explain neurotic behavior by attributing it to an unhappy childhood. But *all* childhood is unhappy; all childhood is charged with uncertainty and fear, with conflict and frustration, with unbearable rage and unattainable desire. It makes little sense to talk about unhappy childhoods unless we ask why some people emerge from childhood with their productive capacities enriched, while others remain paralyzed by unresolved and infantile dilemmas" (Leo Rosten, *The Many Worlds of Leo Rosten* [New York: Harper & Row, 1964], p. 207).

27 Orlansky, "Infant Care and Personality"; Benjamin Spock, *Baby and Child Care* (New York: Pocket Books, 1963).

lished a book on unmarried mothers, in which she concluded that these girls had almost invariably come from homes in which the mother was dominant.[28] But a few years later, Clark Vincent matched a group of unmarried mothers with a group of girls who were not unmarried mothers, and he could not determine any significant difference in the family dynamics of the two groups.[29] He also could not isolate any particular personality pattern that would distinguish the unmarried mothers from the matched sample from the general population.

The art of sampling is relatively new in behavioral science and probably even newer in psychoanalysis and related psychiatric disciplines. Yet almost anything can be proven and believed if the sample is sufficiently unrepresentative.[30]

It seems clear that this extremely tentative view of psychosexual development in children resulted in parents feeling more anxious and fearful—one could no longer rear children by tradition. Instead, parents were supposed to become "experts."

5. *Freudian theory took the romance out of parenthood.* Any parent who knows the Freudian conceptual system very well must approach his parental role with some foreboding, being convinced that, even with the best of luck, the most he can hope to produce is a "mild neurotic."

The complexity of human behavior

It seems clear that human behavior is the result of the interaction of at least three basic sets of variables: the organism and its genetic components, the cultural norms of the social world in which the person lives,[31] and the psychodynamic (the unique experience of any given person). There is also another factor, which is seldom mentioned in books on personality but which parents talk about quite often—the unpredictable and improbable combination of events. This is what earlier generations of fathers and mothers called luck or fate. It is literally true that the best efforts of parents can sometimes be nullified by some rare circum-

---

[28] Leontine R. Young, *Out of Wedlock* (New York: McGraw-Hill Book Co., 1954). Her data are based on interviews with unmarried mothers, but she does not compare this group with a control group from the general population. Thus, her findings may well be true of the unmarried mothers she interviewed, but the same characteristics might be found in a matched sample from the general population.

[29] See Clark E. Vincent, "Psychological and Familial Factors," *Unmarried Mothers* (New York: Free Press, 1961), Part III.

[30] The classic example of poor sampling that produced totally misleading findings was the famous poll taken by the now defunct *Literary Digest* which predicted that a man named Alf Landon would defeat Franklin D. Roosevelt in the 1936 presidential election. Landon carried two states.

[31] In a complex and pluralistic society such as ours, each person is exposed to a variety of subcultural norms, which may deviate from those of the larger society.

stance involving the combination of several events that would normally occur separately and that could be handled better in another sequence.

It is extremely difficult for any one discipline to deal adequately with all of the above variables. As a result, each group tends to emphasize the factors it understands best. Since social, cultural, and interpersonal interactions can literally be *seen* (or felt), behavioral scientists tend to focus on these in their analysis. One prominent biochemist has observed that genetic factors have been "excommunicated" from the behavioral sciences for the last two generations.[32] He goes on to argue this is largely because human genetics are too complex for most social scientists to understand.

Parents suffer from their lack of knowledge of human genetics. They can understand one child and cannot figure out why another one is so different. Robert Ardrey says that except for identical twins, "the chance is one in a trillion that any two siblings will be genetically alike."[33]

All of this means that parents always have an inadequate understanding of their child and have to guess at factors they do not know about.

Some examples of inadequate science and its impact on parents

Parents and schizophrenia

In recent years parents have been held responsible if their children develop schizophrenia.[34] It is argued that this form of mental illness develops because of the "double bind" and other dysfunctional interaction patterns in the family. One mother said to the writer: "Our youngest son had to drop out of the university because he developed schizophrenia. The psychiatrist told us it was because of problems at home. But our three older children went through college without any particular problems—do you think we could have done that badly with the younger one?"

Actually, reputable scientists do not agree about the so-called causes of schizophrenia. Some of them believe that genetic factors play a major role in the etiology of this disease. A well-known sociologist makes this statement: "Although genetic studies of schizophrenia have not yielded

[32] Roger J. Williams, "The Biology of Behavior," *Saturday Review,* January 30, 1971, p. 19; Williams is professor of chemistry and biochemistry at the University of Texas at Austin.

[33] Robert Ardrey, *The Social Contract* (New York: Atheneum Publishers, 1970), p. 47.

[34] See, e.g., Don D. Jackson, ed., *Communication, Family, and Marriage* (Palo Alto, Calif.: Science & Behavior Books, 1968).

consistent results . . . the results obtained have provided as much basis for the heredity theory as there is for any other."[35]

Parents with schizophrenic children will often read newspaper statements such as the following: "A noted psychiatrist and researcher said here Thursday that the tendency toward schizophrenia and related disorders is primarily inherited." The parent will note that the physician quoted is a professor of medicine at Harvard and the editor of a medical journal.[36]

In another newspaper report, two scientists will report that they have found that an enzyme deficiency is the key to schizophrenia. These two researchers have "discovered that an enzyme deficiency in the brains of schizophrenic patients appeared to upset the brains' metabolism, leading to abnormal production of chemicals that are known to have a mentally disturbing effect."[37]

What should parents believe if their child develops schizophrenia? Should they be saddled with guilt for the rest of their lives when the illness is so poorly understood? We do not think so.

Parents and homosexuality in their children

Sexual deviation seems to be increasing in American society. In many cases parents are being accused of "causing" children to become homosexual. One mother gave this account to the writer: "Our youngest son has been discharged from the army as a sex deviate. I went to see a psychiatrist and he said this problem usually represents the way a boy was reared at home. This puzzles me because our other two sons are married, with children, and have never shown any tendency toward homosexuality as far as we know. Why didn't we ruin all three of them?"

Does anybody know what really turns one person to homosexuality while another prefers the opposite sex? One well-known psychiatrist laughs at the idea that some particular family syndrome produces homosexuality. He says: "With perhaps 20 million American men who practice some form of homosexuality, it's inconceivable that all should have emerged from the same set of causes—the stereotype of the domineering, overprotective, femininizing mother and the weak or absent father." He

---

[35] David Mechanic, Mental Health and Social Policy (Englewood Cliffs, N.J.: Prentice-Hall, Inc., 1969), p. 35.

[36] News story in The Milwaukee Journal, May 28, 1971; the researcher being quoted here is Seymour S. Kety, professor of psychiatry at Harvard University and editor of the Journal of Pediatric Research.

[37] Associated Press dispatch, The Milwaukee Journal, May 5, 1972; the researchers quoted here are Professors Jacques Gottlieb and Charles Frohman of Wayne State University.

goes on to say that in over ten thousand interviews with male homosexuals "I've heard . . . every combination and variation of parental history that you can imagine."[38]

Another report in the daily press concludes that biochemical factors are significant in the etiology of sexual deviation. This group of scientists at a well-known university makes this statement: "Preliminary results of a biochemical study of male homosexuals and heterosexuals have challenged the traditional view that all homosexuality is caused by social and psychological factors." They go on to point out that their research method is more sophisticated than that previously employed in this type of study.[39]

Should parents blame themselves if their offspring turn to homosexuality? The writer thinks not.

We have an extensive collection of news stories in which parents are held responsible for drug addiction in their children, alcoholism, and juvenile delinquency. Now it may well be that fathers and mothers do contribute to some of these behavior problems in their sons and daughters; but, in view of the complexity of some of this behavior, it seems only humane to be modest in blaming parents for all of the problems of the next generation. We are aware, of course, that many scientists (if not most of them) urge caution in generalizing from limited data; but it does not always come out that way in the mass media, and parents are often the victims.[40]

Positive contributions of modern science to parents

It is certainly true that some features of modern science have been of great help to fathers and mothers. An example would be modern medicine, with its arsenal of drugs and other treatment facilities. One can only imagine what parents went through in earlier centuries when a child became critically ill and the physician could be of little help.

In the field of mental retardation, modern science has been of great help to parents in being able to diagnose various forms of mental retardation and to offer alternate plans for care and treatment.

A new field is that of genetic counseling—helping couples determine whether it would be safe for them to go ahead with plans for parent-

[38] Psychiatrist Lawrence J. Hatterer of the Payne Whitney Clinic of New York Hospital, New York City, quoted in a *New York Times* dispatch, *Wisconsin State Journal*, February 21, 1971.

[39] Report of a study at the University of California at Los Angeles, *Milwaukee Journal*, April 4, 1971.

[40] A good case study of misreporting in the public press concerns various news stories about the oral contraceptives. See Robert W. Kistner, *The Pill* (New York: Delacorte Press, 1969); Kistner is a professor of medicine at Harvard University.

hood.[41] Although too little is known about human genetics, at least the knowledge now available can be given parents by professionally trained genetic counselors.

In the area of family-relationship problems, many new treatment systems have been developed. Satir and others have evolved "total family" therapy systems, in which the patient is the whole family, not just one of its members. Essentially, this system hypothesizes a "sick family" rather than a disturbed individual.[42]

The behavior-modification group has also developed new treatment systems that are down to earth and relatively short-term in the time required for treatment.[43]

Summary and conclusion

In this chapter we have attempted to analyze the impact of the behavioral sciences on the modern American parent. While the value of scientific research is granted, the results to date in the area of parenthood have not been too impressive. There is an infinite variety of parents and children in any modern pluralistic society such as America, and it is not easy to generalize about them on the basis of limited research, inadequate samples, lack of control groups, and poor research design.

It is true that the better professionals recognize these limitations in the data and urge their application with some caution. But it is also true that the less well trained professionals are not that modest in their consultations with parents. The most serious problem, however, in the opinion of the writer, develops when the research findings are written up for popular consumption by the general public. Newspapers, magazines, and other forms of mass media in the United States are not noted for being reluctant to arouse public interest by sensational methods, and this tendency is compounded by the fact that journalists and other writers for the mass media have usually had no professional training that would equip them to recognize limitations in research method or design.[44] This places

---

41 For a discussion of the field of genetic counseling, see James R. Sorenson, *Social Aspects of Applied Human Genetics* (New York: Russell Sage Foundation, 1971).

42 For an exposition of the family-therapy treatment system evolved by the Palo Alto research group, see Virginia Satir, *Conjoint Family Therapy* (Palo Alto: Science & Behavior Books, 1964).

43 See, e.g., Gerald R. Patterson, *Families: Applications of Social Learning to Family Life* (Champaign, Ill.: Research Press, 1971).

44 The University of Wisconsin School of Journalism now has a grant to bring newspaper journalists to the campus to improve their understanding of social science and thus to upgrade their reporting on the developments in this field. This program is supported by the Russell Sage Foundation. For an interesting analysis of the problems of science reporting for the general public, see Hillier Kriegbaum, *Science and the Mass Media* (New York: New York University Press, 1967), p. 192. He writes: "If

great responsibility on professional researchers in the family field to make sure that their findings cannot easily be misunderstood. This is not easy in the mass society.

The chapter closed by noting some encouraging developments in the sciences of human behavior.

---

there is a major expansion in science reporting in the decade or two ahead, much of this should take place in improved coverage of our social problems and the scientific attempts to overcome them."

chapter
four

Role analysis
of parenthood

The use of role analysis

In recent years a body of knowledge known as "role theory" has come to be widely used by social scientists and some members of the various helping professions.[1] While there are different things that one can do with this approach, one of the most useful is that role analysis can be utilized to dissect small social systems so that we can see how each part is supposed to function and how it is related to the rest of the system. For example: in marriage counseling one can analyze the role of wife in its various subroles, identify those producing problems, and proceed to find out the source of the problems. Is the husband complaining about his wife's failure as a sexual companion, or is it the housekeeping subrole that bothers him? Using this approach, such a complex interaction system as a marriage can be broken down into parts that can be analyzed separately.

---

[1] The definitive source for role theory is Bruce J. Biddle and Edwin J. Thomas, eds., *Role Theory: Concepts and Research* (New York: John Wiley & Sons, 1966); see also Robin Williams, *American Society*, rev. ed. (New York: Alfred A. Knopf, 1960), pp. 55–73.

Essentially, a role is a task that some person is supposed to perform.[2] Roles have to be defined, assigned, perceived, performed, and integrated with other role tasks. Every role carries with it a position in the interaction system that relates to status and prestige. In a well-organized family, the major roles have been identified, assigned, and performed with some degree of competence. Where this does not occur, the family may be said to be disorganized to a certain extent. Minor roles may be ignored or performed indifferently without producing too much difficulty, but major roles (such as care of young children) require constant and at least adequate role performance.

In the modern American family, male and female roles have been shifted and reorganized extensively since about 1920, and some families appear to be disorganized in that nobody seems to know who is supposed to do what. An analogy can be made here to bureaucratic theory: a business firm or an academic department may be said to be disorganized when major tasks have not been properly assigned or are not being performed adequately.

In this chapter we seek to apply role theory and role analysis to modern parents. We believe that this approach is helpful in understanding the problems that many American fathers and mothers appear to have.

Our procedure will be to state the major points and to comment on them briefly. More extensive analysis will be given some of the points later in this chapter, and other points will be elaborated on in other chapters.

Role analysis of modern parenthood

1. The role of parent in modern America is not well defined. It is often ambiguous and hard to pin down.

2. The role is not adequately delimited. Parents are expected to succeed where even the professionals fail.

3. Modern parents are not well prepared for their role as fathers and mothers. Brim demonstrates this rather conclusively in a study conducted for the Russell Sage Foundation.[3]

4. There is a romantic complex about parenthood. The writer has published a paper on this, and Lerner discusses it at some length.[4] In some

---

[2] Biddle and Thomas have found over 250 different concepts used by role analysts; see "The Nature and History of Role Theory," *Role Theory*, chap. 1. For a good brief introduction to role analysis, see Edwin J. Thomas, ed., *Behavioral Science for Social Workers* (New York: Free Press, 1967), pp. 15–50.

[3] Orville G. Brim, Jr., *Education for Child Rearing* (New York: Russell Sage Foundation, 1959), various chapters.

[4] E. E. LeMasters, "Parenthood as Crisis," *Marriage and Family Living* 19 (1957): 325–55; see also Max Lerner, *America as a Civilization* (New York: Simon & Schuster, 1957), pp. 560–70.

ways, the romantic complex surrounding parenthood is even deeper and more unrealistic than that relating to marriage.

5. Modern parents are in the unenviable position of having complete responsibility for their offspring but only partial authority over them. Our thesis on this point is that parental authority has been eroded gradually over the past several decades without an equivalent reduction of parental responsibility.[5]

6. The standards of role performance imposed on modern parents are too high. This arises from the fact that modern fathers and mothers are judged largely by professional practitioners such as psychiatrists and social workers rather than by their peers—other parents who are "amateurs" and not professionals.

7. Parents are the victims of inadequate behavioral science—as was discussed in the previous chapter. They have been told repeatedly by psychiatrists, social workers, sociologists, ministers, and others that nothing determines what the child will be like but the influence of the parents. As Brim makes clear, this is obviously not true.[6] It is a form of Watsonian environmentalism made so popular in the 1920s and later repudiated by many students of personality. Freudians have had a hand in this deception also.

8. Parents do not choose their children, unless they are adoptive parents.[7] Thus, they have the responsibility for children whether they find them congenial or not. This, or course, is nothing new in parenthood the world over, but the expectations of role performance for modern American parents are such that the nature of the child can impose severe strain. Middle-class college-graduate parents, for example, are supposed to get their children through college regardless of the child's intellectual interest or desire for learning. In an earlier America, college attendance was less compulsive, and such children could be apprenticed to the local banker or placed in some business operated by one of the relatives. This sort of parental maneuvering is becoming harder and harder. Fortunately, a new type of college that specializes in the delicate task of giving college diplomas to students who do not want them is beginning to emerge.[8] There is every reason to think that their future is bright.

9. There is no traditional model for modern parents to follow in rearing their children. The old model has been riddled by critical studies, yet

---

[5] See J. M. Mogey, "A Century of Declining Paternal Authority," *Marriage and Family Living* 19 (1957): 234–39.

[6] Brim, "The Influence of Parent on Child," *Education for Child Rearing*, chap. 2. See also Dennis H. Wrong, "The Over Socialized Conception of Man in Sociology," *American Sociological Review* 26 (1961): 183–93.

[7] Various studies have concluded that 20–30 percent of American pregnancies are unplanned.

[8] The writer does not wish to identify these colleges—the reader can supply his own names.

no adequate new model has developed. Instead, we have had a series of fads and fashions in child rearing based on the research of the moment. Wolfenstein has an interesting paper on this.[9] Brim, in a very careful survey of the literature, concludes that parent educators have been unconsciously presenting their middle-class values for all parents to emulate.[10] This has not been much help to parents who probably need the most help—parents from low-income groups.

10. Contrary to what some may think, parenthood as a role does not enjoy the priority one would expect in modern America. The needs of the economic system, in particular, come first, as can be seen in the frequency with which large firms transfer young managers and their families around the country. One college girl interviewed by the writer said that her family had moved 16 times in the first 18 years of her life. The armed forces and their manpower needs often frustrate the efforts of modern fathers and mothers. Hours of employment in many retail businesses involving work at night and on Sunday sometimes defeat the best efforts of parents to maintain close family ties. Employed mothers as well as fathers face this problem. Many tax laws are unfair to families and in particular to the woman who works outside of the home. School hours and school vacations often do not coincide with the needs of parents. All of this reflects the fact that we do not have a national policy on the family in the United States—various social institutions formulate their own policies.

11. Other new roles have been assumed by modern parents since World War I which are not always completely compatible with the role of parent.[11] The clearest and most striking example of this would be the occupational roles assumed by millions of American mothers. And for those who regard these women as frivolous, it might help to remember that our schools, our social service agencies, and our hospitals could simply not be operated without these employed mothers. Yet they are usually given little sympathy or public support if anything happens to their children. The Nye and Hoffman book makes all of this very clear.[12]

12. The parental role is one of the few important roles in contemporary America from which one cannot honorably withdraw. Most of us can escape from our jobs if they are too frustrating; many of us escape from

---

[9] See Martha Wolfenstein, "Trends in Infant Care," *American Journal of Orthopsychiatry* 33 (1953): 120–30.

[10] Brim, *Education for Child Rearing,* chaps. 4 and 5.

[11] See Biddle and Thomas (*Role Theory,* pp. 273–310) for a discussion of role conflict; see also Talcott Parsons, *The Social System* (New York: Free Press, 1951), pp. 280–83; and Arnold W. Green, "The Middle-Class Male Child and Neurosis," *American Sociological Review* 11 (1946): 31–41.

[12] F. Ivan Nye and Lois Wladis Hoffman, eds., *The Employed Mother in America* (Chicago: Rand McNally & Co., 1963).

our parents when we marry; and a considerable number of husbands and wives manage to withdraw with some honor from marriages that they no longer find enchanting. But it is harder to pull out of parenthood, especially for mothers, even when the parent knows he or she is failing. This is a difficult spot to be in and not an enviable one.

13. And, last but not least, it is not enough for modern parents to produce children in their own image: the children have to be reared to be not only different from their fathers and mothers but also *better*. This point is commented on at some length later in the chapter.

Summary to this point

So far, 13 features of the parental role which produce problems for some parents have been presented. The writer is aware that some fathers and mothers go blithely about their way not reading Dr. Spock or going to PTA and seem quite contented in their role as parent. Whether these parents are typical or deviant is not very clear. Miller and Swanson reported that most of their parents were happy and contented in their role[13]—but these were mothers *looking back* on their experience. This does not mean that on any particular day (or night) that they were having a good time.

In the next section, some of the above 13 features of the parental role will be discussed in more detail.

The role is poorly defined, ambiguous, and not adequately delimited

It is impossible to interview modern parents without concluding that large numbers of them are confused, frustrated, and discouraged. They have been robbed of the traditional ways of rearing children without having an adequate substitute; they feel that they cannot achieve what they are expected to achieve; the standards for child rearing are too high; the authority of parents has been undermined by mass media, school officials, courts, social workers, and the adolescent peer group.

When should children be punished? Is it legitimate to use physical punishment anymore? Has fear been outlawed as a tool to be used by fathers and mothers when it seems appropriate? What is meant by "harsh" child-rearing methods? Should fathers try to assume more authority with their children or less? Do parents have a right to defy public authorities when they are convinced the authorities are wrong? What

---

[13] Daniel R. Miller and Guy E. Swanson, *The Changing American Parent* (New York: John Wiley & Sons, 1958), p. 216. It needs to be remembered that these mothers (fathers were not interviewed) were looking *back* at the early years of child rearing from the vantage point of the future.

rights do parents actually have in modern America? Is it true that there are no bad children, only bad parents? Is it true that the first few years determine what an adult will be like 30 years later? Is it true that the violence so common on television has no negative effect on children? Is it true that modern parents are largely responsible for the increase in juvenile deliquency in the United States? Are parents responsible for the new type of violence and sadism characteristic of juvenile crimes today? Are parents the main cause of the increase in premarital sexual relations reported by some studies? Is it true that mothers who work outside of the home are virtually sentencing their children to juvenile delinquency or mental illness or both? Is the American mother as bad as the best sellers say she is? Do psychiatrists know as much about people as they think they do? Do parents ever have the right to be different whether society or the child's peer group likes it or not?

The writer submits that few, if any, of the above questions can be answered with any degree of certainty in modern America. Parents have been made the bad guy in the drama of modern living and have been blamed for the failures of all of the other basic social institutions in our society—the school, the church, the government, the mass media, the economic system, the armed forces, and so forth.

Responsibility without authority

In American industry one of the cardinal principles of management is that responsibility should be tied in with authority. In other words, a person in a position of responsibility should be given the authority to carry out his (or her) assignment. This is not true of modern parenthood.

In his history of the family in Western society, Zimmerman of Harvard University points out that the father in Roman society during the golden era of the empire was absolute lord and master of his children as well as his wife.[14] We will not dwell in this book on the delicate subject of the relationship of husbands and wives in modern America, but it would be a crude joke (or travesty) to suggest that the modern father is any lord or master over his children—indeed, he is lucky if they are not lord and master over him.

It is easy, of course, to blame this condition on the modern American male, but the matter is not that simple. American society in almost every respect has become feminine—even sports, to some observers[15]—and the

---

[14] Carle C. Zimmerman, *Family and Civilization* (New York: Harper & Bros., 1947).

[15] When the writer played semiprofessional baseball in the 1930s, the players chewed tobacco. Today many of them chew bubble gum. See the discussion in Myron Brenton, "Notes on the Femininization of Society," *The American Male* (New York: Coward-McCann, 1966), chap. 3.

reasons are not entirely clear. From the outside toilet in the dead of winter to the two-bathroom home is a long stretch, but Americans have made it in little short of a century—and plumbers have done even better than that. Automobiles have been designed for women, saloons have given way to cocktail lounges, and so on. How would fathers escape such a massive assault on masculine dominance?

On a more sober note, it seems clear that the rights of fathers and mothers over their children have been seriously proscribed in the past several decades. Parents in Wisconsin, for example, are no longer permitted to prepare their infants for burial in the event of death—yet their ancestors were allowed to do so.[16] And in states such as Minnesota, even university professors are not considered qualified to educate their children at home unless the state education department says so.[17] Parents who oppose medical procedures on the basis of religious faith have consistently had their pleas denied by the courts; parents who punish their children physically are often called into court to answer for their behavior. There seems little doubt that parents today are as responsible as ever —and even more so—for their children but have much less authority over them. And what power has not been usurped by the formal society has been grabbed by the informal society of the child's peer group, especially at the adolescent level.

We do not wish to belabor the point. But in our own family we have the distinct feeling that many agencies (including the church) are anxious to influence our children, but that none of them wish to assume any final responsibility for them. That delightful bit is reserved for parents.

The best illustration of all of this is provided by those guardians of the public morals, the owners of the mass media in modern America: the magazines, the movies, radio, and television. Whenever some public agency questions the content of the mass media, these groups always cry that they do not influence children—they only entertain them. And yet many parents are shocked when they take the time to examine the nature of the material their children are exposed to by these groups. If advertisers have reason to believe that the mass media influences adults, what reason is there to believe that it does not also influence children?

---

[16] In 1964 a married couple of low income was prosecuted in Wisconsin for burying an infant without employing a mortuary (news story in the *Wisconsin State Journal*, April 10, 1964). Ancestors of the writer living in rural Ohio always buried their own dead without consulting authorities of any kind—unless a minister was called in to help with the burial rites.

[17] In the 1960s a celebrated case in Minnesota resulted in a court order requiring that a university professor enroll his child in either a public or private elementary school approved by the state. The parents in this case had argued that they could give their child a superior education at home. We have lost the news story citations on this case, but it was widely publicized nationally. Compare this with the era of the poet Robert Frost, who sent his children to school only when he felt like it (see Lawrence Thompson, *Robert Frost* [New York: Holt, Rinehart, & Winston, 1966]).

The usual reply is that good parents do not permit their children to see or read or hear such stuff—but on the same grounds why prohibit the sale of marijuana or the sale of alcoholic beverages to minors? Is it not true that in the same sense good parents would make it impossible for their children to use such services?

The answer is that even conscientious and capable parents can not rear their children properly in an evil environment—and the basic solution is to make the society fit for children to be reared in.

Urban parents can never hope for the control and authority over their children that rural parents had. But at least they can hope that the urban neighborhood and the metropolitan community can be made a decent world in which to bring up children. And any person or any group which makes this impossible should be made to shoulder at least *some* of the responsibility for what happens to young Americans. Parents should not always have to be the bad guys in the modern world.

Judgment by professionals—not your peers

It is a basic principle in Anglo-Saxon law that persons charged with some offense are entitled to be judged by their peers, and especially so when the charge is serious. Parents in modern society, however, are seldom given this consideration: they are judged by professional practitioners. As a rule these professionals represent fields such as psychiatry, clinical psychology, social work, the teaching profession, or the law. In the opinion of the writer, this is one of the reasons why parents in modern America feel so threatened and insecure.

If one analyzes the situations in which parents in trouble find themselves, it seems clear that they are usually facing one or more of the above professional groups. If the problem relates to school work, the teachers, the school guidance counselors, and/or the school administrators will be sitting in judgment.

Often the problem will involve either some public welfare agency or a juvenile court, in which case a professional social worker or a judge will be evaluating the parental effort.

In metropolitan areas, a child-guidance clinic or a mental health facility will be involved in the assessment of parental role functioning.

Regardless of the professional agency involved, the father and mother will be judged against the professional norms of the practitioners. In few instances are the parents evaluated by other parents. And yet this is the essence of the law of our land.

The writer has been impressed with this matter in listening to professional workers discuss parents and their failures. Very often some specialized knowledge of the practitioner is advanced to show what the parents should have or should not have done with some particular child.

And often it seems to be assumed that modern parents have no right to be amateurs: they should practice parenthood as if it were a profession.

It might be argued that parenthood is becoming professionalized. The writer would argue just the reverse: parents today are just as confused (if not more so) than ever, and their preparation for parenthood is just as poor as ever, but they are being *judged* by professionals. And this is an uncomfortable position at best.

One can argue, of course, that this has always been the case, but the fact is that parents in the 18th and 19th centuries were closer to public officials in terms of values and background than they are today—social work, psychiatry, juvenile courts, and schools in modern America reflect professional subcultures much more today than they did yesterday. Schoolteachers in 1900, for example, had only a high school diploma or, at best, one or two years of college education; but, when the writer is summoned to the local school to discuss his children, the guidance counselor is a specialist, the teacher is often a specialist, and even the school principal has had fairly elaborate training in child development, school guidance, and related matters.

It is easy to overlook changes of this nature in thinking about parents in modern society, and yet they are very real. And for some parents they are quite frustrating and threatening.

One parent interviewed by the writer said his son had come home from school with a note that he needed to have his eyes examined. The school nurse had given all of the pupils a vision test, and this particular child had scored below the acceptable norm. A visit to the local oculist resulted in glasses being prescribed at a total cost of approximately $50. The parents were glad that the vision problem of their child had been identified, but at the moment they did not have the money to pay for the glasses. When the child appeared in class two weeks later without them, a note was sent home from the school asking why the corrective work had not been taken care of. The mother finally went to a small-loan company and borrowed the money for the glasses.

One can appreciate the fact that school nurses are trying to be helpful to parents, but it is not always possible for fathers and mothers to take the action recommended by the school.

It might be pointed out that in some Western societies the school would not only have identified the vision problem in this case but would also have corrected it through a school eye clinic.[18]

If the parents in this case had been receiving public welfare, the glasses could have been provided at public expense, but they fell into that economic no man's land in which they did not qualify for public

---

[18] A professor from Sweden told the writer that in his country the school not only identified vision problems but provided the glasses at a very nominal charge to the parent.

assistance but at the same time could not afford good medical care for themselves and their children.

In a sense parents in the above bind are caught in a mass affluent society in which fathers and mothers at all economic levels are held to the same standards but are not given the means to live up to the standards. As Harrington says, it is more painful to be poor in a wealthy society than in a poor one.[19]

Ethically, it is cruel to call such matters to the attention of parents unless the school or some other social agency is prepared to help correct the situation.[20]

One could illustrate endlessly the ways in which modern parents are judged by professional practitioners, but perhaps the point has been made.

No margin for error

In most areas of life there is some margin for error—even those of us who have never had a serious automobile accident will admit that at times we have been lucky, or that the other driver made it possible to avoid a serious collision.

One certainly feels in a profession such as teaching that some students will simply not learn—or at least they will learn very little. Yet if most (or even some) of the students learn, the average teacher or professor will find it not too hard to rationalize his failure to make the material meaningful to all of his students.

This same philosophical acceptance of some defeat is certainly found in medicine, law, the ministry, nursing, and social work. Nobody expects these professionals to save everybody who presents himself at their office. It is recognized and accepted that some people are "too sick" or "too maladjusted" to make effective use of the service provided. Parents, however, are expected to succeed with every child. This is disturbing to some parents. The writer talked with one mother who put it this way: "I am scared to death when I think that what happens to my children rests on my shoulders—it makes me feel so inadequate."

One factor has been the smaller family. It is one thing to fail with one or two children if you have five or six, but failure in the smaller family is more absolute. As an only child put it to us in a college class, "My parents only have one child and if I fail them *all* of their children will have failed

---

19 Michael Harrington, *The Other America* (New York: Macmillan Co., 1963).

20 In some ways, this situation reflects the odd mixture of the welfare state and the free enterprise system in modern America: the free clinic identifies the problem, but one has to turn to the private medical fraternity to correct the problem.

them." She went on to say that this was a frightening spot to be in and that she hoped to have several children when she married.[21]

The late John Kennedy said that one of the awesome burdens of being president in the nuclear age was that the chief executive could not afford to make an error in starting a war—hundreds of millions of people would be dead in a nuclear exchange before the error could be corrected. He pointed out that this was not the case in an earlier period of our history.[22]

It seems to this writer that the same thing has happened to parents: with the large family of the 18th and 19th centuries, an error with one child still left three or four other children that might turn out to be respectable representatives of the family. But the smaller family of the 20th century has left less room for error, and this has produced more anxiety and more guilt in parents.

Parents cannot quit

In our lives many of us find ourselves in roles that are not congenial: occupational roles, religious roles, military-service roles, community-volunteer roles, kinship roles, even marital roles—and one of the comfortable features of living in an urban, pluralistic society is the mobility available to us. If we do not like our home town or our home state, we move on somewhere else. As Mead says, Americans love their home towns as long as they do not have to live there.[23] One could even go further and say: Americans love their relatives as long as they do not have to live near or with them.

Some roles, however, even in our fluid society, are hard to escape if they are not comfortable. One of these is the military-service role for men in certain age and status categories, but, even here, conscientious objectors and persons not suited for military duty are usually given special consideration.

Some of our kinship and family roles are not always comfortable, but the mobility of modern America makes it possible as a rule to reduce these to manageable levels. A daughter leaves the small town of birth where most of her family and other relatives live and moves to the great

---

[21] The writer has never talked with an only child who would wish this experience on anybody else.

[22] This was during the famous crisis with the Soviet Union over the Russian nuclear missiles being installed in Cuba.

[23] Margaret Mead, *And Keep Your Powder Dry* (New York: William Morrow & Co., 1942). In a provocative paper Alice Rossi refers to the parent role being "irrevocable"; see Alice S. Rossi, "Transition to Parenthood," *Journal of Marriage and the Family* 30 (1968): 26–39.

city or its suburbs; a son migrates from Ohio to California; married couples often live far from all of their in-laws, and sometimes by design.

Most of us find it possible to try on for size and comfort many occupational roles before settling into one for life. In an earlier America, where most people were farmers, this was harder to manage. It is still true that some Americans get trapped in jobs not exactly tailored to their fit, but this usually represents a series of decisions that did not turn out well.

It is even true that a modern American can withdraw from his or her marital role if it is too uncomfortable, and the statistics show that an increasing number of men and women have been availing themselves of this new role flexibility since the end of World War I.[24] Many persons do not approve of this new-found freedom to try again, but divorce is now legal in all 50 states and is to be found in some of the best families.[25]

It is the writer's impression that the role of parent is one of the hardest to give up in our society once it has been assumed. And this is especially true for mothers.

The law in most states says that natural and adoptive parents are responsible for their children until the children attain legal adulthood.[26] A considerable number of American fathers take this obligation somewhat lightly, judging by divorce, desertion, and separation statistics, but the vast majority of American mothers stick it out, for better or worse. Some observers, such as Ashley Montagu, believe that mothers in all of the mammals and primates are more reliable parents than are the fathers, and it certainly is true at the human level.[27] In the sense of being a permanent parent, the old saying is true: the woman pays and pays and goes on paying until the child is no more.

Even among fathers, however, there is a lot of reluctance to desert or abandon children, and undoubtedly many American men preserve their marriages and homes for the sole purpose of "doing what is right for the children." Whether their sacrifice really benefits the children may be debated, but their intentions are clear: they feel obligated to do what they can to provide their children with a stable home. American wives, of

---

[24] For an interesting study of the gradual shift in attitudes toward divorce in our society, see William L. O'Neill, *Divorce in the Progressive Era* (New Haven: Yale University Press, 1967).

[25] This list now includes the Henry Ford II family, the Franklin D. Roosevelt family, the Rockefeller family, and the Kennedy family.

[26] For a review of the legal framework within which parents in our society operate, see Alfred Kadushin, *Child Welfare Services* (New York: Macmillan Co., 1967), chap. 6; see also Helen Clarke, *Social Legislation*, rev. ed. (New York: Appleton-Century-Crofts, 1957).

[27] Ashley Montagu, *The Natural Superiority of Women* (New York: Macmillan Co., 1968).

course, feel this even more strongly and often continue their marriages for the above reason.[28]

It is a truism that the human infant has by far the longest period of dependency of any of the so-called higher animals, but the fact remains that the period has been getting even longer in modern America. The age of marriage was later in earlier centuries in the United States—especially for men—but the period of dependence was shorter. And the frontier offered avenues of escape not available to modern young Americans.

It is not true, of course, that modern parents can never quit, because some of them do, but the fact remains that public disapproval of child neglect is probably as strong as that for any kind of deviance in our society—and the courts symbolize this by their attitude toward parents who do not fulfill their obligations as fathers and mothers.

One point usually made in discussing this matter is that "after all they did not have to have children; nobody forced it on them." Well, maybe not, but in the same sense the writer does not have to contribute to the March of Dimes when the neighbor lady comes knocking on the door—but we always do. There is a very thin line between "voluntary" and "involuntary" behavior at the human level—and the line seems to be getting even thinner in the mass homogenized society.

Modern parents are expected to rear children that are not only different from the parents but *better*

Probably the title of this subsection makes the point as well as it can be made. Both Riesman and Lerner, as well as Brim, point out that it is not enough for modern parents to simply produce children who will replace them in the larger society, one reason being that the larger society is changing so rapidly that the old models will no longer suffice.[29]

This point is aptly demonstrated by the dilemma facing rural parents today: rural society as the parents know it is disappearing from modern America—there is no place in rural America for the majority of the children growing up there. Modern agriculture is becoming big business. The capital investment, the managerial skills, and the technology required today to succeed in almost any phase of farm production are beyond the reach of most of the children growing up in rural communities.[30] This

---

[28] Mrs. Eleanor Roosevelt has been quoted to the effect that she did not believe that marriages should be preserved for the sake of the children; see Joseph P. Lash, *Eleanor and Franklin* (New York: W. W. Norton & Co., 1971), p. 491.

[29] Brim, *Education for Child Rearing;* Lerner, *America as a Civilization;* see also David Riesman et al., *The Lonely Crowd* (New Haven: Yale University Press, 1961), pp. 37–65.

[30] See chap. 11, "Parents and Social Change," for further discussion of the problems of rural parents.

means that these rural fathers and mothers are rearing their children for a world the parents have never lived in: the urban world of commerce and industry, the world of the city and the suburb.

Arthur Pearl has developed the concept of "the credentialed society" to describe modern America.[31] He refers to the fact that even to drive a garbage truck today a person needs a high school diploma. This was not true in earlier periods of our history. In such a social system, there is no place in the economy for the school dropout: he is forever barred from gainful employment. This places great stress on parents to force their children to remain in school—even when the school situation is negative.

It is not enough for parents to produce carbon copies of themselves; they have to do what some of the new copying machines are supposed to do—turn out copies better than the originals.

It would seem that this is one of the reasons why modern parents feel so inadequate. They are not sure they are able to do what is required. And their children are not sure either.

To some extent, of course, American parents have always faced this problem, at least the immigrant groups did. But the country was expanding then, the frontier was still open, and individual ability rather than formal education was the main ingredient required for economic and personal success.

It is possible that parents will not be able to meet this challenge and that some social institution other than the family will have to assume more of the burden. In the recent effort of the federal government to strengthen local school programs, especially in low-income areas, there is emerging a strategy of helping parents in these areas give their children a better chance.[32] Perhaps the function of the family in urban-industrial society will be delimited even more than it has to date, with the government and the school becoming more dominant in the socialization of children and their preparation for adult life. Some of the programs designed to enrich the lives of preschool children from deprived families seem to represent this approach to the problem.

There is a truism in political sociology that societies undergoing major social revolutions almost always (if not always) deemphasize the family and its influence on the next generation until the major changes sought in the revolution have been achieved. Russia did this in the 1920s, Nazi

---

31 See Arthur Pearl, "The Poverty of Psychology—An Indictment," in *Psychological Factors in Poverty*, ed. Vernon L. Allen (Chicago: Markham Publishing Co., 1970), pp. 357–59.

32 Some of these possibilities are explored in Peter Schrag's study, *Village School Downtown* (Boston: Beacon Press, 1967); see also Benjamin Fine, *Underachievers: How They Can Be Helped* (New York: E. P. Dutton & Co., 1967), chap. 11. There are also some interesting illustrations of new school programs in an earlier study by James Conant, *Slums and Suburbs* (New York: McGraw-Hill Book Co., 1961).

Germany did this in the 1930s, and Red China is doing this today.[33] To the extent that America is now in another socioeconomic revolution, perhaps the same strategy will be employed here—at least for a generation or so. And maybe the results will be better than some expect—the family, after all, is basically a conservative, if not a reactionary, type of group. It prepares much better for the past than it does for the future. In a society oriented toward the future, as is the United States, this inevitably produces certain problems. Perhaps some of these can be resolved or reduced by strengthening other social institutions rather than the family itself. To the extent that parents are relieved of some of their parental responsibility, the results may be therapeutic for all concerned.

Role theory and parenthood

With the arrival of the first child, the married couple assume a brand new role—that of father and mother. Even though most of them have looked forward to having a child, a significant proportion of them will find that they are poorly prepared for this new role, and some of them will even find that they are unable to function adequately as a parent.

Some of the difficulty experienced by many new parents will be related to what Wright calls "the discrepancy of expectations"—the role of parent will not be exactly as they had imagined it to be.[34] For some of them being a father or mother will be more satisfying than they had anticipated, while for others parenthood will be more frustrating than they could have imagined.

One source of difficulty related to the arrival of the first child is the fact that all through courtship and the childless years of marriage the young couple have functioned in a two-person (dyad) group, but now with the beginning of parenthood they find themselves in a three-person group (the triad). There is an old bit of folklore in our society which says that "two is company but three is a crowd"—the point being that a triad is infinitely more complex than a dyad.[35]

In a three-person group there is always the possibility that the group will subdivide. Two persons will form a subgroup and leave the third person more or less stranded.[36] The young wife, for example, may be so

---

[33] For a discussion of this point, see William J. Goode, *World Revolution and Family Patterns* (New York: Free Press, 1963).

[34] See Beatrice A. Wright, "Disability and Discrepancy of Expectations," in *Role Theory*, ed. Biddle and Thomas, pp. 159–64.

[35] For a discussion of the dyad and triad types of groups, see Theodore Caplow, *Two Against One: Coalitions in Triads* (Englewood Cliffs, N.J.: Prentice-Hall, Inc., 1968), p. vi: "In the primary triad of father, mother, and child, the foundation of a coalition may undermine paternal authority before the child is out of the cradle."

[36] While serving as a dean of students, the writer was impressed with the number of complaints received from students assigned to three-person rooms. Quite often two

enamoured of her new role as mother that she begins to neglect her role as wife. If this happens the husband-father may feel left out of the charmed circle.

It is quite easy for an American mother to overload her parental role and become a mommy—a woman who always gives priority to her children over her husband. This is a problem of "role balance"—dividing one's time and energy among the various roles that make claims on fathers and mothers.

In family counseling, one gets the impression that role balance for the American husband is most often jeopardized by his occupation, his male peer group, or some hobby such as fishing or golf. When this happens the wife feels neglected.

With the American wife it seems that role balance is often upset by becoming a mother. The baby is so small and helpless, and its needs are so great, that the husband loses all of the priority he formerly enjoyed with his wife. Whether it is sex or social companionship, he may begin to feel neglected and be jealous of the new child.

Toman has identified 64 basic types of conflict possible between a child and his or her parents.[37] It is literally true that children destroy some marriages, but the proportion is difficult (if not impossible) to determine. It is also true that children save some marriages, but here again the precise statistics are not available.

Arnold Green has argued that there are basic conflicts between the role of parent and other fundamental roles at the middle- and upper-class levels in our society.[38] The parent's drive for occupational mobility is often frustrated, Green thinks, by the presence of children. Green believes that parents at these class levels develop a deep ambivalence about their roles as mothers and fathers.[39]

Unfortunately, feelings of this nature are not uncovered in the house-to-house surveys of parents so often published in professional journals.[40] Being a parent is a sacred trust, one of life's deepest experiences, and

---

of the occupants would gang up on the third person and that student would request a new room assignment. This appeared to happen much less often in two-person rooms.

[37] Walter Toman, *Family Constellations* (New York: Springer Publishing Co., 1964).

[38] Green, *Middle-Class Male Child and Neurosis;* see also David F. Aberle and Kaspar D. Naegele, "Middle-Class Fathers' Occupational Role and Attitudes toward Children," *American Journal of Orthopsychiatry* **22** (April 1952): 366–78.

[39] It would seem that young fathers in the middle class are especially prone to role conflicts in that they are attempting to establish themselves in their occupational role at the very moment when their wives and children need them most. One can see this clearly on the college campus in talking with the wives of junior faculty members.

[40] We have reference to the material on parents found in survey studies such as Robert O. Blood, Jr., and Donald M. Wolfe, *Husbands and Wives* (New York: Free Press, 1960); this is a valuable study but it does not delve into the depths of parental feelings and conflicts.

persons do not readily admit the full range of their parental feelings. One mother said to us: "I love all of them and yet on certain days I felt like killing each and every one of them." The amazing thing about this statement is that this mother is actually a very competent parent—she has reared five children with what appears to be above-average results.

It may be that the stress of becoming a parent in our society is related to the fact that parenthood (not marriage) actually represents the last step in the long process of becoming an adult in American society. This may seem obvious, but the writer has the distinct impression that many young Americans feel that marriage itself is the last step into the adult world. This may indeed be the case legally, but is certainly is not true psychologically or socially. If this line of reasoning is sound, it would mean that the role of parent would present somewhat of a surprise to many young married couples—they may think they are fully grown up when in fact they have to prove it all over again when they become parents.

In the paper cited earlier, Green argues that the father's occupational role is often in conflict with his parental role. If this is true, a similar conflict would be found among employed mothers who still have children at home. We discuss this matter elsewhere and do not want to consider it here at any length, but it certainly seems to be true that economic efficiency is given so much priority in our society that it is difficult to imagine an American father neglecting his job (or refusing a promotion) out of deference to the needs of his children. Mothers undoubtedly do this, at great sacrifice to their occupational success, but fathers who did so would have to be regarded as deviants.

We do not wish to romanticize the farm family, but some observers have felt that the farm father has had an advantage over urban-industrial fathers in that his parental role is easier to integrate with his occupational role. This may be true, but farm parents have other problems in modern America that are analyzed in chapter 11.

Parents who run away

It is common to read in the daily press about children (mostly teen-agers) who have run away from their parents. It is not often, however, that one reads about parents who have run away from their children. Desertion of children, of course, is well known to social workers, but reference here is not to desertion but *escape:* parents who are willing to go on helping their children but who no longer wish to live with them.

In upper-class families, the above situation has never produced any problems—the annoying child was simply shipped off to somebody's boarding school. In the middle and lower classes, however, matters have never been that simple.

In the family described below a middle-class father and mother felt that they could not go on living with their three semiadult children. After much soul searching, the father accepted a position in another country for several years—in other words, until the children would be grown up and no longer living at home. The parents offered financial aid for the children who stayed in college and paid room and board for a high school youngster who chose not to go away with his parents.

The mother explained the situation to the writer as follows: "My husband had an excellent offer to work in this other country. At first we felt it was impossible because the children were still at home. Then we realized that the older ones no longer shared our values or our way of life— they had all become hippies of one kind or another and cared very little for what we thought or felt. We offered the youngest one a chance to go with us and he turned down the offer. It seemed to us that we had done what we could for the children and that the time had come to think of ourselves. So we decided to go."

These parents were criticized in their community for "deserting" their children, but the father and mother seem to have very little (if any) guilt over their action. They say that the children seem not to have been affected one way or another by the absence of the parents.

One of the deficiencies in our social structure is that we have no way for parents and children to separate "with honor" when they are not getting along—with the exception of the upper-class boarding-school system mentioned above. The same problem exists in our marriage system: husbands and wives cannot take a vacation from each other without gossip and criticism.

In any intense human relationship, such as that between parent and child, there are times when either the child or the parent (or both) need to get away for a time to think things over. In some human societies, this appears to have been provided for. A graduate student of the writer's claims, for example, that in an American Indian community in which she did social work it was not uncommon for a youngster to live with somebody else for a year when the home situation became too tense. Margaret Mead describes a society in which the young semiadult males have bachelor houses in which they live.[41]

The situation in our society is especially acute at the high school level, when the child is so close to adult status and yet so far. Some homes are literally armed camps during this period, with parents and children scarcely speaking to each other. With many states now lowering the age of adult status to 18, it would seem that some means will have to be

---

[41] See Margaret Mead, *Male and Female* (New York: William Morrow & Co., 1949).

devised to give adolescents a more secure move toward manhood and womanhood.

Summary and conclusion

In this chapter the position has been taken that the parental role in modern America is poorly defined, not well delimited, and that most fathers and mothers have had inadequate preparation for the role.

It was also suggested that parental authority has been eroded in our society over a period of several decades, without any reduction in parental responsibility. This development apparently reflects the "rights of children" movement since World War I and has resulted in some confusion as to the rights of parents.

Another major point is that the parental role in our society is harder to withdraw from than other major roles. The best illustration of this is the new right of Americans to discontinue marriages that they no longer find congenial. There has been no comparable development for parents.

The chapter closed with some consideration of role theory as related to parenthood and noted the appearance of a new type of American parent—fathers and mothers who are still willing to help their children but who no longer are willing to live with them.

chapter
five

Parents and
social class

In the past several decades, American social scientists have produced a mass of research on the behavior of the various socioeconomic levels in our society.[1] It is not implied in this material that all individuals or families at a given social level are identical in their beliefs and overt behavior, but simply that they tend to reflect a subculture or way of life evolved by the group over time. Some persons may be marginal members of their social class and reflect only partially its subculture. There may also be subcultures within subcultures: dentists and physicians, for example, are both members of the upper middle class in our society, but they each also have unique group-behavior patterns related to the different nature of their occupations. Dentists have regular hours, to cite one difference, while most physicians do not.

It should be understood clearly that, while the terms *upper* and *lower* are used to designate positions in the American social class structure, these are not meant by social scientists to reflect value judgments—they designate, for the most part, power and prestige, not moral worth.

Some levels of the social class structure have been studied more in-

---

[1] Herbert Gans has an extensive analysis of social class subcultures and family life in his study *The Urban Villagers* (New York: Free Press, 1962); see also Robin Williams, *American Society*, 3d ed. (New York: Alfred A. Knopf, 1970).

tensively than others: the middle class, for example, tends to be over-represented in much research, while the upper class is often missing entirely in many studies. In recent years special efforts have been made to reach low-income groups and to record their way of life.[2]

To the extent that American society is becoming a mass or homogenized society, the social class differences considered in this chapter may be diminishing, but at the moment this is a difficult matter to assess. Rural subculture, for example, may be disappearing, but at the same time other and new subcultures related to social class position may be evolving.[3] The reader needs to keep this in mind in considering the material presented in this chapter.

Our analysis will begin with parents at the bottom of the social class structure—fathers and mothers rearing their children at the poverty level.

Parents at the poverty level

The average American knows very little about persons at the poverty level.[4] Most college students have never met such a person or known such a family. In the affluent society, poor people are viewed as deviants —they really have no place in the society, and most of us do not know how we should view them. As Harrington pointed out long ago, most Americans would prefer not to see the poverty group and would like to forget that they exist.[5]

There is no universally accepted figure on the percentage of families living at the poverty level in American society. The problem is that authorities differ about what income a family needs to sustain a decent way of life in contemporary United States. It would appear, however, that at

---

[2] There is now a mass of material about poverty groups in American society; for an extensive summary, see Salvador Minuchin et al., *Families of the Slums* (New York: Basic Books, 1967); also Lee Rainwater, *Behind Ghetto Walls* (Chicago: Aldine Publishing Co., 1970); and David A. Schulz, *The Changing Family* (Englewood Cliffs, N.J.: Prentice-Hall, Inc., 1972).

[3] The black nationalist group illustrates an emergent subculture, see Stokely Carmichael and Charles V. Hamilton, *Black Power* (New York: Alfred A. Knopf, 1967). Another example of an emergent family subculture would be the commune; see Ross V. Peck et al., *The New Families* (New York: Basic Books, 1972); Richard Fairfield, *Communes USA* (Baltimore: Penguin Books, 1972); and Keith Melville, *Communes in the Counter Culture* (New York: William Morrow & Co., 1972).

[4] Rainwater has attempted to analyze the stance taken by the average American when he or she stops to think about the poverty group; see Lee Rainwater, "Neutralizing the Disinherited: Some Psychological Aspects of Understanding the Poor," in *Psychological Factors in Poverty*, Vernon L. Allen, ed. (Chicago: Markham Publishing Co., 1970).

[5] Michael Harrington, *The Other America* (New York: Macmillan Co., 1962); some people credit this book with having inspired the so-called war on poverty.

least a fourth of all American parents are rearing their children in some degree of poverty.[6]

The poor have often been romanticized in our society. As Rainwater points out in the paper cited above, the poor are viewed as being different biologically from the rest of us, or they are portrayed as happy and contented with their lot. Max Lerner comments on this as follows: "One image that we shall have to discard . . . is the romantic image of the lower lower class family as stable, integrated, and happy, while the middle-class is divorce ridden and neurotic."[7]

A mass of data can be cited to contradict the romantic folklore image of the lower class family—we cite only a few representative studies. In his classic analysis of divorce in Detroit after World War II, Goode found divorce highest in the low-income groups, and higher among black poor people than among white people of the same income level.[8] In their study of mental illness and social class, Hollingshead and Redlich found psychosis rates higher in lower-class families than in the middle or upper class.[9] In his analysis of school dropouts, Conant found much higher rates among the lower class.[10] Except for embezzlement, almost all forms of crime in modern America are highest in low-income groups.[11] Studies of physical disease find most ailments more frequent among low-income groups—this is especially true of such outmoded diseases as tuberculosis.[12] Surveys of dental care report over half of low-income children and adults to suffer from serious dental neglect.[13] Alcoholism has always been common among low-income groups, but in modern America it may be almost as common among middle- and upper-income groups.[14] Kinsey found premarital sexual experience to be highest among the lower class

---

[6] For one estimate of poverty in the United States, see Louis Ferman, Joyce Kornbluh, and Alan Haber, eds., *Poverty in America* (Ann Arbor: University of Michigan Press, 1965).

[7] Max Lerner, *America as a Civilization* (New York: Simon & Schuster, 1957), p. 558.

[8] See William J. Goode, *After Divorce* (New York: Free Press, 1956), chap. 4.

[9] See August B. Hollingshead and Frederick G. Redlich, *Social Class and Mental Illness* (New York: John Wiley & Sons, 1958); see also the analysis of Paul M. Roman and Harrison M. Trice, *Schizophrenia and the Poor* (Ithaca: New York School of Industrial Relations, 1967).

[10] See James Conant, *Slums and Suburbs* (New York: McGraw-Hill Book Co., 1961).

[11] See Marshall B. Clinard, *Sociology of Deviant Behavior,* rev. ed. (New York: Rinehart & Co., 1968), chaps. 6–9.

[12] This material is summarized in Alvin L. Schorr, *Slums and Social Insecurity* (Washington, D.C.: Government Printing Office, 1963), pp. 13–14.

[13] News release from Wisconsin Department of Public Health, Madison, Wisc., August 24, 1967.

[14] For an analysis of alcoholism and social class, see Harrison M. Trice, *Alcoholism in America* (New York: McGraw-Hill Book Co., 1966), pp. 21–24.

(persons who had not gone beyond the eighth grade in school).[15] Rejection rates for the armed forces are almost three times as high in the poverty group as they are for the middle and upper classes.[16] Public welfare recipient rates are, of course, highest among the low-income families.[17]

Poverty involves a host of conditions that low-income parents have to cope with in rearing their children. Some of their specific disadvantages are summarized in the next section.

High birth rates

As a group, poverty parents have more than their share of children to rear. As Rainwater and others have documented, low-income groups have less knowledge about family planning and less access to birth-control facilities than do middle- or upper-class parents.[18] This means that, in addition to their other handicaps, poverty parents are struggling with more children per parent than other social class groups in the society.

Slum neighborhoods

Studies have shown for a long time that certain behavior characterizes slum areas, regardless of what group happens to be living in the area at any given time. In their study, *Beyond the Melting Pot*, Glazer and Moynihan document the various behavior difficulties that have been endemic in certain slum areas of New York City, regardless of whether the area was inhabited by Italians, Negroes, Irish, or Puerto Ricans.[19]

Parents at the poverty level have little choice about what neighborhood they live in. They must enter the urban community at what the sociologists used to call "the point of least resistance." It is undoubtedly true that some low-income parents are quite adept at getting the best out of their social environment—as Pearl and Riessman argue—[20]but the fact remains that rearing children in a slum area is a challenge most parents would be happy to escape.

---

[15] Alfred C. Kinsey et al., *Sexual Behavior in the Human Male* (Philadelphia: W. B. Saunders Co., 1948), chap. 10; also Kinsey et al., *Sexual Behavior in the Human Female* (Philadelphia: W. B. Saunders Co., 1953), various chapters.

[16] See Alvin L. Schorr, *Poor Kids* (New York: Basic Books, 1966).

[17] Ibid.

[18] Lee Rainwater, *And the Poor Get Children* (Chicago: Quadrangle Books, 1960); also Leslie Westoff and Charles Westoff, *From Now to Zero* (Boston: Little, Brown & Co., 1971).

[19] Nathan Glazer and Daniel Patrick Moynihan, *Beyond the Melting Pot* (Cambridge, Mass.: Harvard University and M.I.T. Press, 1963).

[20] Arthur Pearl and Frank Riessman, *New Careers for the Poor* (New York: Free Press, 1965).

Inferior employment

Lower class mothers are more likely to seek outside employment if it is available; and, if they find it, the working hours, the wages, and the conditions of employment are apt to be less than ideal. Low-income black mothers in Chicago, for example, according to Drake and Cayton in *Black Metropolis*, are likely to be domestic servants, commuting long distances to the suburbs and working long hours, six days a week, with little or no vacation time off.[21]

These mothers face almost insuperable problems in rearing their children properly, regardless of their devotion to them. The proper conditions for good parenthood are simply not available.[22] The three-generation or extended-family system, with a grandmother or other relative in the home, has probably been the best defense these mothers have had for coping with their parental problems. But the three-generation or extended-family system has never been very popular in urban America, and this tends to mitigate against these mothers using this coping device.

If the lower-class father is living with the family, his employment is also likely to be sporadic and not of the best nature. His wages are relatively low, his skills are limited, and his unemployment rate is generally high.[23]

A majority of the poor white families live in poverty-striken rural areas, such as Appalachia, which offer very few, if any, public welfare or health services that might help these parents with their children.[24] The urban poor, bad as the ghetto is, have at least some public and private agencies to help them with some of their parental problems.[25]

One concludes that it is not only the low income that poses problems for lower-class parents; it is also the other conditions they have to contend with.

---

[21] St. Clair Drake and Horace R. Cayton, *Black Metropolis* (New York: Harcourt Brace & Co., 1945).

[22] One problem facing these mothers is the lack of adequate day-care facilities for their preschool children; see *Report on Day Care*, Child Welfare Report, no. 14 (Washington, D.C.: Government Printing Office, 1964). This report shows that in the 1960s for 3 million children under the age of six whose mothers worked outside of the home, there were only 185,000 places available in approved child-care centers for preschool children. There has been some improvement in this situation in the 1970s.

[23] For an excellent study of lower-class men, see Elliot Liebow, *Tally's Corner* (Boston: Little, Brown & Co., 1967).

[24] For a good summary of these problems, see Harry Caudill, "Appalachia: The Dismal Land," in *Poverty: Views from the Left*, ed. Jeremy Larner and Irving Howe (New York: William Morrow & Co., 1968), pp. 264–79.

[25] The writer is of the opinion that urban slums, bad as they are, offer some advantages over rural slums—chiefly in the superior welfare services offered in metropolitan areas; for an illustration, see Camille Jeffers, *Living Poor* (Ann Arbor, Mich.: Ann Arbor Publishers, 1967)—a participant-observation study of life in an urban low-income housing project.

Inadequate education

These lower-class parents do not usually have a high school education —if that is the right word for what American high schools have been giving their graduates since the 1920s. Many of them have not even completed the eighth grade. Some of them can not read or write. All of this means that they face almost insuperable handicaps in trying to understand the world they and their children live in, to say nothing of trying to cope with that world.[26]

There is another dimension to this handicap: they find it difficult, if not impossible, to retain the respect of their children, most of whom have more formal schooling than their parents, and this discrepancy is made more devastating by the fact that these children are living in a world in which a high school diploma is taken for granted.

It is certainly true, as Handlin and others have pointed out, that most of the earlier immigrant groups in America had this same sort of problem,[27] but those immigrants and their children were living in a very different kind of world—a world in which poverty was taken for granted and formal education was unusual rather than typical. The world of the earlier immigrant and his children was also less dangerous and less complicated: there were fewer laws to violate, there was (apparently) less serious juvenile delinquency, and certainly the expectations applied to these immigrant parents were lower and less harsh than those applied today.

The fact is that these low-income parents need desperately to get their children through the school system, yet they themselves usually did not graduate and they lack knowledge of how the system works. In a famous study, Hollingshead demonstrated how middle- and upper-class parents manage to keep their children in school, regardless of the child's mental capacity or his social behavior.[28]

Poor health

With a few exceptions such as heart attacks, there seems to be overwhelming evidence that the lower-class parent has more illness, both mental and physical, has less resistance to various diseases, has inferior

---

[26] Gans (*Urban Villagers*, chap. 11) says the lower class views the outside world with suspicion and distrust. In 1966 the median years of formal schooling completed by nonwhites in the United States was 9.2 years for persons over 25 years of age, see *U.S. Book of Facts* (Washington, D.C.: Government Printing Office, 1968), p. 116, table 158.

[27] Oscar Handlin, *The Uprooted* (Boston: Little, Brown & Co., 1952).

[28] August B. Hollingshead, *Elmtown's Youth* (New York: John Wiley & Sons, 1949).

medical and hospital care, and dies earlier than parents who hold a more favorable position in the class structure.[29]

Any person who has ever been a parent knows what it is like to try to take care of young children when the parent is not feeling well, and the situation is no different when trying to cope with an adolescent youngster under similar circumstances. In over a hundred parent-discussion groups conducted by the writer in the past several years, ill health was one of the items most often cited by fathers and mothers for not being able to live up to their own standards of parental performance.[30]

In some types of illness, such as tuberculosis, the illness often results in the afflicted parent being out of the home for considerable periods of time. This might also be true of mental illness.

For financial reasons, lower-class parents often go to work when ill when other parents would stay home. For the same reasons, they (and their children) often do not have medical attention when they should. These parents, because of their poor education and relatively low "social intelligence," are also preyed on by all sorts of medical quacks, such as patent-medicine vendors, chiropractors, and witch doctors. The money they do have to spend on medical care is often poorly spent.

Unstable marriages

It would seem that one of the crucial factors for the parental team is a stable marriage. If so, there appears to be evidence that marital instability rates are highest at the low-income levels. In one of the more impressive studies of divorce in our society, Goode concluded that divorce rates are inversely correlated with socioeconomic status—in other words, that divorce rates increase as income declines.[31] There also seems to be evidence that desertion rates are higher at the lower-class level.[32] To this list must be added the fact that the absent-father syndrome is also more common a low-income levels.[33] All this adds up to the fact that poverty parents are more than normally plagued with marital problems as they struggle to rear their children.

---

[29] For an analysis of the inferior health and inadequate medical services found among American black families, see Thomas F. Pettigrew, A Profile of the Negro American (Princeton, N.J.: D. Van Nostrand Co., 1964); also David R. Hunter, The Slums (New York: Free Press, 1964), chap. 7.

[30] The other item mentioned most often involved the problem of rearing children when spouses disagree about how they should be reared.

[31] Goode, After Divorce, chap. 4.

[32] See William M. Kephart, The Family, Society, and the Individual, 3d ed. (Boston: Houghton Mifflin Co., 1972).

[33] See Leonard Benson, "Fatherlessness," Fatherhood: A Sociological Perspective (New York: Random House, 1968), chap. 10.

Inadequate legal services

Numerous studies have demonstrated that low-income parents and their children do not receive their fair share of justice in America.[34] Children in the poverty group are more apt to be arrested for minor offenses in the community; when arrested they receive relatively poor legal defense; and when convicted the children of poverty families tend to receive more severe punishment.

Low-income parents have less knowledge of the legal system and are unable to afford the legal services that would protect them and their children against unfair treatment in the courts. This is in sharp contrast to parents at the middle- or upper-class levels.

Blue-collar parents

This section focuses on the stable, employed blue-collar parents: factory workers, plumbers, truck drivers, school custodians, and the like.[35] These persons work largely with their hands. As a rule their work involves the handling of physical objects rather than the manipulation of people. A good illustration would be the difference between a television-set repairman and a television-set salesman.

For most blue-collar jobs in modern America, a high school diploma would suffice. Incomes, however, often exceed those of white-collar workers. In the writer's suburban community, to cite only one example, licensed plumbers average $10,000–$12,000 a year, whereas public school teachers earn about $8,000 per year. (Income, of course, does not necessarily determine life style.)

There is considerable income range within the blue-collar world: some long-distance truck drivers may earn $20,000 per year, whereas other truck drivers may average less than $9,000. In some metropolitan centers, such as New York City, electricians may earn $30,000 per year or more if they get enough overtime. It needs to be remembered that if they are members of a trade union, these workers usually receive premium wages

---

[34] See Jacobus Tenbroek, ed., *The Law of the Poor* (San Francisco: Chandler Publishing Co., 1966); also *The Extension of Legal Services to the Poor* (Washington, D.C.: Government Printing Office, 1965); also the *U.S. Riot Commission Report* (New York: Bantam Books, 1968).

[35] A very useful collection of material on blue-collar workers will be found in Arthur B. Shostak and William Gomberg, eds., *Blue Collar World* (Englewood Cliffs, N.J.: Prentice-Hall, Inc., 1964); see also Arthur B. Shostak, *Blue-Collar Life* (New York: Random House, 1969). Mirra Komarovsky, in *Blue-Collar Marriage* (New York: Random House, 1964), has a detailed analysis of marriage at this social class level. Much of the material in the work by Gans (*Urban Villagers*) deals with blue-collar workers and their families.

for all time over 40 hours per week, plus double time for Saturdays, Sundays, and holidays.

One great advantage that many blue-collar workers have over most white-collar employees is their protection by powerful trade unions. Seniority rights protect them against persons lower in the hierarchy; fringe benefits cover their medical expenses; and dismissal must be for very specific violations of work rules.

In spite of the above advantages, however, blue-collar fathers and mothers have some very real problems in our society. These are analyzed in the next section.

Special problems of blue-collar parents

It was indicated earlier that there is considerable range of income, status, and security in the blue-collar world in contemporary America. The following discussion will have to be read with this in mind.

Some of the special problems of blue-collar parents are the following.

1. *The declining proportion of this segment of the population.* America is becoming increasingly a white-collar world. This is forcing the sons and daughters of these parents to move into white-collar occupations, which are increasing. For example, the steel workers' union has actually lost membership since World War II as the steel mills have been automated. The same situation prevails among printers, dock workers, and many other blue-collar work groups.[36] This means that the father may not be able to get his son into his union or into an apprenticeship; it also means that the blue-collar fathers and mothers are not as able to guide their children as the children move into a white-collar world. Such parents do not know as much about colleges, and they often do not push their children as hard in elementary or secondary school. It is simply harder for blue-collar parents to launch their children into the white-collar world than it was to help them get into a trade at the blue-collar level. Basically, such parents face the same problems farm parents face: most farm children will not be able to find a niche in agriculture, yet both they and their parents have grown up in a rural world.

2. *The percentage of mothers employed outside of the home tends to be somewhat higher at the blue-collar level.* Nye and Hoffman point out that this differential is not as pronounced as it was before World War II, but the fact remains that blue-collar mothers work outside of the home

---

36 For a brief summary of these trends, see George Meany, *Labor Looks at Capitalism*, AFL–CIO Publication, no. 139 (Washington, D.C., 1966). In 1956 the number of white-collar jobs exceeded blue-collar jobs for the first time in the United States; see Michael Harrington, "The Politics of Poverty," in *Poverty: Views from the Left*, ed. Jeremy Larner and Irving Howe (New York: William Morrow & Co., 1968), p. 18.

considerably more often than do mothers at some of the middle-class levels.[37] There is not much difference at the lower-middle-class level.

Blue-collar mothers have some compensating factors to offset their outside employment, however: they do not belong to as many voluntary organizations as do middle-class women and when they do belong they do not carry as much responsibility.

3. *Blue-collar parents have some social distance problems with their children.* All American parents have this problem to some extent because of rapid change and the vast amount of social mobility in the United States. But blue-collar parents suffer more from this situation due to the fact that their children are being forced to move into the white-collar world. This is quite different from the lower class, where vertical social mobility is relatively rare.

The value stretch between blue-collar fathers and mothers

There is some evidence that blue-collar fathers and mothers do not share the same goals and aspirations.[38] When employed, the mothers at this social level are usually in white-collar occupations, whereas the fathers are in blue-collar jobs. The mother, for example, may be a waitress or sales clerk—jobs that involve handling people—while the father spends his life handling physical objects. In addition, the mothers are constantly exposed to white-collar values and norms via the mass media, material that the fathers tend to ignore.

To the extent that the above is true, blue-collar parents may have more difficulty than white-collar parents in agreeing on goals for their children.

Blue-collar parents and the mass media

The vast majority of television programs, radio shows, magazine articles, and advertisements in our society focus on the white-collar world. An afternoon spent watching the traditional "soap opera" should confirm this for any reader. In the early 1970s CBS Television did develop a successful series featuring a blue-collar husband-father, but some labor leaders objected that the main male character, Archie Bunker, did not reflect credit on blue-collar workers.[39] In any event, blue-collar fathers and

---

[37] These data are reviewed in F. Ivan Nye and Lois Wladis Hoffman, *The Employed Mother in America* (Chicago: Rand McNally & Co., 1963), pp. 7–16.

[38] See Nathan Hurvitz, "Marital Strain in the Blue-Collar Family," in Shostak and Gomberg, *Blue-Collar World*, pp. 92–109. In a study of a blue-collar tavern (not yet published), the writer found only one wife in a blue-collar job.

[39] Reference is made to the CBS TV series, "All in the Family." Various labor leaders have been quoted in the daily press as not liking the character part of Archie Bunker.

mothers, and their children, seldom see their world reflected in the mass media.

It is difficult to assess the net impact of this virtual exclusion from the mass media; but, in the past, minority groups in the United States have complained that similar treatment of them has made it more difficult to achieve a positive self-image. Another possible effect is to make one unhappy with his world—if it is not worth portraying on television or in the movies, is it worth perpetuating?

Blue-collar parents are becoming a minority group

In the 19th century, America was essentially a blue-collar society—the millions of immigrants entered the social class system at the bottom and it often took them two to three generations to work their way up to the middle class.

This has now changed. The most rapidly expanding segments of the economy are white-collar, and blue-collar persons are becoming a minority group—just as farm parents have become. In the writer's metropolitan community, the public school superintendent has been quoted as saying, "We must stop counseling all high school students to go to college and remind them that blue-collar jobs are also rewarding and worthy of consideration."[40]

When all of the social leaders are white-collar, when the mass-media idols are white-collar, how does a blue-collar father or mother portray his or her way of life as something for a child to emulate or admire? It is a good question.

Middle-class parents

Some social scientists have argued that parental stress is greatest at the middle-class level.[41] Actually, there is a vast social distance within the white-collar middle class: it is a long way from clerking in a shopping center to being a surgeon, yet both are considered members of the "middle class."

In one sense it is always difficult to be in the middle—alternate models of behavior exist above and below and you have to carve out your own way of life. And yet, how many middle-class parents would be willing to trade places with parents at the poverty level?

In this section, attention will be focused on two segments of the mid-

---

[40] *Wisconsin State Journal*, July 5, 1972.

[41] See e.g., Arnold Green, "The Middle Class Male Child and Neurosis," *American Sociological Review* 11 (1946): 31–41; although based on very inadequate data, this paper has been widely cited as evidence that the middle-class family is "neurotic." See also Robert F. Winch, *The Modern Family* (New York: Holt, Rinehart & Winston, 1952); Winch's criticism of middle-class parents was considerably softened in later editions of this text.

dle class: parents at the bottom of the white-collar world, the so-called lower middle class, and parents at the top of the white collar world, the so-called upper middle class. There are also "middle" middle class parents, but space prohibits discussion of them in this volume.

Lower-middle-class parents

The lower middle class, the fastest growing social class in America, includes the woman who checks out your groceries at the supermarket, the receptionist at the motel registration desk, the waitress in your favorite restaurant, and the government clerk who checks your income-tax return. There are literally millions of new jobs at this level in the "consumer society."[42]

These lower-middle-class people may not have unions to bargain for them or protect them; hence, they are frequently subject to low wages, long hours, and job insecurity. To the extent that they can be unionized, they represent one of the largest labor pools available to the mass trade unions.

Some observers of modern America, such as Max Lerner, regard the lower middle class to be one of the least enviable positions in the contemporary social class system.[43] These people lack the pride of the old blue-collar aristocracy; they make less money; they have less skill to sell; and they lack job security. At the same time, they tend to identify with the more highly educated and prosperous white-collar groups above them.

Lower-middle-class parents are apt to face some very real problems. The wife-mother often works full time in an attempt to achieve the standard of consumption the family aspires to.[44] The marital failure rate at this socioeconomic level is relatively high.[45] These fathers and mothers tend to be ambitious for their children, pushing them toward college even though the parents themselves are not usually college graduates. If the children succeed in climbing the social class ladder, the family ties often suffer from vertical social class mobility.[46] The ability of the parents to guide their mobile children is limited by the fact that the par-

---

[42] Some of the features of the consumer society are discussed in John Kenneth Galbraith, *The Affluent Society* (Boston: Houghton Mifflin Co., 1958); see also Alvin Toffler, *Future Shock* (New York: Random House, 1970).

[43] Lerner, *America as a Civilization,* pp. 488–95.

[44] There is also a tendency for the father at this class level to moonlight (hold a second job) to achieve a decent standard of living.

[45] See Goode, *After Divorce,* chaps. 4 and 5.

[46] See E. E. LeMasters, "Social Class Mobility and Family Integration," *Marriage and Family Living* 16 (1954): 226–32. For a different version of this matter, see Eugene Litwak, "Extended Kin Relations in an Industrial Society," in *Social Structure and the Family,* ed. Ethel Shanas and Gordon F. Streib (Englewood Cliffs, N.J.: Prentice-Hall, Inc., 1965), pp. 290–323.

ents have never lived in the social world the children are moving into. As socialization for the child's new position proceeds, some of the ideas and values inculcated by the parents have to be discarded. This sometimes hurts the parents or the child or both. And in the process, sibling relationships are often weakened also.

It is never easy to be at the bottom of a social class—the people above you have many advantages that you can see (almost touch), and yet many of these patterns of life are beyond your reach. This produces a tendency for the lower middle class to spend more than it should and to strive for a way of life that may not be realistic for them. It is a wise father and mother who can foresee the pitfalls in the lower-middle-class world.

In one lower-middle-class family studied by the writer, the husband-father was manager of a meat department in a small supermarket. In order to earn more money, he worked four evenings a week, or about 80 hours every seven days. He also "moonlighted" as a bartender on week ends. The couple had purchased a beautiful house with heavy mortgage payments and a high interest rate (the interest rate was high because they did not have enough savings to make an adequate down payment on the house).

In addition to the new home, the couple were making payments on a new automobile, wall-to-wall carpeting, and a color television "console" ($800). When the husband could not make all of his monthly payments, the wife took a job at an all-night restaurant as a waitress. In addition to their excessive work schedules, this young couple (in their 30s) were attempting to rear four children.

Disaster was almost inevitable in this situation. One of the children became involved in a glue-sniffing incident, and when the juvenile-court judge learned of the work patterns of the parents he ordered them to spend a certain number of hours a week at home with their children. This, of course, made it impossible for the couple to sustain their standard of living—if it can be called "living." The crisis was finally resolved when the couple sold their expensive home and moved to a smaller community where the husband could earn an adequate living as a meat cutter.

It is not implied that this couple are typical of lower-middle-class parents. The case is presented to show what can happen when persons at this social class level become enamoured of a way of life beyond their reach.

Upper-middle-class parents

Gans takes the position that the upper middle class is perhaps the most confortable position in the American social class system.[47] Most of these

---

[47] See Gans, *The Urban Villagers,* p. 264.

parents are physicians, lawyers, accountants, business executives, or owners of successful moderately small enterprises (drug stores, for example). Incomes are comfortable but not large enough to make the family conspicuous in the community. The vast majority of the fathers and mothers in the upper middle class are college graduates, often with advanced degrees in some profession.[48]

With their income, these parents can choose the community in which to rear their children, can afford to send them to college, and, in general, can launch them into the competitive society.

It seems that stable marriages are another advantage enjoyed by these parents. In the survey cited above, less than 5 percent of the parents of upper-middle-class college students were reported to be divorced or separated.[49]

In spite of their many advantages, parents at the upper-middle-class level have some very real problems:

1. These parents have usually won their socioeconomic position by virtue of high levels of personal effort and achievement. Physicians, for example, have gone to college and medical school for 10–15 years before completing their training. Business executives have often begun their careers at modest levels and have worked their way up through some large corporate structure to get where they are—a process that often involves a decade or more of perseverance after completing college.

All of this effort pays off in the sense that these fathers and mothers can give their children many advantages, but they *cannot* assure them of a position in the upper middle class: the child has to win this position in the same way that the parents won it, through hard effort.

Here is an example: at the private college referred to earlier, the writer was adviser to a young man whose father was a gynecologist. It had always been the father's dream (shared by the son) that someday the boy would go through medical school and come home to join the father's medical practice. This dream became a nightmare when the son completed two years of a premedical program with a C average. At that point he was notified by the college's premedical counselor that he would never gain admission to a medical school and that he should explore other careers.

Notice that there is simply no way for a physician or an attorney to get his son or daughter into his own profession unless the child has at least some minimum level of ability and perseverance. This problem is

---

[48] These observations are based on a survey of 540 upper-middle-class students attending an expensive private liberal arts college where the writer was teaching (unpublished study completed in the late 1950s).

[49] For a more pessimistic view of marriage at the upper-middle-class level, see John Cuber and Peggy Haroff, *The Significant Americans* (New York: Appleton-Century, 1965); these authors believe that "psychological divorce" is common at this social class level.

not faced by upper class parents, who usually control enough wealth that they can guarantee the child's social position.

2. The other problem faced by upper-middle-class parents is the revolt on the part of their children that began in the 1960s and had become massive by the early 1970s. In this revolt the sons and daughters renounced the way of life of their parents as being too materialistic and sought other values and other goals.[50] Many of the upper-middle-class youngsters dropped out of college or refused to pursue long professional training programs. They dressed differently from their parents, used drugs other than alcohol for relaxation, and many of them experimented with sexual and marital patterns not approved by their parents. In sum, many of the children of upper-middle-class parents in the last several years have not found the way of life of their parents attractive.

Some of the difficulty in this parent-child gap is related to the fact that the children have relatively little faith in the future of human society as it is presently organized. They are not willing to struggle for 10–15 years to enter some profession, when they read almost daily in the press that the year 2000 may see the end of the world as we now know it. Their parents were not faced with such a catastrophic view of man's future—they felt that you could go to college for a decade or so and still have plenty of time to enjoy the rewards that would surely come when the training period was over. Their children, very often, are not convinced that this is the case. The children are also not convinced that the big house and the big cars are worth the rat race they involve.

It is not clear, as yet, how this dilemma of the upper-middle-class parent in the 1970s will be resolved.

Upper-class parents

On the surface it would seem that upper class parents have all the advantages: they have money, they have power, they can afford to hire persons to help with the care of their children, and they can assure their child of a secure place in the society, regardless of the child's ability. Actually, the situation is not that simple.

Hardly any systematic research appears to have been done on upper-class parents,[51] but some idea about their advantages and disadvantages can be gained from the numerous books about these people. For example, the various studies of the life of Winston Churchill reveal that as an infant he was cared for by a nanny (for whom he retained a lifelong affection), that he received his early education from a series of governesses

---

[50] Some features of this revolt are analyzed in Charles A. Reich, *The Greening of America* (New York: Random House, 1970).

[51] Even a superficial review of the literature on parents will reveal that almost all of the studies have focused on either the middle-class or blue-collar groups.

and tutors, that he was sent off to boarding school at the age of nine, and that he spent the rest of his youth either in boarding schools or in summer tutorial programs until he was ready for his military education.[52] The young Churchill's letters are full of pleadings that he be permitted to spend Christmas or the summer holidays at home instead of going off to France or Germany with some tutor.

The upper classes in Western society have never really reared their own children—they have always employed other persons to do most of the actual work in caring for their offspring. The late Duke of Windsor describes how he used to be permitted to spend exactly one hour a day with his parents (the king and queen) when he was a child.[53]

In the United States, Franklin D. Roosevelt was sent off to Groton preparatory school after having had a number of nurses, governesses, and tutors at Hyde Park.[54]

The upper classes in Western society have always been convinced that sons must be protected from their mothers. The current Prince of Wales, for example, has been sent to a number of spartan boarding schools with all-male faculties to assure that he would not be "spoiled" by his mother.[55]

One of the reasons why upper-class parents have had to have help with their children has been the heavy societal responsibilities that such parents carry. In Lash's study of the marriage of Eleanor and Franklin Roosevelt, he points out how difficult these parents found their child-rearing responsibilities when FDR was governor of New York State and later president of the United States.[56]

For the American upper-class child who does not behave properly, there have always been the military preparatory school for the boy and Miss Somebody's School for the errant daughter. This is an advantage that middle- and lower-class parents have never had.

In spite of all their advantages, upper-class parents in America appear to have the following problems:

1. "The shadow of the ancestor" often haunts the children of illustrious parents. Father or grandfather or grandmother or somebody among the ancestors left a legacy of accomplishment that the children (or the grand-

---

[52] All of the details will be found in the study of Churchill's mother: Ralph G. Martin, *Jennie*, 2 vols. (Englewood Cliffs, N.J.: Prentice-Hall, Inc., 1969–71).

[53] See Edward VIII, *A King's Story* (New York: G. P. Putnam's Sons, 1951).

[54] See John Gunther, *Roosevelt in Perspective* (New York: Harper & Bros., 1950). A very good discussion of how upper-class parents educate their children will be found in George C. Kirstein, *The Rich: Are They Different?* (Boston: Houghton Mifflin Co., 1968).

[55] Geoffrey Wakeford, *The Heir Apparent* (New York: A. S. Barnes & Co., 1967).

[56] See Joseph P. Lash, *Eleanor and Franklin* (New York: W. W. Norton & Co., 1971).

children) can not match. John D. Rockefeller, Jr., describes how he decided to leave the business world because he knew that in no way could he compete with the reputation of his father—the world's first billionaire. The son eventually achieved a significant and meaningful life in the field of philanthropy, establishing the Rockefeller Foundation.[57]

The children of Franklin and Eleanor Roosevelt faced this same problem of achieving some sort of self-identity: if you are a girl, what do you do with your life when your mother has been voted to be the outstanding woman of the world in her generation? And, if you are a boy, what do you do when your father has been elected president of the United States four times?[58]

Middle- and lower-class children have an advantage in that they have a chance to surpass the accomplishments of their parents. This is usually not possible at the upper-class level.

2. Wealthy parents have always had the problem of not spoiling their children. This is one reason why upper-class boarding schools have usually been known for their spartan characteristics—small rooms with little furniture; cold showers; modest food; early rising; and stern schoolmasters.[59]

Another related problem of upper-class parents is that of motivating their children to "do something" in this world, when the children already have everything that most people spend their lives struggling for.

3. Finally, upper-class parents and their children face the problem of notoriety—the merciless glare of publicity that hovers over them from cradle to grave. One of the writer's students in recent years was the daughter of the state governor (her father was also one of the wealthiest men in the state). This girl talked at length about newspaper photographers and reporters following her car, some of them hoping for material that could be used against her father politically. She described a minor automobile accident that made headlines all over the state when the reporter wrote that the governor's daughter had the accident "while returning from a wild cocktail party." The girl claimed that she had actually been attending a very mild social event at her sorority house.

While the writer was working on this chapter, the daily press was full of reports of a plot to kidnap John F. Kennedy, Jr., for ransom purposes. While such events may be relatively rare, prominent parents worry constantly that "something might happen" to their children.

---

[57] See Raymond B. Fosdick, *John D. Rockefeller, Jr.* (New York: Harper & Bros., 1956).

[58] These matters are considered in Lash, *Eleanor and Franklin.*

[59] See Kirstein, *The Rich.*

Summary and conclusion

In this chapter attention has been centered on parents at five different levels of American society: parents at the poverty level; blue-collar parents; lower- and upper-middle-class parents; and parents at the top of the social class system.

Students should remember that there are endless variations within these social class levels. The attempt here was to extract some general patterns that would often (but not always) be found at the different social class positions.

chapter
six

Minority-group
parents

"God knows how I ever raised them kids in that hell-hole," one
black mother said to us, "but somehow I got 'em raised and none of them
turned out too bad."[1]

This woman had migrated to the Middle West after her husband had
died in Mississippi. Friends and relatives helped her finance the move
(no furniture—just herself and her three children and a few personal
possessions).

She was fortunate in that she hit the North during World War II,
when labor was scarce, and she obtained immediate employment as cook
and baby-sitter for a wealthy white family. This family became fond of
her, and through them the two sons obtained employment when they
completed high school. A daughter is now married to a career man in the
armed forces. Thus, in one generation, this family moved up from the
rural South to the urban North and achieved solid blue-collar status.

The hell-hole referred to by the mother was the urban ghetto in which
she was forced to rear her children. While her actual living quarters were
not too bad, by her account, the neighborhood itself was dilapidated and
dangerous. She felt that in some ways it was harder to rear children in
the urban North than in the rural South, and yet she did not regret making the move.

---

[1] Statement by a woman who migrated from rural Mississippi to Wisconsin during
World War II.

To a certain extent this mother's story is typical of all minority-group parents: they move because conditions are not good where they are, and then they find that the situation in the new community is far from ideal also. Some of them, such as a great many Puerto Rican parents, decide that the move was a mistake and return to their former home.[2] But the vast majority stay and make the best of it in the new community.

For some, the move is disastrous. For others, if they can survive the first "culture shock," the move may prove eventually to have been a wise decision.[3]

In this chapter we wish to explore some of the problems that all minority-group parents have to struggle with in American society. In addition, attention will be given to the specific problems presented to the parents of particular minority groups.

First, however, let us look at the concept of minority group as the sociologists use it.

The concept of minority group

The main thing about minority-group status is that it always involves prejudice and discrimination.[4] Whether the parent is a Jew, a Roman Catholic, an American Indian, a Puerto Rican, an Afro-American—no matter what minority group a person belongs to, prejudice and discrimination are always involved.

Statistically, a minority group may actually constitute a majority of the population, as blacks do in many counties of the South (and as they now do in Washington, D.C.).

In terms of power, the minority group is always at a disadvantage. The dominant group controls the economic system, the political system, the police force, and so forth.

The basic image of the minority group which is projected by the dominant group is always one of inferiority, worthlessness, and potential violence.

And lastly, the dominant group always feels morally superior. It is not that they have ever mistreated the minority group. On the contrary, they

---

[2] Oscar Lewis, in the introduction to *La Vida* (New York: Random House, 1965), reports that in 1960 there were perhaps a million moves by Puerto Ricans to and from the United States with a net in-migration of about 20,000.

[3] In a beautiful book about an Italian village during World War II, there are several descriptions of peasants who had emigrated to the United States and then had returned to their village for one reason or another. Most of these people regretted not staying in America. See Carlo Levi, *Christ Stopped at Eboli* (New York: Farrar, Strauss & Co., 1947).

[4] For an analysis of the concept of minority group, see J. Milton Yinger, "Minority Groups, Castes, and Classes," *A Minority Group in American Society* (New York: McGraw-Hill Book Co., 1965), chap. 3.

have always been good to the minority group and cannot understand why these people are not grateful.

With this background, let us look at the generic problems experienced by all minority-group parents. This will be followed by a discussion of some of the relatively unique situations faced by parents in specific minority groups.

Generic problems of minority-group parents

All minority groups have problems, but they are not always the same problems. Jews in modern America, for example, do not usually suffer from lack of money or education, yet they face overt and covert prejudice and discrimination that take many forms—Jewish quotas in some of the better private colleges; restrictive deeds that in the past (and perhaps even today) have excluded them from desirable suburbs; anti-Semitic clauses in fraternity and sorority membership requirements that have forced Jewish students to form their own campus fraternal groups; country clubs that deny membership to Jews; private dining clubs that limit membership to Gentiles; resorts that are sold out if the person requesting reservations has a Jewish name; and even virtual exclusion from entire industries.[5] Jewish parents have to help their children cope with anti-Semitism as part of the process of growing up.

Briefly, what are the generic problems common to all minority-group parents in our society? They seem to the writer to be: residential segregation, slum housing, poverty, inadequate schools, unemployment (or under-employment), poor health (mental as well as physical), loss of civil rights, prejudice, discrimination, and the problem of self-image.[6]

An exception to most of the above, as we indicated earlier, would be the American Jewish parents of today, but their predecessors in the United States had their full share of ghetto life and all that goes with it.[7]

Space does not permit the full discussion of these generic problems of minority-group parents, but some of their dimensions will be dealt with as we look at the problems of specific groups.

---

[5] For an excellent study of how Jewish persons are discriminated against, see Judith R. Kramer and Seymour Leventman, *Children of the Gilded Ghetto* (New Haven: Yale University Press, 1961).

[6] For a good analysis of the problems of minority groups in general, see Yinger, *A Minority Group*. An excellent discussion is also to be found in Nathan Glazer and Daniel Patrick Moynihan, *Beyond the Melting Pot* (Cambridge, Mass.: M.I.T. Press, 1963).

[7] In various books, Harry Golden, the popular writer, has described conditions faced by early Jewish immigrants on the lower East Side of New York City; see also the autobiography of Alfred Kazin, *Starting Out in the Thirties* (Boston: Little, Brown & Co., 1965).

Afro-American parents

One scarcely needs to document the statement that black parents in the United States have faced severe problems in rearing their children since the day the first Afro-American walked ashore.[8] In the days of slavery, these difficulties were largely those of the mother, since black marriage was not recognized under slave law and black fathers were not accorded the status of parent.[9]

American society and the position of black parents have changed drastically since slave days, but the stresses on these parents remain severe. It is the purpose of this section to make these explicit.

1. *The generation gap between black parents and their children.* What would it be like to have grown up in rural Mississippi and be rearing your children in New York City or Denver or Los Angeles?

What would it be like to spend all of your early life in a rigidly segregated society and then try to rear your children in a partially integrated society?

What would it be like to grow up in the so-called lower lower class and then help your children work their way up into the world of a college education and a middle-class position in the society?

Black parents can best answer the preceding questions, for only they have lived through the racial revolution in the United States.

The so-called generation gap results from rapid and deep social change, which explains why the gap has been so prominent in the black family in our society since 1940.[10]

The "Uncle Tom" type of black parent who is afraid to insist on his rights as an American citizen can no longer retain the respect of his children; he must either join the revolt or be cast on the pile of discarded elders. It is not easy for parents to change their outlook on life, nor is it easy to watch your children man the barricades. These dilemmas are part

---

[8] For historical perspective on the problems of the black family in America, see E. Franklin Frazier, *The Negro Family in the United States* (New York: Dryden Press, 1966). Afro-Americans are by far the largest minority in the United States, constituting approximately 10–11 percent of the population in the 1970s.

[9] For an excellent discussion of the conditions under slavery in the United States, see Frank Tannenbaum, *Slave and Citizen* (New York: Alfred A. Knopf, 1946). The problems of the black father are considered in William H. Grier and Price M. Cobbs, *Black Rage* (New York: Basic Books, 1968); esp. chap. 4, "Acquiring Manhood."

[10] Some idea of the progress made by blacks in the United States since 1940 may be found in Thomas F. Pettigrew, *A Profile of the Negro American* (Princeton, N.J.: D. Van Nostrand Co., 1964). See also Andrew Billingsley, *Black Families in White America* (Englewood Cliffs, N.J.: Prentice-Hall, Inc., 1968); Billingsley argues that the black family has been amazingly stable in view of the conditions that black parents have had to cope with.

of the social gulf that separates the generations in the American black community.

2. *Geographical migration.* In the past several decades, several million Afro-Americans have moved—but not in the same way that most of us move. Many of these families went from the rural South to the urban ghettoes of the North and West—Washington, Philadelphia, New York, Boston, Chicago, Denver, Los Angeles, and Seattle.[11]

This constitutes one of the great migrations in the history of Western society. Beginning in World War I, it reached a peak during and after World War II.

Some of these parents had been urbanized in the South, but observers seem to think that it is still a long jump from Nashville or Birmingham to Chicago or Denver.[12]

In certain aspects, these migratory families are similar to the great waves of immigrants who moved to the United States from Europe during the era 1870–1920.[13] They are similar in that they tear up their roots and seek a new life in a new place. They are similar in that the parents grew up one place and the children will be growing up in the new place. They are also similar in that the migrant usually enters the social structure in the new home at the bottom—what the urban sociologists call the point of least resistance. This, of course, has always been the urban slum.

But the big difference between these black migrants and their white predecessors is that these people originally came from Africa, not Europe, and for this reason their reception in the new community was less than enthusiastic.

It is true, of course, that the black Americans were not the only new arrivals in American cities to meet with a cool reception. The "yellow" Chinese and Japanese were not exactly met by cheering crowds when they arrived on the West Coast and eventually moved inland, nor was the "red man" (the American Indian) ever greeted with any emotion except distrust and suspicion.

It is also true that the "swarthy" immigrants from Italy met with great hostility—partly because they were Roman Catholics but also because they were from southern Europe rather than northern Europe.[14]

---

[11] The net migration of blacks from the South to other parts of the United States is estimated to have been about 5 million from 1910 through 1966; see the *U.S. Riot Commission Report* (New York: Bantam Books, 1968), p. 240.

[12] Some material on the complicated move from the South to a city such as Chicago may be found in St. Clair Drake and Horace R. Cayton, *Black Metropolis* (New York: Harcourt, Brace & Co., 1945).

[13] Some of these problems are looked at in Oscar Handlin, *The Uprooted* (Boston: Little, Brown & Co., 1952).

[14] On Italians in the United States, see Glazer and Moynihan, *Beyond the Melting Pot;* on the American Indian, see William A. Brophy and Sophie D. Aberle, *The Indian: America's Unfinished Business* (Norman: University of Oklahoma Press,

six. Minority-group parents 91

But the black parents *were* unique in that their ancestors had been slaves, and part of the terrible price of slavery was that the black person's cultural heritage from Africa was literally obliterated. This was not true of the Italians or the Chinese or the Japanese—all of whom could pass on to their children the glory that had once been theirs. The black father or mother could not do this; all they knew was that they had once been slaves.[15]

3. *A negative self-image.* Afro-American parents, as we have just indicated, were not in a position to help their children achieve a positive self-image. In the United States they had only slavery to remember, and of their ancestral achievements in Africa they knew nothing.[16] Modern psychotherapy has demonstrated that a positive self-image is one of the prerequisites of mental health.[17] This was a gift that few black parents could give their children.

4. *A matriarchal family system.* Under slavery the black family was inevitably matriarchal because the black father was not recognized biologically, legally, or socially.[18]

Both Billingsley and Scanzoni, in their studies of the contemporary black family in America, stress the fact that the mother-centered family is *not* the dominant pattern of the black family in the United States of today —they claim that approximately 70 percent of black families have both parents present.[19]

5. *Residence in urban ghetto or rural South.* Relatively few black parents in America have ever enjoyed the privilege (or the advantage) of rearing their children in well-organized communities, with good housing, good schools, adequate recreation facilities, efficient police protection, and so forth.[20] Only a parent who has attempted to function in

---

1966); on the Japanese-Americans, a good discussion is available in Albert Q. Maisel, *They All Chose America* (New York: Thomas Nelson & Sons, 1957); on the Chinese-Americans, see B. L. Sung, *Mountain of Gold* (New York: Macmillan Co., 1967); also Gunther Barth, *Bitter Strength* (Cambridge, Mass.: Harvard University Press, 1964).

15 Another crucial difference is that the Afro-Americans did not choose to come to the United States; they were forced to come, while the other immigrants chose to come. Since the American Indian was already here and then had the land taken from him, his situation is different from all of the other minority groups.

16 Pettigrew (*Negro American;* see index: self-esteem), discusses the problem of the black's self-image in a number of places.

17 For an extensive discussion of the self-image and its relationship to personality adjustment, see Calvin S. Hall and Gardner Lindzey, "Rogers' Self Theory," *Theories of Personality* (New York: John Wiley & Sons, 1957), chap. 12; see also Lee Rainwater, "Crucible of Identity," *Daedalus* 95 (1965): 172–216.

18 Glazer and Moynihan (*Beyond the Melting Pot,* chap. 1) discuss the matriarchal family system; see also Frazier, *Negro Family.*

19 See Billingsley, *Black Families;* also John H. Scanzoni, *The Black Family in Modern Society* (Boston: Allyn & Bacon, 1971).

20 An excellent study of living conditions in an urban slum is that of Lee Rainwater, *Behind Ghetto Walls* (Chicago: Aldine Publishing Co., 1970); see also Alvin L.

either a rural slum or an urban ghetto can testify to the heroic efforts required of fathers and mothers to prevail against such odds.

6. *Outside employment of mothers.* In the United States about one family out of three has both parents in the labor force. In black families, however, the percentage is much higher, from 70 to 80 percent in the lower socioeconomic levels.[21]

This, of course, does not mean that such mothers necessarily neglect their children, but it certainly does mean that these mothers have to juggle a complex set of roles to fully discharge their parental responsibilities.

7. *Social welfare support.* In the early 1970s it was estimated that approximately 30 percent of black families in the United States were in the so-called poverty group.[22] This is about three times the rate for the general population. Scanzoni points out that this poverty tends to be correlated with mother-only family situations.[23]

Not all American families in the poverty group receive welfare aid, contrary to public belief, but to those that do receive welfare benefits the level of payment is extremely low. In the average state, a budget for a family of a certain size is adopted, and then the state determines what percentage of that budget they will pay—and seldom do they pay 100 percent.[24]

One of the results of such public policy is the failure of black children (and other children on welfare) to receive an adequate diet, which in turn affects growth and development in various ways.[25]

Puerto Rican parents

The Puerto Ricans are relatively unique among American minority groups in that most of them entered the United States as *citizens* (citizenship was conferred on all Puerto Rican residents in 1917).[26] Thus,

---

Schorr, *Slums and Social Insecurity* (Washington, D.C.: Government Printing Office, 1963).

[21] See Scanzoni, *Black Family;* also Alphonso Pinkney, *Black Americans* (Englewood Cliffs, N.J.: Prentice-Hall, Inc., 1969); and Charles V. Willie, ed., *The Family Life of Black People* (Columbus, Ohio: Charles E. Merrill Publishing Co., 1970).

[22] U.S. Census Bureau report, *New York Times,* July 12, 1972; this poverty figure uses a cut-off point of $4,150 income per year for a family of four.

[23] Scanzoni, *Black Family.*

[24] Schorr discusses this process of determining welfare budgets and payments in *Poor Kids* (New York: Basic Books, 1966).

[25] On the effects of diet on the growth of children, see Herbert G. Birch and Joan Dye Gussow, *Disadvantaged Children: Health, Nutrition, and School Failure* (New York: Grune & Stratton, 1970). On the general effects of poverty on black families, see Louis Kreisberg, *Mothers in Poverty* (Chicago: Aldine Publishing Co., 1970); also Andrew Billingsley and Jeanne M. Giovannoni, *Children of the Storm* (New York: Harcourt Brace Jovanovich, Inc., 1972).

[26] On the citizenship status of the Puerto Ricans and other relevant data about

they are different from the Afro-Americans, most of whom entered America as slaves, and also from the American Indian, who was conquered and not granted citizenship until 1924.[27]

Minority groups such as the American Chinese or the American Japanese had difficulty getting into the United States because of anti-Asian immigration laws, while the Puerto Ricans, being citizens, could enter and leave as they wished.

The American Indian had no choice about living in America since he was already here when the European whites got off the boats. The American blacks also had no choice because they were enslaved and transported to wherever the slave market was active.[28]

Tannenbaum makes an interesting point that the Indian in North America was never enslaved, at least not in large numbers.[29]

Puerto Ricans enjoyed two advantages when they migrated to the mainland, not only were they citizens on arrival, they also were accepted as *whites*, thus avoiding the racial caste barrier that has always plagued the Afro-American and the American Indian.[30]

Actually, some Puerto Ricans are a mixture of three different biological stocks—European, Indian, and African. But for the most part they are accepted as whites by the average American.

It is difficult to state exactly how many Puerto Ricans are in the United States at any given time due to the tendency for families to return to the island when economic conditions deteriorate in the United States. In the 1960s the estimate was about 1 million.[31]

Puerto Ricans have never been evenly distributed over America but have been concentrated in a few urban centers such as New York City.[32] This uneven distribution has produced two effects: (1) a feeling in the

them, see the following: Glazer and Moynihan, *Beyond the Melting Pot,* chap. 2; Lewis, *La Vida,* the lengthy introduction; Clarence Senior, *The Puerto Ricans* (Chicago: Quadrangle Books, 1965); and Oscar Handlin, *The Newcomers* (Cambridge, Mass.: Harvard University Press, 1959).

[27] For a discussion of the citizenship status of the American Indian, see Brophy and Aberle, *The Indian,* p. 16.

[28] Persons with very little knowledge of the slave trade and the conditions it imposed on blacks might find the following books useful: Daniel P. Mannix and Malcolm Cowley, *Black Cargoes: A History of the Atlantic Slave Trade* (New York: Viking Press, 1962); also James Pope-Hennessy, *Sins of the Fathers* (New York: Alfred A. Knopf, 1968.)

[29] For a discussion of the fact that Indians were seldom enslaved in the Americas, see Tannenbaum, *Slave and Citizen,* p. 41.

[30] Senior (*Puerto Ricans,* p. 46) reports that about 80 percent of the Puerto Ricans in the United States are classified as white by the Bureau of the Census.

[31] Lewis (*La Vida,* introduction) estimates that there were about 1 million Puerto Ricans in the United States in the 1960s.

[32] Lewis (*La Vida,* introduction) reported approximately 600,000 Puerto Ricans in New York City.

areas of concentration that the Puerto Ricans were invading the country, and (2) almost complete ignorance in the rest of the country of what a Puerto Rican is like.[33] This sort of situation tends to produce not only fear but widespread ignorance and misinformation.

1. *Language*. With a native language derived from Spanish, the Puerto Rican parent faces his first handicap. He can not help his child learn English (or American) because he does not speak the language himself. This puts the child at a serious disadvantage in the school system and perhaps in the labor market.

The language barrier also creates problems for the father or mother. They have difficulty communicating with the school officials, the public welfare workers, the police, and so on. Language problems have always plagued immigrant parents in America, and the Puerto Ricans are no exception.

2. *Matriarchal family system*. Oscar Lewis reports that among low-income Puerto Rican families the mother is the stable, dominant parent.[34]

There is nothing inherently wrong with a mother-centered family system, but with the father absent and the mother employed outside of the home this family system can be extremely vulnerable. This possibility is accentuated in the United States by the absence of the extended-kin network found in Puerto Rico itself.[35]

Among middle- or upper-class Puerto Ricans, of course, the family system is patriarchal; but these are relatively rare in the United States.

3. *Poverty*. Puerto Rican families in the United States are often at or near the poverty level.[36] This is nothing new to most of these parents because they were also poor in Puerto Rico—that was the main reason for migrating to America.

But being poor in your native land, surrounded by friends and relatives, is quite different from being poor in Spanish Harlem in New York City or the slum areas of Chicago.

It hardly needs to be repeated here that poverty symbolizes a host of related problems for parents, such as poor housing, inadequate schools, deteriorated neighborhoods, marginal jobs, less than average health, and skimpy police protection. Parents who can cope successfully with this list of problems deserve some sort of medal.

4. *Excessive fertility*. Most minority groups in the United States have

---

[33] See Senior, *Puerto Ricans*, pp. 37–40, for a discussion of this point.

[34] Lewis (*La Vida*, introduction) reports that 26 percent of the sample he studied in New York City had households headed by a woman; about half of the marriages in his New York sample were of the consensual or "free union" type.

[35] A comparison of the kin network and its functions in Puerto Rico versus that in New York City may be found in Lewis, *La Vida*.

[36] Senior (*Puerto Ricans*, p. 97) reports that Puerto Ricans in New York City are overrepresented in the poverty group about two and a half times.

higher than average birthrates.[37] In view of the setting in which these parents operate, the rearing of large families poses extremely difficult problems for Puerto Rican parents. Being Roman Catholics, these fathers and mothers lack the support of their church in using modern contraceptives, but some observers report a failure of Puerto Ricans to observe the Church's teaching on birth control.[38]

There is every reason to believe that Puerto Rican parents in the United States do a good job in view of the negative factors they have to cope with.

American Indian parents

As a group, American Indian parents probably face the most difficult situation of any parents in the United States. In some areas, as many as 90 percent of the Indian families are reported to be dependent on public welfare.[39] The infant mortality rate is several times the national average, depending on the particular disease.[40] School dropout rates, illiteracy rates, marital instability rates—all are greatly in excess of the national average.[41] Longevity is substantially lower than that of the Afro-Americans.[42]

Conditions vary, of course, from one tribe to another, but even the relatively well-to-do tribes, such as the Menominee in Wisconsin and the Navaho in the Southwest, are reported to be suffering from hunger and severe poverty.[43]

---

[37] The low-income birthrate of American blacks is about 30 percent higher than that of comparable whites according to Kingsley Davis; see his paper, "Some Demographic Aspects of Poverty in the United States," in *Poverty in America*, Margaret S. Gordon, ed. (San Francisco: Chandler Publishing Co., 1965), pp. 299–319. Brophy and Aberle (*The Indian*, pp. 162–63) say that the American Indian birthrate is about double that of the general population. Handlin (*The Newcomers*, pp. 57–58) says that the birthrate of the Puerto Rican in America is "high."

[38] Senior (*Puerto Ricans*, pp. 108–9) says that, while Puerto Ricans in America are largely Roman Catholic, only about 25 percent attend church—hence their attitude toward birth control does not necessarily reflect that of the church.

[39] Brophy and Aberle (*The Indian*, pp. 70–72) report that for the period 1959–60 three times as many Indian families were dependent on public welfare as compared with the rest of the nation.

[40] Brophy and Aberle (*The Indian*, p. 163) report that in 1944 infant mortality among American Indians was three times that of the national average; by 1957–59 the rate had dropped to about twice the national average.

[41] For a general review of the current status of the American Indian, see Brophy and Aberle, *The Indian;* this is the final report of the Commission on the Rights, Liberties, and Responsibilities of the American Indian.

[42] Pettigrew (*Negro American*, p. 99) reports that in 1900 average nonwhites in the United States had a life expectancy of 32–35 years. By 1960 this had increased to 61–66 years, which is still 6–8 years less than that of whites. Indian longevity lags behind that of American blacks, however.

[43] On the precarious condition of the Menominee, reported to be one of the more affluent tribes, see Joyce M. Erdman, *Wisconsin Indians* (Madison, Wisc.: Governor's

The American Indian has never been accepted as an equal by other Americans. He was not even granted full citizenship until 1924—seven years after Puerto Ricans were given their citizenship and over a half century after the blacks in America had been granted citizenship.

Tragically, the American Indian found, as did the Afro-American, that legal rights and actual rights are far from being the same thing.

The following problems would seem to face Indian fathers and mothers as they try to accept their parental responsibilities in modern America.

1. *Language problems.* The children often learn a language at home that is not used at school or in the larger society. As Brophy and Aberle point out, the Indian languages view the world in ways quite foreign to most Americans, and this greatly complicates the adjustment of the Indian child in the public school system.[44]

Language problems have always plagued new arrivals in America, except for the English-speaking settlers of the colonial era. But most of these other groups learned English (or American) rather rapidly because they had to in order to survive in the open society. The Indian, however, the first to arrive on these shores, was not forced to learn the language of the invaders because he was shunted off to isolated reservations, where he continued to use his own language. This may have helped to preserve some small part of his cultural heritage, but it also complicated his dealings with the outside world.

2. *The reservation system.* About three fourths of all American Indians were still living on reservations in the early 1970s.[45] The other one fourth have migrated to metropolitan centers.

The reservation system accomplished its original purpose: it put Indians away, where the rest of Americans would not have to interact with them and, in effect, could forget about them.

From the Indian's point of view the reservation system has been a disaster: it did not really preserve Indian cultures; it did not produce viable Indian communities; and, at the same time, it prevented the Indian from participating in the larger American society.[46]

3. *Culture conflict.* Among the hundreds of Indian tribes in the United States, there are innumerable conflicts between the historic cul-

---

Commission on Human Rights, 1966); some of the problems of the Navaho are discussed in Brophy and Aberle, *The Indian,* various chapters.

[44] The language problems of Indian school children are reviewed in Brophy and Aberle, *The Indian;* see also William T. Hagan, *American Indians* (Chicago: University of Chicago Press, 1961).

[45] For a discussion of reservation Indians and urban Indians, see Vine Deloria, Jr., *Custer Died for Your Sins* (New York: Macmillan Co., 1969).

[46] On the failure of the reservation system, see Dale Van Every, *Disinherited* (New York: William Morrow & Co., 1966).

ture of the tribes and that of the larger society.[47] These include not only language but also marriage and family systems, child-rearing practices, property ownership, religious faith, and so on.

Parents face the difficult task of living in and rearing their children for two different worlds. The more the child learns about his tribal culture, the stranger the outside world appears to be. Some minority groups in the United States, such as the Jews, seem to be able to preserve their own subculture while competing successfully in the larger society. To date few American Indians have been able to do this.

4. *Poverty.* The amount of poverty among American Indians is almost beyond belief. In some counties in the United States, some 80 percent of all Indian families are eligible for public welfare. It has been estimated that the Indian has a poverty rate approximately four times higher than that of the general population in American society.[48]

It is not only the inconvenience and the embarrassment of not having money—it is also the self-degradation. As Harrington makes clear, the day of the "honest and deserving poor" has long since departed in the United States.[49] Poverty today has a moral tone it did not have in an earlier America. Only the hippies, it seems, can live at the poverty level in our society and feel superior, but this is partly because they came from affluent homes. It is extremely difficult to laugh at money if you have never had much of it.

Poverty affects all phases of Indian life, such as housing, food, medical and dental care, education, and clothes.[50] Welfare programs help Indian parents meet some of these needs, but only at a bare subsistence level.

5. *Self-image.* Psychotherapists tell us that a negative self-image is one of the traits found in the emotionally disturbed person in our society.[51] In view of the Indian's position in modern America, it would be odd if he did not have a self-image that was destructive.

---

[47] For a discussion of culture conflict between Indians and white society, see Aberle and Brophy, *The Indian;* also Dee Brown, *Bury My Heart at Wounded Knee* (New York: Holt, Rinehart & Winston, 1970).

[48] The poverty data on American Indians is discussed in Brophy and Aberle, *The Indian.*

[49] One of Harrington's main points in *The Other America* is that being poor in our society is no longer respectable. The "honest but deserving poor" have been obliterated in affluent America.

[50] Surveys of the Menominee Indians in Wisconsin have revealed that, in the late 1960s, at least 70 percent of the children in this group were in immediate need of dental care (Wisconsin Department of Health and Social Service, personal communication). In the book by Erdman, (*Wisconsin Indians,* p. 57) the statement is made: "Indian health is approximately a generation behind that of the non-Indian population in Wisconsin."

[51] For an interesting discussion of identity problems among American Indians, see Erik H. Erikson, "Childhood in Two American Indian Tribes," *Childhood and Society,* 2d ed. (New York: W. W. Norton, 1963), Part II.

98   Parents in modern America

The late Senator Robert Kennedy, in 1968, reported that in one Indian tribe in Idaho the suicide rate was 100 times the national average.[52] If true, this is in sharp contrast to the suicide rate among Afro-Americans, which Pettigrew reports to be lower than that of whites.[53]

The American black community is in the process of rediscovering its African heritage and is using this to help restore self-respect and a sense of identity. It would seem that the American Indian needs very much to do this also.

5. *Excessive fertility.* It is reported that the birthrate of the American Indian in the 1960s was approximately double that of the general population.[54] It is difficult to see how Indian parents can hope to solve their problems at this fertility level. Perhaps new contraceptive methods and new attitudes toward planned parenthood will help to solve this problem.

6. *Smallness of group.* It is difficult to obtain accurate figures on the total number of Indians in America. One reason is the difficulty of defining who is an American Indian.[55] In the 1960s the United States Bureau of Indian Affairs calculated that there were 500,000–600,000 Indians on and off of the reservations, but by the 1970 census the number of persons listing themselves as Indians had jumped to approximately 1 million.[56] One theory about the increase is that Indians are beginning to recover pride in their cultural heritage and are now willing to identify themselves as being of Indian descent.

Being less than 1 percent of our population, Indians find that most other Americans have never known a real live Indian; ideas about them are formed from television programs and Hollywood movies.[57] This, of course, produces gross distortion of what Indians are like. Most college students, for example, have never had a high school or college friend from the Indian community.

The smallness of their population also places Indians in a power deficit: there literally are not enough Indians for the rest of the population to be afraid of. There are also not enough Indian votes in most states to be a decisive factor in political elections. This type of problem can only

---

[52] In a *Milwaukee Journal* news release, April 5, 1968, it was stated that the Indian suicide rate in Idaho is 100 times the national average. The writer has been unable to confirm this figure from other sources.

[53] Pettigrew (*Negro American,* pp. 77–78) reports that for the period 1949–51 the black suicide rate in the United States was only 42 percent that of the white.

[54] Brophy and Aberle (*The Indian,* pp. 162–63) state that the Indian birthrate is at least twice that of the national average and perhaps higher.

[55] Brophy and Aberle (*The Indian*) discuss the problem of defining who is an Indian and of determining the number of Indians in American society.

[56] Census Bureau news release, *New York Times,* April 17, 1971.

[57] See Deloria, *Custer,* for a discussion of white stereotypes about Indians.

be solved by Indians forming a political alliance with other minority groups. In the past this has proved to be very difficult.[58]

Van Every points out that historically Indians have found it very difficult to work effectively as a group—because there are several hundred distinct tribes with different languages, diverse cultures, and separated by thousands of miles.[59] In recent years valiant efforts have been made to unite the American Indians, but that has proven to be a difficult task.[60]

Problems of American Jewish parents

1. *Religion.* Regardless of what other cultural differences they may have, most of the minority groups in America are nominally Christians. The society was founded and populated largely by Protestants and Catholics, and these groups have shaped the basic institutions and are largely responsible for its tone.[61] Jews, no matter what their degree of orthodoxy, are thus a distinct religious minority. At one time or another, Jews have been persecuted in almost every nation in Western society.

It is easy to underestimate the depth and strength of anti-Semitism in the modern world, but those who do have forgotten too soon the atrocities of World War II.

Jewish parents are not naïve about their tenuous position in a civilization founded by the followers of Christ. Most of their ancestors suffered at one time or another at the hands of Christians who profess nothing but love for their fellowman.

The problem, then, for American Jewish parents is to somehow help their children preserve their own cultural heritage without seeming to feel odd in the society. One Jewish father said to the writer: "At times I am inclined to doubt that it is worth the trouble (and the potential danger) of preserving our Jewish subculture—I am tempted to join the Methodist church and not even have my boy circumcised."

It takes a nice balance and a gentle touch for American Jewish parents

---

[58] The "poor people's march on Washington," in the summer of 1968, represented one of the first efforts of the American Indian to work with American blacks to solve or alleviate their mutual problems. Steiner, chap. 19, has an extensive discussion of this matter.

[59] Van Every argues that the Indians could have defeated the Europeans when they first invaded America if they had been united.

[60] Deloria, *Custer,* and Steiner, discuss the effort to combine all Indians into one effective political force.

[61] A good analysis of the three major religious groups in our society may be found in Will Herberg, *Protestant, Catholic, Jew* (New York: Doubleday & Co., 1956). A very useful recent book on Jews in America is the work of Sidney Goldstein and Calvin Goldscheider, *Jewish Americans* (Englewood Cliffs, N.J.: Prentice-Hall, Inc., 1968); see also Glazer and Moynihan, "The Jews," *Beyond the Melting Pot,* chap. 3.

to help their children become not only good Americans but also good Jews. It is the perennial plight of the small religious minority that faces Jewish parents in our society.

2. *Racism.* The average American thinks of Jews as a separate race in the same way that Afro-Americans are considered to be a distinct race. Social scientists have argued for decades that Jews are a cultural group, not a separate and distinct race, but this message seems not to have filtered down to the average citizen.

Thus, in a very real sense, Jews in our society have suffered from racism as have the blacks and the American Indians.

All sorts of negative qualities have been attributed to Jews by racists, and Jewish parents have the problem of helping their children understand the nature of those Americans who hold such beliefs.

It is no accident that the Ku Klux Klan in the United States has always been bitterly anti-Semitic. This is part of the racist attack on minority groups.

3. *The problem of success.* American blacks, as well as American Indians, have usually been accused of being lazy or lacking in ambition. Jews in our society are criticized for being just the opposite. They are condemned for being too aggressive, too clannish, and so forth.

In a sense, the ability of the American Jew to compete in our society has been used against him. Although as a group they have one of the highest standards of living in the United States today, many Americans forget that the average Jewish immigrant entered our society at the bottom and that their affluence today often represents several generations of effort.[62]

4. *Miscellaneous problems.* Jewish children, as other minority-group children, never know when they will run into prejudice and discrimination. When this happens, the child is confused and hurt. Parents have to help their children understand such treatment and to respond appropriately.

The problem of interfaith marriage is a constant one for American Jewish parents. In some communities their children can simply not find suitable marriage partners of their own faith. One Jewish college girl put this to the writer in these words: "I come from the deep South. My father owns a beautiful clothing store in this town of 35,000 and we are the only Jewish family in that town. I was sent up here to meet 'a nice Jewish boy' and you know what happened? I fell in love with a Protestant boy whose

---

[62] Glazer and Moynihan (*Beyond the Melting Pot*), have a treatment of Jewish history in New York City; Goldstein and Goldscheider (*Jewish Americans*) have an analysis of three generations of Jews in Providence, Rhode Island. Kramer and Leventman (*Children of the Gilded Ghetto*) have a three-generation analysis of Jews in the Saint Paul–Minneapolis metropolitan area.

parents don't have a dime. We are engaged and my mother is about to have a stroke."

These are real problems for any small minority, and parents have to be flexible and imaginative to cope with them.

The American Jewish community is by no means united or homogenous. There are wide variations in religious orthodoxy as well as vast differences in social class position. This heterogeneity within a relatively small minority poses its own problems for Jewish parents.

Problems of other minority-group parents

It is an interesting and puzzling fact that Chinese and Japanese parents have done quite well in the United States in the face of extreme prejudice and discrimination.[63] It is true that these people did not enter the society as slaves, as the Afro-Americans did, but as Asiatics they suffered from the same racist attitudes that have plagued American blacks and American Indians. As late as World War II, the Japanese-Americans were confined to what were essentially concentration camps, no matter what the government called them.

Another minority group, the Mexican-Americans, have not done nearly so well, the bulk of them still being at the poverty level.[64]

Why have some minority group parents done so well, while others have made relatively little progress? It seems to the writer that social scientists are not, as yet, prepared to answer this question, but an analysis of the strategies employed by the successful minority parents may provide some clues.

Successful strategies for coping with problems

1. *Reduction of family size.* The minority group having the highest standard of living in the United States, the Jews, also has the lowest

---

[63] On the phenomenal success of the Japanese in the United States, see Maisel, "The Japanese," *They All Chose America,* chap. 9, p. 133; Maisel reports that in recent decades almost 50 percent of American-Japanese children of college age have been enrolled in college. In their study of Jews in Providence, Rhode Island, Goldstein and Goldscheider (*Jewish American,* p. 65) found that 41 percent of the Jews in this community had attended college, compared with 13 percent of the general population in Providence. In her study of the American-Chinese, Sung (*Mountain of Gold,* p. 125) reports considerably above average educational attainment for this minority group—as of 1960 16.7 percent of the males in this group had completed four or more years of college, compared with 8.0 percent for American whites and 2.2 percent for American blacks.

[64] In the famous CBS television broadcast called "Hunger in America," June 16, 1968, the statement is made that in San Antonio, Texas, with a Mexican-American population of about 400,000, "a quarter of San Antonio's Mexican-Americans, 100,000 people, are hungry all the time" (see p. 1 of the script released by CBS).

birthrate.[65] The four groups with the lowest standard of living—Negroes, Indians, Puerto Ricans, Mexican-Americans—all have relatively high birthrates.[66]

Middle-class blacks, in contrast, are reported to have birthrates below that of middle-class whites.[67]

In an urban society in which children are an economic liability, only the most capable parents seem to be able to rear large families with any degree of success. In a provocative book, Schorr argues that four children seem to be the maximum number that most low-income American parents can manage—above that number problems seem to predominate.[68]

Religious affiliation may be a factor in the relatively high birthrates of the Puerto Rican or some American Indians, but this is not the case with most American blacks. It would seem that the relatively high fertility of this group reflects two basic factors: (1) recent migration from the rural South, and (2) lower-class subculture.[69]

Whatever the causes of high birthrates for various minority groups, it seems unlikely that these parents can cope with their problems unless (and until) they have smaller families.

2. *Major stress on education.* As of 1955 about 62 percent of all Jewish children of college age were reported to be in college in the United States; this compares with 26 percent of the general population in college.[70] About the same time, the percentage of Chinese and Japanese

---

[65] Goldstein and Goldscheider (*Jewish Americans*, p. 118) report that Jews in America have consistently used contraceptives more widely and more efficiently than any other population group in the United States. They say: "Jews have the smallest families, marry later, expect and desire to have the smallest families, approve the use of contraception, are most likely to plan the number and spacing of all their children, and are most likely to use effective methods of contraception."

[66] Brophy and Aberle (*The Indian*) were cited previously to the effect that American Indian birthrates are at least twice the national average; Kingsley Davis, "Some Demographic Aspects of Poverty in the United States," in Margaret S. Gordon, ed., *Poverty in America* [San Francisco, Chandler Publishing Co., 1965], pp. 299–319, reports that the black birthrate in the United States is about 30 percent higher than that of whites at lower class levels; Maisel (*They All Chose America*, pp. 172–84) discusses the relatively high birthrate of the Mexican-Americans. Handlin (*The Newcomers*, pp. 57–58) points out that both the Negroes and the Puerto Ricans in New York City have higher than average birthrates.

[67] American black families at the middle-class level do not have excessive birthrates. In fact they may average fewer children than white families of the same social class level (see Davis, *Poverty in America*, pp. 299–319).

[68] On family size and family disorganization at lower levels, Schorr (*Poor Kids*, p. 38) says: "There is a sprinkling of evidence that the fourth or fifth child represents a point of no return for poor families." He goes on to point out that about seven out of every ten youths rejected for the armed forces come from families with four or more children.

[69] For a good study of birth control at lower-class levels, see Lee Rainwater, *And the Poor Get Children* (Chicago: Quadrangle Books, 1960).

[70] Maisel, *They All Chose America*, p. 133.

children of college age actually attending college was estimated to be 40–50 percent.[71]

In recent years in the United States, nonwhites have averaged only about 7.9 years of formal education.[72] There was a time in America when parents and their children did not need extensive schooling, but that time has long since passed.

It is true, of course, that Afro-Americans, Indians, and other minority groups have not found the American educational system well suited to their needs,[73] but unless they can work out some solution to their educational problems their competitive chances in the society do not appear very bright.

3. *Urban residence.* In the last 75 years the immigrant groups that have moved up into the mainstream of American society have found their opportunity in urban America. Once the frontier was closed and the free land exhausted, there was relatively little opportunity for new arrivals in rural America.

Afro-Americans and American Indians are not, of course, new arrivals, but since World War II the Negro has become one of the most urbanized groups in the United States. The cities have not solved his problems, but substantial improvement in his condition can be shown for the period since 1940—when the mass move to the city began.[74]

Groups that have done quite well in America, the Jews, Chinese, and Japanese, are all highly urbanized. In fact, nine out of ten Jewish families are reported to live in cities.[75]

It is an interesting fact that the minority group with the lowest standard of living in modern America—the Indians—are overwhelmingly rural in residence.[76]

Immigrants and migrants do not find the cities of America waiting with open arms, but if they can resist the initial culture shock they seem

---

[71] Ibid.

[72] Kenneth B. Clark and Talcott Parsons, eds., *The Negro American* (Boston: Beacon Press, 1966), p. 84, report that in 1960 nonwhite males had an average of 7.9 years of schooling compared with 10.6 for whites. On the inequalities in our educational system, see James Coleman, *Coleman Report on Equality of Educational Opportunity* (Washington, D.C.: Office of Education, 1965).

[73] For an extensive analysis of the failure of the New York City public schools to meet the needs of minority group children, see David Rogers, *110 Livingston Street: Politics and Bureaucracy in the New York City School System* (New York: Random House, 1968).

[74] Pettigrew (*Negro American*) has data on the progress made by American blacks since 1940.

[75] See Milton M. Gordon, *Assimilation in American Life* (New York: Oxford University Press, 1964), pp. 174–75, for a discussion of urbanization and American Jews.

[76] The evidence on the lack of urbanization among the American Indian may be found in various chapters of the Brophy and Aberle study (*The Indian*). About two thirds of the Indians still live on or near a reservation.

to move up within two or three generations. The Irish did it; the Italians did it; the Jews did it; so did the Chinese and Japanese. All of these groups were despised by the White Anglo-Saxon Protestants (WASPS) at one time, yet today hold a respected place in American society.

Perhaps the writer is too optimistic and underestimates the depth of racism in our society. Yet any one who lived through the anti-Catholic hatred of the 1920s, as the writer did,[77] can hardly believe the peaceful coexistence of Protestants and Roman Catholics today. And anybody who saw the hatred of the Japanese-American during World War II would find it difficult to see the position of this group in American society today.

With all of its faults, the large city has been the most receptive community in our society to families that were different. It is to be hoped that this welcome has not worn out.

4. *Extended-family system.* Some of the ethnic minorities, such as the Italians and the Jews, seem to have survived their first encounter with the large city by a process of doubling up—new arrivals moved in with relatives already established; mothers held outside jobs; older brothers and sisters helped younger children to get a start.[78] This system of mutual aid seems to be extremely functional for low-income families. Resources are shared until each family can care for its own.

5. *Political power.* Some of the earlier minority groups, such as the Irish and the Italians, achieved power and respectability by means of political activity. They infiltrated the political machines of the metropolis and literally took over. Now that blacks are winning the right to vote and are becoming politically astute it would seem that they too could make themselves felt in the legislative halls and the city council chambers.[79] With a population of 10–11 percent of the total electorate (when they are all permitted to vote), the blacks are almost in the position of deciding who shall be president of the United States. The two major political parties are so equal in strength—outside of the South—that the black vote can make the difference.

The smaller minorities, such as the Indian, can only hope to exercise political influence by forming a coalition with other underprivileged

---

[77] The writer witnessed hatred of Catholics and violence toward them while growing up in a Ku Klux Klan home in a small city in Ohio in the 1920s. Returning to this community in the 1960s, one finds that many of the children of these parents who hated each other have intermarried and the community itself reflects little tension between Protestants and Roman Catholics.

[78] In the word by Kazin (*Starting Out*) this doubling-up process among early Jewish immigrants is described; see also the same extended-family system as it worked in the home of Richard Wright, the black writer, as described by Constance Webb in *Richard Wright* (New York: G. P. Putnam's Sons, 1968).

[79] Kenneth Clark, in *Dark Ghetto* (New York: Harper & Row, 1965), pp. 154–68, analyzes the political possibilities and some of the related problems in the political efforts of blacks in the urban ghetto.

groups. If such an alignment could ever be worked out, it would constitute a formidable political force.[80]

Conclusion and summary

In this chapter an attempt was made to identify the generic problems
of all minority group parents as well as those of specific groups.

To some extent, these problems resemble those of all lower-class parents, discussed in the previous chapter, but there are also differences.
Frequent reference was made in this chapter to the struggles of earlier
immigrant groups, such as the Italians, who in their day had to cope with
suspicion, hostility, prejudice, and discrimination also.

The chapter closed with a review of some of the strategies that have
been proven effective by minority-group parents who are now firmly
established in American society.

---

[80] Senior (*Puerto Ricans*, p. 18) states that about one sixth of all Americans belong
to one minority or another.

chapter
seven

The American
mother

This chapter will focus on the role of the mother in American society. Since World War II some very severe attacks have been directed at mothers in the United States and these will be analyzed in detail. The chapter will close with a discussion of the revolt against motherhood in the 1960s and the 1970s.

Background

Following World War II American mothers were subjected to an attack so vicious that one wonders why they were willing to go on bearing and rearing children. A famous psychiatrist, Strecker, accused them of almost causing the United States to lose World War II by emasculating their sons.[1] A popular writer, Philip Wylie, wrote an even more devastating book called *A Generation of Vipers*, in which he charged American mothers with the psychological castration of their sons.[2] His reference to *Vipers* refers to the child-rearing practices of the American mother by which she sucks the life blood out of her male children. This is strong language and one might dismiss it as being merely the bitter reminis-

---

[1] Edward A. Strecker, M.D., *Their Mothers' Sons* (New York: J. B. Lippincott Co., 1946).

[2] Philip Wylie, *A Generation of Vipers* (New York: Rinehart & Co., 1942).

cences of an unhappy man except for the fact that the book became a runaway best seller—some 400,000 copies of the book were sold within the first few years of publication. It is difficult to imagine a book of this nature selling well unless it met with a responsive chord in the minds and hearts of its readers. It would be interesting to know *who* bought the book—mothers? fathers? sons? daughters? Unfortunately, we do not know.[3]

In commenting on the Strecker book, Gorer, the English anthropologist, has this to say:

According to this book, Mom, the clinging, possessive mother, not only causes psychoneurosis, she is the main cause of every unpleasant phenomenon, from schizophrenia, through lynching to National Socialism and Japanese Emperor Worship! . . . reading it, one would almost think that Americans were produced by parthenogenesis, so vestigial is the role given to the father in forming his children's characters.[4]

Although Gorer's own critique of the American mother is more moderate and more humane than that of Strecker or Wylie, it is interesting that he labels this chapter, "Mother-Land."[5]

In 1965 Robert Ardrey, the anthropologist, joined in on the attack on the American mother. He wrote: "She is the unhappiest female that the primate world has ever seen, and the most treasured objective in her heart of hearts is the psychological castration of husbands and sons."[6] Ardrey goes on to argue that the American mother "has everything" but that she is trying to escape the roles that human evolution prescribes for her. This last statement did not win any friends for Ardrey in the women's liberation movement.

Vicious as these attacks are, they are all by men, and one is tempted to dismiss them as the anguished cry of males who did not like their particular mothers. But in the 1960s the attack was joined by at least two women—Friedan and Rossi. Friedan wrote a best seller in which she argued that the American mother had been trapped into motherhood, with disastrous results for her children, her husband, society, and herself.[7] In essence, this book launched the contemporary women's liberation movement in the United States.

In 1964 Rossi wrote a paper with an anti-mom tone that reminds one

---

[3] The writer has been unable to locate any research on the readership of controversial books such as this.

[4] Geoffrey Gorer, *The American People*, rev. ed. (New York: W. W. Norton & Co., 1964), p. 64.

[5] See chap. 2.

[6] Robert Ardrey, *African Genesis* (New York: Atheneum Publishers, 1965), p. 165.

[7] Betty Friedan, *The Feminine Mystique* (New York: W. W. Norton & Co., 1963); this book has been a continuous best seller for several years.

of the masculine attacks on the American mother. Rossi says: "It is a short-sighted view indeed to consider the immature wife, dominating mother or interfering mother-in-law as a less serious problem to the larger society than the male homosexual, psychoneurotic soldier or ineffectual worker, for it is the failure of the mother which perpetuates the cycle from one generation to the next, affecting sons and daughters alike."[8] This statement leads one to think that America could solve most of its problems if we could just get rid of mothers.

Mothers and society

In the attacks on the American mother cited above, it appears that mothers were being regarded as if they were an independent variable—that they either operate outside of the larger society or cause that society to be the way it is.

A family system cannot be evaluated apart from the society in which it functions. If American mothers are as devastating as their critics would have us believe, then it is difficult to see how the nation has survived. Lerner is making this point when he writes: "If the American family is sick, then the class system must also be sick, and the whole economy, the democratic idea, the passion for equality, the striving for happiness, and the belief that there can be free choice and a future of hope . . . the point is that the American family is part of the totality and reflects its virtues as well as weaknesses."[9]

Erikson takes a more reasonable position when he argues that American parents have to be given some credit for the accomplishments of American society in the last several decades. He writes: "It seems senseless to blame the American family for the failures, but to deny it credit for gigantic human achievement."[10]

One has the impression that somehow the American mother has been made "the bad guy" in the contemporary family. If so, this is a dramatic reversal of the situation in the 19th century when the father was the tyrant and the producer of neuroses in children. How did this change come about?[11]

---

[8] Alice S. Rossi, "Equality between the Sexes," *Daedalus* (Spring 1964): 607–52. For another pessimistic view of the role of the American wife-mother, see Jessie Bernard, *The Future of Marriage* (New York: World Publishing Co., 1972).

[9] Max Lerner, *America as a Civilization* (New York: Simon & Schuster, 1957), p. 551.

[10] Erik H. Erikson, *Childhood and Society*, 2d ed. (New York: W. W. Norton & Co., 1963), p. 289.

[11] The writer has attempted to analyze this family revolution in a paper written for UNESCO; see E. E. LeMasters, "The Passing of the Dominant Husband-Father," *Impact of Science on Society* (Paris, 1971), 21: 21–30.

It seems to us that the steam (or the feeling) behind the attack on the American mother is related to the emancipation of women, which began in the United States during World War I and continued during the 1920s.[12] This was a period of massive social change—or revolution—in our society. The great wave of immigration from Europe was dwindling to a trickle; millions of farmers and their children were moving into cities; the new jobs were industrial jobs; and women were invading not only the world of politics but other pockets of American society more or less closed to them before—colleges and universities, all sorts of community activities, industry and business, and even that male sanctuary, the saloon (known as a speakeasy during Prohibition). Out of all of this social explosion not only a new American woman emerged, but also a new American male and a new American family.

The new American male will be discussed in another chapter. Here we wish to concentrate on the new American woman and the new family system.

As we see it, the American father either abdicated or was pushed out of his position as head of the family during the process of female emancipation. In a sense he was kicked upstairs, as they say in industry, and was made chairman of the board.[13] As such he did not lose all of his power—he still had to be consulted on important decisions—but his wife emerged as the executive director or manager of the enterprise which is called the family. The extent of this shift of responsibility can be seen in the wife-mother's new role or position as director of the family budget. If there was any one symbol of the Victorian father's power and glory it was his complete control of family finances. In many Western societies prior to the modern era, married women (mothers) could not even own property in their own names; if they worked, their income belonged to their husband; and most of them were regarded as being too emotional to handle money.[14] Only big, strong men could do that.

Today, in modern America, the wife-mother is responsible for over 80 percent of the family's consumer expenditures—almost a complete revolution from the pre-1920 era.[15]

It is not clear whether the American father abdicated from his throne

---

[12] A very readable analysis of social change in our society since 1900 may be found in Frederick Lewis Allen, The Big Change (New York: Harper & Bros., 1952).

[13] For a discussion of how business kicks worn-out executives upstairs, see Alfred P. Sloan, Jr., My Years with General Motors (New York: Doubleday & Co., 1964); also Peter F. Drucker, Concept of the Corporation (Boston: Beacon Press, 1946).

[14] For a good brief summary of the changing position of women in American society, see Margaret Mead and Frances Balgley Kaplan, American Women (New York: Charles Scribner's Sons, 1965), pp. 78–95.

[15] For a detailed analysis of the role of the wife-mother in the economics of the modern American family, see Robert O. Blood, Jr., and Donald M. Wolfe, "The Economic Function," Husbands and Wives (New York: Free Press, 1960), chap. 4.

or was the victim of a palace revolution, but when the shooting and shouting of the 1920s and the 1930s were all over, the Little Woman had emerged as the power behind the throne, so to speak.

At this point we are not concerned with an evaluation of this transformation but are merely trying to understand what happened.

By the beginning of World War II, the American mother had become the bad guy in our family system. As the executive and administrator of the family, she assumed more and more responsibility, made more and more decisions, and aroused more and more hostility.

This change can be seen in the psychiatric literature from 1890 to 1960.[16] In the early days of psychoanalytic theory, it was the strong, patriarchal father who was the bad guy in the family system of Europe, the system inherited by the United States. It was the father that children feared; he made the crucial decisions; he handed out punishment; he dispensed money. Any hostility that was available could readily be focused on the old man. One can see this pattern in the play about his own family written by Eugene O'Neill.[17] The mother is sweet, loving, and forgiving, while the father is stern and forbidding.

In modern American psychoanalytic literature, the typical father is seen as a passive dependent type—not very strong and not very sure of himself.[18] On television he looks even worse—pathetic and confused.

It is difficult to hate the current American father; he merits your sympathy and understanding. It is the American mother who draws the hostility; she is the one who hands out money and says yes or no.

When any group of human beings in a society battles its way out of an inferior social position, hostility is always generated. This can be seen clearly in the current struggle of the American blacks for equality; white backlash is very apparent. It appears that a considerable amount of male backlash against women is still to be seen in American society.[19] Some men take the position, "OK, they wanted to wear the pants, now let them see what it is like." It is difficult to determine how widespread such an attitude is among American men, but it is certainly not rare.

---

16 One has only to compare Freud's analysis of the father in Victorian society with that of Ackerman to see the startling change in the position of fathers since the 19th century; see Nathan Ackerman, *The Psychodynamics of Family Life* (New York: Basic Books, 1958).

17 See Eugene O'Neill, *Long Day's Journey into Night* (New Haven: Yale University Press, 1956). Other interesting material on O'Neill's parents may be found in Arthur and Barbara Gelb, *O'Neill* (New York: Harper & Bros., 1962).

18 See, e.g., the description of the American father in Ackerman, *Psychodynamics of Family Life*, pp. 177–81.

19 For discussions of the American male, see Myron Brenton, *The American Male* (New York: Coward-McCann, 1966); Elaine Kendall, *The Upper Hand* (Boston: Little, Brown & Co., 1965); also Charles W. Ferguson, *The Male Attitude* (Boston: Little, Brown & Co., 1966).

The foregoing analysis leaves many questions unanswered—some of which will be taken up in the chapter on the American father—but it seems to us that something of this nature must have taken place to explain the venom and the popularity of books such as Strecker's and Wylie's.

How does one explain the attacks on American mothers by women such as Friedan and Rossi? In some ways they represent the type of person who looks back at a social revolution and is bitter because its basic goals were not achieved. Friedan and Rossi are *disenchanted* with the present plight of American women; they fought for their freedom, won it, and then did not know what to do with it.

It is interesting to note that E. Franklin Frazier has accused the new American black middle class of the same error. They have won social equality, says Frazier, and all they can do with it is play bridge and drink martinis.[20]

It is quite possible that American mothers have achieved more equality than they really wanted. It seems clear that what was originally intended to be a 50–50 partnership in parenthood has turned out to be closer to 70–30 or even 80–20, with the American father having all the fun with the children and the mother all of the headaches.

It seems clear that urbanization is related to many of the basic changes in the modern American family, and it undoubtedly played a part in the shift of power from the American father to the American mother. Although, theoretically, the urban father had more time to spend with his children than the farm father had—because of the eight-hour day and the five-day week—the fact remains that the urban father's job was *away* from the home while the farmer's was not.

In the early days of the move to the city, before metropolitan areas became so dominant, city fathers could often go home for lunch, but this pattern rapidly disappeared as cities became larger.

It is our hypothesis that the assumption of power by the American mother took place between 1920 and 1940, an era that produced feminine equality but had not yet drawn women into jobs and the myriad of community roles they sustain today. This was actually the heyday of the full-time mother that Rossi writes about—a woman who no longer had a farm to distract her and had not yet gone to work outside of the home. With her husband away at work all day, this mother had ample time and opportunity to pervade the lives of her children.[21]

It is our belief that this picture no longer fits the American mother—either she works outside of the home, engages in community activities, or

---

[20] E. Franklin Frazier, *Black Bourgeoisie* (New York: Free Press, 1957).

[21] A more extensive analysis of the impact of urbanization on parents will be presented in chap. 11, "Parents and Social Change."

serves as companion to her husband when he wants her to. In any event, she lives a rather busy, hectic life. One might say that the doting mother in American society has been replaced by the distraught mother.

Other socioeconomic changes were also involved in this shift of power. A woman who had as much education as her husband and had won legal and political equality was no longer content to be a second-class parent at home. She wanted as much to say about money and children as her husband. If she held an outside job, not common for mothers in the 1920s or the 1930s, this was another reason for demanding equality in the home. And as the divorce rate increased, mothers increasingly served as both mother and father.

Insofar as there ever was a possessive or smothering type of American mother, the lower birthrate of the 1920s and the 1930s might have been a factor—as families become smaller each child becomes statistically more precious.

The economic catastrophe of the 1930s, blandly referred to as the depression, apparently reduced the prestige and power of the American father, judging by the research of Cavan and others.[22] This, then, must have strengthened the position of the mother. Even in recent years the charge has been made that the nationwide AFDC child welfare program has favored mothers over fathers in low-income families.[23]

The last socioeconomic force to be cited here is *war*. During the several decades under discussion here, America fought two world wars. Millions of husbands and fathers were away from their wives and families for periods of two to five years. It seems only logical (and necessary) that while the men were away the women took over and did things that had to be done, not only in the home but in the community and larger society also.[24] And when wars end, things never entirely return to their prewar state.

We have now completed our attempt, inadequate as it may be, to explain the reasons for the bitter attacks on the American mother. Next we turn to an examination of some of the evidence used in these attacks.

---

[22] The basic research on the impact of the depression on families will be found in: Ruth Shonle Cavan and Katherine Howland Ranck, *The Family and the Depression* (Chicago: University of Chicago Press, 1938); Mirra Komarovsky, *The Unemployed Man and His Family* (New York: Dryden Press, 1940); Robert C. Angell, *The Family Encounters the Depression* (New York: Charles Scribner's Sons, 1936).

[23] See Alvin Schorr, *Poor Kids* (New York: Basic Books, 1966); also his more recent study of public welfare policy and its impact on low-income families: *Explorations in Social Policy* (New York: Basic Books, 1968).

[24] For an excellent discussion as to how mothers take over male roles when their husbands are in the armed forces, see the research reported in Reuben Hill, *Families under Stress* (New York: Harper & Bros., 1949).

The nature of the data used in the attack

A considerable proportion of the data used to condemn the modern mother has been taken from the clinical files of psychiatrists and psychiatric clinics. Strecker, for example, a psychiatrist, used data collected on men discharged from the army for psychiatric reasons during World War II.[25]

In an attack by Lundberg and Farnham, the data were drawn from the files of a woman psychiatrist in private practice.[26] In a chapter on the American woman as mother, entitled "Mother and Child: The Slaughter of the Innocents," the following statement is made: "The spawning ground of most neurosis in western civilization is the home. The basis for it is laid in childhood, although it emerges strongly later, usually from late adolescence until middle age, provoked by circumstances and conditions encountered in life. And as we have pointed out, the principal agent in laying the groundwork for it is the mother."[27]

On the surface, there is nothing wrong with using psychiatric case material in analyzing American society. But unless the person doing the analysis has had good research training, a number of dangerous pitfalls will seriously damage the value of the findings. Some of these are as follows.

1. *The sample.* It should be remembered that psychiatric case material is drawn from a very limited and biased sample. The general population that copes with its problems is automatically excluded from the clinic or private practice sample. Furthermore, such samples are heavily biased in their social class composition, as Hollingshead and Redlich have demonstrated.[28]

The crucial error committed by the users of psychiatric data is to generalize from the clinic or private-practice population to the general population in the society. A classic example of this would be the Lundberg and Farnham volume cited earlier.

2. *The failure to use a control group.* In social science research design, a control group serves to check on our findings. Are the variables used to explain the behavior actually responsible for the behavior? If the Strecker book, for example, had utilized proper research design, a sample

---

[25] See Strecker, *Their Mothers' Sons.*

[26] Ferdinand Lundberg and Marynia A. Farnham, *Modern Woman: The Lost Sex* (New York: Grosset & Dunlap, 1947). This is one of the most hysterical attacks on the American mother the writer has seen.

[27] Ibid., p. 303.

[28] For an extensive discussion of social class bias in clinic and private-practice case records, see August B. Hollingshead and Frederick C. Redlich, *Social Class and Mental Illness* (New York: John Wiley & Sons, 1958).

of soldiers who were *not* discharged from the Army for psychiatric reasons would have been matched with the cases Strecker was using. In this way it might have been determined whether there was a significant difference in maternal patterns between the men who broke down psychologically in the army and those who did not. Without such a control group, we really do not know what factors produced the psychiatric casualties.[29]

This may not impress the reader untrained in research methodology, but some amazing results have been obtained when psychiatric data has been subjected to control-group analysis. In a study of unmarried mothers, for example, Vincent matched a group of girls who were *not* unmarried mothers with a group who were, in order to test the findings of an earlier study that had concluded that the unmarried mothers had suffered from a maternal syndrome that was relatively abnormal or unique.[30] The analysis of the control group revealed that these so-called normal girls reported a relationship with their mothers that was not significantly different from that reported by the unmarried mothers.[31]

3. *Failure to seek for other explanations of the behavior.* If you are convinced that the American mother is what is wrong with our society, then you do not need to look for other possible explanations of the problems under consideration. It seems that most of the critics of the mother in our society are guilty of this error. They simply do not grant the fact that forces other than mothers influence children and that it is extremely difficult to rear a healthy child in a sick society. The American value system itself—hardly created by mothers—may be one of the major factors producing personality disorganization in the United States.[32] Our highly competitive economic system subjects youth and parents alike to great stress. Conflicts in our culture related to sexual ethics, racial relations, or science versus religion, probably have some relationship to schizophrenia, the most common psychosis in our society.[33] But, except for

---

[29] On the use of control groups, see Claire Sellitz et al., *Research Methods in Social Relations* (New York: Henry Holt & Co., 1959), pp. 114–22.

[30] For a dramatic illustration of the value of good research controls, see how Clark Vincent's analysis of the unmarried mother in our society differs from that of Leontine Young. The two studies are Clark Vincent, *Unmarried Mothers* (New York: Free Press, 1961), and Leontine Young, *Out of Wedlock* (New York: McGraw-Hill Book Co., 1954).

[31] A striking example of the value of a well-designed control group will be found in Henry J. Meyer, Edgar F. Borgatta, and Wyatt C. Jones, *Girls at Vocational High* (New York: Russell Sage Foundation, 1965).

[32] See Karen Horney, *The Neurotic Personality of Our Time* (New York: W. W. Norton & Co., 1937), for a discussion of the interaction of culture conflict and personality conflict.

[33] A famous analysis of culture conflicts in American society is that of Robert S. Lynd, *Knowledge for What?* (Princeton, N.J.: Princeton University Press, 1948), pp. 60–63.

writers such as Lerner, Riesman, Erikson, or Brim, one seldom sees these other factors considered by the critics of the American mother.[34] Brim was struck by this anomaly when he wrote his classic analysis of the family-education movement in the United States. He writes: "As a social scientist, one is struck by the fact that parent education seems to operate as if the parent existed in a social vacuum."[35] One certainly has this impression reading the attacks on the American mother.

4. *Failure to look for contrary data.* A basic principle of scientific method is that every effort should be made to identify and assess data that might contradict your tentative conclusions. Even a single case that does not fit the theory may require a totally new approach to the analysis. Such niceties of scientific method do not bother the critics of the American mother. They simply ignore data that might contradict conclusions they have already reached. This may make exciting reading, but it is hardly science.

This concludes our analysis of the evidence used against the American mother. If we were on a jury trying this case we would have to vote "not guilty." Most of the indictment is based on circumstantial evidence that will not bear careful scrutiny, in our opinion.

We now turn to a role analysis of the American mother with the hope that this will give the reader insight into some of the dilemmas faced by mothers in our society.

Role analysis of the American mother

It is our thesis that one of the problems of the contemporary American mother is that she is "overcommitted." Far from being the full-time mother that Rossi writes about, the American woman has expanded almost all of her roles since the end of World War I. Some observers even claim that today's mother puts in longer hours than her grandmother did.[36] It is certainly true that she is trying to do more things than her grandmother ever did—with no more hours available in the week.

It is true, of course, that modern appliances have lightened the burden of house cleaning and laundry, but as one woman said: "That machine does not take the diapers off of the baby and rinse them out. Nor does it put the diapers away or put them back on the baby. The machine *only washes* them."

It is also true that prepared foods have been a great boon to the American mother. But, to balance the picture, we wish to show in the next few

---

[34] Lerner, *America as a Civilization;* Davis Riesman et al., *The Lonely Crowd* (New Haven: Yale University Press, 1961); Orville G. Brim, Jr., *Education for Child Rearing* (New York: Russell Sage Foundation, 1959).

[35] Brim, *Education for Child Rearing,* p. 68.

[36] News story, *New York Times,* August 4, 1969.

pages how the role commitments of today's mother in our society have been expanded.

1. *The role of wife.* Being a wife today is not the same as being a wife in 1900. In the area of sex alone, today's wife is supposed to be a sexual *companion* for her husband; she is not supposed to just submit to him as the Victorian wife did. She is supposed to share her husband's enthusiasm for sex. This is part of the total partnership that modern American marriage is dedicated to.

In many other ways, her role as companion to her husband has been expanded—bowling, golf, fishing, hunting, smoking, drinking—the modern wife's place is not "in the home" but out in the world with her husband.[37]

It is true that this "togetherness" pattern is not found at lower-class levels, as Gans and others have pointed out; but insofar as America is becoming increasingly a white-collar society, the ideal of husband-wife togetherness would seem to be spreading.[38]

To the extent that the modern American wife-mother commits herself to being a companion to her husband she has expanded her role as wife.

2. *The role of mother.* We argued in an earlier chapter that modern American parents are operating under higher standards.[39] Mothers today are expected to be informed about new medical findings, such as new vaccines, and to make sure that their children receive them; they are supposed to be alert to new community programs for children, such as those available at the YMCA or some other community service agency, and to get their children interested and enrolled. Schools, PTAs, Girl Scouts, Boy Scouts, Little League baseball—all of these child-centered organizations expect (and even demand) more from today's mothers than ever before in our society.

It is true, of course, that today's mother will not be criticized by her neighbors or her family if she buys a child's birthday cake at the supermarket—she has an advantage here over the mothers of yesterday. But it seems that she has paid dearly in time and serenity for such conveniences.

3. *Expansion of the home-management role.* In taking over the family budget and the job of purchasing agent, the American mother got herself into more work than she bargained for. The writer's mother had her gro-

---

[37] It is recognized by the writer that lower-income males do not usually subscribe to the cult of "togetherness." For an extensive discussion of working-class family subculture, see Herbert Gans, *The Urban Villagers* (New York: Free Press, 1962); also Mirra Komarovsky, *Blue-Collar Marriage* (New York: Random House, 1964).

[38] For other studies of lower-class family life, see Lee Rainwater, *And the Poor Get Children* (Chicago: Quadrangle Books, 1960); also Elliot Liebow, *Tally's Corner* (Boston: Little, Brown & Co., 1967).

[39] See chap. 4.

ceries delivered to her home daily, but today's woman has to go to the supermarket and bring the family groceries home herself. And if she wishes to shop economically she has to visit more than one store to take advantage of specials.

Mothers today shop for the men in the family as well as for their daughters and themselves.

It is not uncommon today to see an American mother mowing the lawn with the power mower, and even painting the house. But in an earlier America, at least in the cities, this was man's work.

4. *Expansion of the community role.* In an interesting book called *The Gentle Legions,* Carter[40] has described the massive effort of American wives and mothers to raise funds for the voluntary health organizations. These efforts have often been lampooned by comedians, but as Carter says, the triumph over polio was no joke.[41] The $160 million raised for these health organizations by American women is no joke either.[42]

Hill, of the Family Study Center at the University of Minnesota, points out that the American mother has taken on the "community liaison" role in our family system.[43] She is the major line of communication and contact with the schools, the welfare agencies, the youth organizations, the church, and the various health services.

This community role of the American mother is often taken lightly by her critics, but as one minister said: "Without the mothers this community would collapse." He may have been thinking of his own church but we feel that he had a point.

5. *Expansion of her breadwinner role.* Many critics of the American mother seem to forget that for the past several decades she has increasingly held an outside job while rearing her children. Nye and Hoffman, in their analysis of this revolution in our society, make this statement: "Few, if any, single changes in family life have as profoundly affected so many families in so few years as the movement of mothers into paid employment. Since 1940 there has been an estimated net increase of 10 million mothers in the labor force."[44] By 1955, according to Nye and Hoffman, over one third of mothers *with school-age children* were employed outside of the home.[45]

---

[40] Richard Carter, *The Gentle Legions* (New York: Doubleday & Co., 1961).

[41] Ibid., "The Polio Triumph," chap. 4.

[42] Ibid., p. 21.

[43] Reuben Hill, "Sociological Frameworks for Family Study," paper presented at a meeting sponsored by the Department of Psychiatry, School of Medicine, University of Wisconsin, December 1967.

[44] F. Ivan Nye and Lois Wladis Hoffman, *The Employed Mother in America* (Chicago: Rand McNally & Co., 1963), p. 3.

[45] Ibid., p. 6.

It is interesting to note that as of 1900 only one wife in 20 was in the labor force, but by 1950 the ratio was one out of five.[46] One has the impression that some of the critics who accuse American mothers of smothering their children have not read the U.S. labor statistics reports for several decades.

In view of the expansion of the contemporary American mother's basic roles, we find it difficult to accept Rossi's description of these women as full-time mothers. This may have been partially true of the 1920s or the 1930s, but beginning with 1940 the American wife-mother got herself involved in quite a rat race. And she is still running, it seems to us.

We now turn to a brief defense of the American mother.

In defense of the American mother

We believe that a good defense can be presented for the contemporary American mother. Some of that defense has been or will be discussed in detail in other chapters and need not be considered at length here.[47]

In our opinion the record of the American mother in recent decades needs to be judged against the following background.

1. *The depression of the 1930s.* America has seldom experienced a catastrophe more devastating to individuals and families than the economic disaster of the 1930s.[48] In a society dedicated to making and spending money, few things are more disturbing than unemployment. The studies of Cavan, Komarovsky, and Angell (see n. 22 above) reveal some of the demoralizing effects of the depression on family life.

The magnitude of the depression is often forgotten—15–20 million people were unemployed at one time or another in the 1930s.

The writer was a social worker visiting families on relief during the period 1934–36. In this capacity we had the opportunity to enter homes and interview hundreds of families suffering from unemployment. It was perfectly obvious to anyone but those unwilling to look or listen that the lives of these men, women, and children were being twisted out of shape by years of unemployment and economic deprivation.

Some of these children were the ones that Strecker found discharged from the Army for psychiatric reasons a decade later. Is it any wonder? Who was so naïve as to think that a social disaster such as the depression would not exact its toll in human lives?

---

[46] U.S. Census Bureau news release, *Wisconsin State Journal*, August 29, 1968, sect. 2, p. 14.

[47] In the sense that this book takes into account the conditions under which American parents operate, every chapter contains some defense of their record.

[48] A good source book on the depression of the 1930s is David A. Shannon, ed., *The Great Depression* (Englewood Cliffs, N.J.: Prentice-Hall, Inc., 1960).

The writer saw firsthand the heroic efforts being made by mothers in the 1930s to hold their families together. But one seldom reads about these mothers; as a rule we hear about those that failed.

Parents do not operate in a social vacuum—they function in a world of reality. And when that world is as sick as it was in the United States in the 1930s, only the exceptional father or mother can function effectively. The critics of American parents would do well to remember this.

2. *The increase in marital instability.* America no longer has one marriage system, lifetime monogamy, but two: serial monogamy now involves at least one fourth of our married couples.[49] If one adds desertion, separation, and the chronically unhappy married couples to the divorce rate, the total marital failure rate exceeds one fourth.[50] Simon reports that 15 million Americans have now been divorced.[51]

No one questions that divorce and other forms of marital failure pose excruciating problems for parents.[52] Even though parents know that their children may be better off psychologically after the divorce, they often hesitate to separate because of their concern for their children.[53] In doing this, they often damage themselves as adults.

In about 95 percent of the cases, it is the American mother who retains custody of the children after a marital failure, and it is she who has to help the children through this crisis.[54]

In about 10 percent of American homes there is no father present.[55] This type of mother will be considered in a separate chapter, so it is only necessary to point out here that this woman is usually serving as *both* mother and father.

---

[49] The best empirical study of divorce to date in our society is that by William J. Goode, *After Divorce* (New York: Free Press, 1956). Even this study, however, is marred by the fact that no husbands were interviewed. For a careful statistical analysis of divorce, see Paul H. Jacobson, *American Marriage and Divorce* (New York: Rinehart & Co., 1959).

[50] Marriages that have failed by any reasonable standards but have not been terminated are analyzed in a paper by the writer; see E. E. LeMasters, "Holy Deadlock: A Study of Unsuccessful Marriages," *Sociological Quarterly* 21 (1959): 86–91.

[51] Anne W. Simon, *Stepchild in the Family* (New York: Odyssey Press, 1964); these statistics are reviewed in chap. 4, "It's a New World," pp. 50–68.

[52] In addition to the studies of Goode and Simon, see also Morton M. Hunt, *The World of the Formerly Married* (New York: McGraw-Hill Book Co., 1966). A good history of divorce in America is that of William L. O'Neill, *Divorce in the Progressive Era* (New Haven, Conn.: Yale University Press, 1967).

[53] Goode's divorced women felt that their children were better off emotionally after the divorce (see Goode, "The Children of Divorce," *After Divorce*, chap. 21).

[54] Hunt (*World of the Formerly Married*, pp. 260–61) has a discussion of parents after divorce.

[55] For a discussion of the American families with a female head, see Alvin Schorr, *Poor Kids*, pp. 20–22.

In some low-income groups, and among some minority groups, as many as 60 percent of the homes may have no father present.[56]

Simon points out there are 7 million stepchildren in the United States —one child out of every nine has a stepparent.[57] The role of stepparent has historically been viewed as an unenviable job, and especially so for stepmothers.

The high rate of marital failure in the United States since the end of World War I has complicated the role of the mother in our society no end.

3. *The failure of the American father.* Most of the data on personal disorganization indicates that the American male has a higher rate than the American female.[58] If one looks at data on crime, alcoholism, drug addiction, desertion, and so on, the male rates are significantly higher than those for the female. In reviewing the record of the two sexes, Montagu has concluded that females are superior to males at the human level.[59] While material of this nature is subject to various interpretations, the fact remains that men in modern America pose more problems for public authorities than women do.

One can argue that this male-female differential in social adjustment reflects dysfunctional child-rearing methods, as the psychiatrists do; that it reflects genetic differences between the two sexes, as the ethologists do; or that it reflects greater cultural strain on the male, as sociologists usually do.[60]

More will be said about the American father in a separate chapter, but it does seem clear that he has failed quite often as a parent in our society in recent decades.

4. *The feminine revolution in the United States.* In the preceding role analysis of the American mother, an attempt was made to illustrate the expanded function of women in our society. We only wish to state here that American women have been involved in a social revolution since World War I and that this has inevitably complicated their parental

---

[56] See "Unemployment, Family Structure, and Social Disorganization," *U.S. Riot Commission Report* (New York: Bantam Books, 1968), chap. 7.

[57] See Simon, "The Child's World Changes," *Stepchild in the Family*, pp. 69–83.

[58] On social disorganization rates for men, see Harrison M. Trice, *Alcoholism in America* (New York: McGraw-Hill Book Co., 1966); also various chapters in Marshall B. Clinard, *Sociology of Deviant Behavior* (New York: Rinehart & Co., 1968).

[59] Ashley Montagu, *The Natural Superiority of Women* (New York: Macmillan Co., 1968).

[60] Some of the psychiatric literature on this has been cited in this chapter. For the ethologists see Desmond Morris, *The Naked Ape* (New York: McGraw-Hill Book Co., 1967); also Robert Ardrey, *The Territorial Imperative* (New York: Atheneum Press, 1966); also Konrad Lorenz, *On Aggression* (New York: Harcourt, Brace & World, 1963).

role.[61] Once this revolution has been completed—and this may soon be the case—the maternal role in the United States should be less difficult.

5. *The record of American mothers in recent decades is itself open to debate.* The critics of the American mother would have us believe that we *lost* World War II. The fact is that most Americans performed well during the war and that the nation since then has gone on to become one of the most powerful in the history of the human race. It is recognized that the United States has innumerable domestic and international problems, but to say that American parents are failing to produce competent adults is to ignore the accomplishments of this society in the past few decades.

6. *Miscellaneous observations in defense of the American mother.* In the Strecker and Wylie books the major criticism of the American mother concerns her rearing of her sons. It is an interesting fact that upper-class families in the United States, also in England, have never trusted mothers to rear sons—these have been sent away to boarding schools to be disciplined by stern male teachers and headmasters.[62] This may represent sound thinking, but most American mothers have had no choice in the matter; they have had to rear their sons for better or worse.

In many of the criticisms of the mother in our society, it is implied that she is too easy on her children—that she smothers them with attention and caters to their every whim. But what about the traditional Jewish mother? She is usually represented as sentimental and gratifying, yet Jewish children in the United States have compiled an enviable record.[63]

The Italian mother resembles the Jewish mother in many respects, and yet her children also seem to have done reasonably well in the relatively short time they have been in this country.[64]

---

[61] For a historian's analysis of the long struggle for equality for women in American society, see William O'Neill, *Everyone was Brave: The Rise and Fall of Feminism in America* (Chicago: Quadrangle Books, 1969).

[62] For descriptions of how English upper-class boys are sent away to boarding schools, see the autobiography of Harold Macmillan, *Winds of Change* (New York: Harper & Row, 1966); also Randolph S. Churchill, *Winston S. Churchill* (New York: Houghton Mifflin Co., 1966). This first volume deals with the childhood of Winston Churchill. For an account of how Franklin D. Roosevelt was saved from a doting mother, see the account of his years at Groton in John Gunther, *Roosevelt in Retrospect* (New York: Harper & Bros., 1950).

[63] On the Jewish mother, see Martha Wolfenstein, "Two Types of Jewish Mothers," in *The Jews: Social Patterns of an American Group*, ed. M. Sklare (New York: Free Press, 1958).

[64] On the Italian mom, see Irving R. Levine, *Main Street, Italy* (New York: Doubleday & Co., 1963), p. 24. Levine, a foreign correspondent for one of the national television networks in the United States who is stationed in Rome, claims that no mothers anywhere spoil their sons as do the Italian mothers; for another treatment of the Italian mother, this one by an Italian, see Luigi Barzini, *The Italians* (New York: Atheneum Press, 1964), esp. chap. 11, "The Power of the Family."

The revolt against motherhood

In the 1960s and the early 1970s a revolt against motherhood developed in the United States. The opening shot in this revolt was fired by Betty Friedan when she published her very popular book, *The Feminine Mystique,* in 1963. Her thesis was that the price of motherhood was too high in contemporary America—that women's lives were being twisted and distorted by a role that forced mothers to become martyrs to their children. Judging by the sales of the book, this argument did not fall on deaf ears.

Freidan's remedies include the following:

1. Not all women should marry; marriage as a way of life has been vastly oversold to modern women.

2. Not all women should have children. The idea that motherhood is the essence of life is ridiculed by Friedan—she argues that this is part of the mystique that confuses modern women.

3. Women who do have children should have fewer children. Friedan points out that the world is already overpopulated and that reproduction should represent a deliberate choice, not some outmoded cultural compulsion.

4. Sex and motherhood should be separated in the sense that women (and men) should have access to better contraceptive methods, and abortion should be readily available to women who become pregnant but do not wish to become mothers.

5. American women should fight for social change that would make motherhood compatible with a free and creative life for all women.[65]

Traditionalists were shocked and angered by Friedan's attack on motherhood, but middle-class women (college graduates) and the younger generation found it most refreshing.

Actually, after World War II, American women were victimized by a number of myths (what Friedan labels *mystique*). The marriage rate went so high that a girl regarded herself as a reject if she had not roped and corralled a man by the age of 25. As Friedan points out, this is nonsense.

Even this was not enough: if she did not bear three or four children (in the 1940s and the 1950s), her contemporaries considered her almost sterile—and she regarded herself in this light also.

Finally, she could not pursue a career while her children were of preschool age because this would make the children neurotic and would saddle the mother with guilt for the rest of her life.

---

[65] A flood of books on the problems of women followed Friedan's work. For representative samples, see Caroline Bird, *Born Female* (New York: David McKay, 1968), and Germaine Greer, *The Female Eunuch* (New York: McGraw-Hill Book Co., 1970).

Part of the revolt against motherhood may be a reaction to the vicious attacks leveled against the American mother and discussed earlier in this chapter. Why persist in being a martyr if the parishioners do not appreciate the sacrifice?

Erikson takes the position that most of the portraits of the American "mom" are really caricatures: they take certain features of the mother role and exaggerate them out of all proportion.[66] Erikson goes on to argue that some features of momism (such as her eternal and complete sacrifice for her family) were useful in frontier America but have become dysfunctional in modern society.

There is much to be said in support of Friedan and her fellow critics of motherhood. No social role (unless it be that of defending one's country) should demand that the rest of life be suppressed or obliterated. Marriage is not worth that price, nor is motherhood (or fatherhood). Family roles should be so designed that they are integrated with other facets of life rather than excluding them.

It is interesting that motherhood is not the only martyr role modern Americans are revolting against—military service is becoming increasingly difficult to impose on young men, and industry is finding it harder and harder to find bright young college graduates who are willing to subordinate themselves and their families to furthering the growth of General Motors or some other conglomerate. The current divorce rate is evidence that comtemporary men and women are not willing to be martyrs to a disastrous marriage.

Young people today do not think it wholesome that one's entire life be centered around parenthood—or anything else for that matter. One university student put it this way to the writer: "I wouldn't want to think that my parents dedicated their lives to me—the idea scares the hell out of me. My mother always worked (she taught school) and I'm glad she did. Kids should be just *part* of life—not all of it."

Summary and conclusion

In this chapter some of the attacks on the American mother have been examined. The net conclusion has been that the attacks have not been based on adequate empirical data. The chapter closed with comments on what appears to be an incipient revolt against motherhood.

---

[66] Erikson, *Childhood and Society*, p. 291.

chapter
eight

The American
father

In this chapter the role of the American father will be examined in some detail. In the previous chapter it was seen that the American mother has been subjected to numerous attacks in recent decades. In contrast, the American father has been almost ignored by behavioral scientists and writers since the end of World War II.

The role of father is closely linked with the role of husband, and it will be seen that this has been one of the major problems of the American father in recent decades—his marital problems often interfere with his paternal performance.

The neglect of the American father in family research

In recent years there have been numerous studies of the American mother, but literature on the American father is relatively sparse. Ferguson has done a historical study of the male in Western society;[1] Kendall has a satirical treatment of the male in American society;[2] Brenton wrote an analysis of the identity crisis of the contemporary male;[3] Mead has a

---

[1] Charles W. Ferguson, *The Male Attitude* (Boston: Little, Brown & Co., 1966).
[2] Elaine Kendall, *The Upper Hand* (Boston: Little, Brown & Co., 1965).
[3] Myron Brenton, *The American Male* (New York: Coward-McCann, 1966).

cross-cultural study of male and female roles;[4] ethologists such as Morris have published studies of males roles in the primate world;[5] and Benson has a scholarly analysis of the scattered research on the human father.[6]

It is in the field studies of American parents, however, that the omission of fathers is most glaring. Sears, for example, in interviewing 379 "parents" did not find it necessary to include one father.[7] Miller and Swanson had 582 mothers in their sample but no fathers.[8] Blood and Wolfe talked with 909 mothers but excluded fathers from the sample.[9] In a study of divorced parents, Goode located 425 mothers but did not attempt to locate any fathers.[10]

In reviewing the research on unmarried parents, Vincent discovered that for every study of unmarried fathers there were 25 studies of unmarried mothers.[11]

In the *Handbook of Socialization Theory and Research*, there are only five specific references to fathers in 1,140 pages of text.[12] In a survey of family research, Ruano and his associates found that of 444 papers published from 1963 through 1968 only eleven utilized data from husbands and/or fathers.[13]

In a study of child-guidance-clinic case records, Pollak discovered that fathers were almost completely ignored by clinicians working with child-behavior problems.[14]

This exclusion of fathers from research on parenthood seems to rest on two assumptions: (1) that mothers can report accurately what fathers think and feel; and (2) that fathers are unimportant in the child-rearing process. Are these assumptions valid? In a study of foster parents, Fanshel discovered that foster fathers emerged with quite a different profile when

---

[4] Margaret Mead, *Male and Female* (New York: William Morrow & Co., 1949).

[5] Desmond Morris, *The Naked Ape* (New York: McGraw-Hill Book Co., 1967).

[6] Leonard Benson, *Fatherhood: A Sociological Perspective* (New York: Random House, 1968).

[7] Robert R. Sears et al., *Patterns of Child Rearing* (Evanston, Ill.: Row, Peterson & Co., 1957).

[8] Daniel R. Miller and Guy E. Swanson, *The Changing American Parent* (New York: John Wiley & Sons, 1958).

[9] Robert O. Blood, Jr., and Donald M. Wolfe, *Husbands and Wives* (New York: Free Press, 1960).

[10] William J. Goode, *After Divorce* (New York: Free Press, 1956).

[11] Clark Vincent, *Unmarried Mothers* (New York: Free Press, 1961).

[12] David A. Goslin, ed., *Handbook of Socialization Theory and Research* (Chicago: Rand McNally & Co., 1969).

[13] B. J. Ruano, J. D. Bruce, and M. M. McDermott, "Pilgrim's Progress II: Recent Trends and Perspectives in Family Research," *Journal of Marriage and the Family* 31 (1969): 688–98.

[14] Otto Pollak, *Social Science and Psychotherapy for Children* (New York: Russell Sage Foundation, 1952); see also idem, *Integrating Sociological and Psychoanalytic Concepts* (New York: Russell Sage Foundation, 1956).

they were actually interviewed rather than being described by foster mothers.[15] Seeley and associates, in an elaborate study of suburban parents, concluded that interviews with fathers yielded significantly different versions of child rearing from those obtained from mothers.[16] In a study of divorce, O'Brien found that divorced men give a different view of the divorce process from that given by women.[17] In a study of domestic court reconciliation cases, Mueller concluded that it was not possible to obtain an accurate account of the reconciliation process by interviewing only the wife.[18] Mueller also says that her study suggests "a serious bias in samples which have included only wives or ex-wives as respondents." In a study of birth-control and abortion practices, de Winter concluded that family-planning programs that exclude the husband-father from interviews make a serious error.[19]

It is the writer's contention that the burden of proof should be on the shoulders of those who exclude the American father from research samples.

Role analysis of the father in modern America

1. *The parental role is a peripheral role for the American male.* For the American mother, the role of parent probably takes precedence over all other adult roles. For some women this may not be the case, since they may choose to give priority to their role as wife or to an occupational role, but these women would seem to be in the minority in our child-centered society. Mrs. John F. Kennedy has been quoted as saying: "If you fail with your children, then I don't think anything else matters very much."[20]

For the American father the situation is quite different. Two roles in particular—that of his job and that of military service—almost always have to be given priority over his role as parent. Since 1940, between 15 and 20 million men in our society have had to go to the corners of the earth to discharge their military obligations, and the fact that they might be fathers does not entitle them to automatic deferment.

Nobody knows how many millions of American fathers have had their family lives disrupted by the long arm of the job, but the total must be

---

[15] David Fanshel, *Foster Parenthood: A Role Analysis* (Minneapolis: University of Minnesota Press, 1966).

[16] John R. Seeley et al., *Crestwood Heights* (New York: Basic Books, 1956).

[17] John O'Brien, "The Decision to Divorce" (Ph.D. diss., University of Wisconsin, 1970).

[18] Jeanne Mueller, "Reconciliation or Resignation: A Case Study," *Family Coordinator* (October 1970) pp. 345–52.

[19] Adrian de Winter, "Family Planning in Uruguay" (Ph.D. diss., University of Wisconsin, 1971).

[20] See Theodore C. Sorensen, *Kennedy* (New York: Harper & Row, 1965), p. 381.

astronomical. In an unpublished study of blue-collar construction workers, the writer was impressed by the frequency with which these men had to work out of town to maintain steady employment.[21] Almost all of these men agreed that such jobs posed real problems for them and their families.

When a man is transferred in our society, he often moves to the new community months before his family is able to join him. During this period his wife has to assume some responsibility with the children that normally would belong to the husband. Then, when the family is reunited, roles have to be redistributed again and lines of authority reestablished. In one research project during World War II, Hill discovered that it was not always easy to "pick up where they left off" when the father returned from the armed forces.[22]

It seems to us that this peripheral nature of the parental role is often overlooked by critics of the American father. They judge him as if children were the center of his life in the way they are for American mothers. In our judgment this is not only unfair to the fathers but also unrealistic.

2. *There is no biological base or imprinting for the father role at the human level as there is for the mother.* In a famous book, Davis puts this point as follows: "The weak link in the family group is the father-child bond. There is no necessary association and no easy means of identification between these two as there is between mother and child."[23] He goes on to point out that almost all human societies have evolved complex social devices for binding the father to his children.

Mead is making this same point when she says that the role of father at the human level is a "social invention"—strictly speaking, he could be dispensed with once conception had taken place.[24] Most societies have chosen not to let the male escape so easily, but to tie him to the child has required elaborate cultural arrangements, whereas these are not usually necessary for the mother.

All of this means that fathers in our society (or any other society) are almost entirely dependent on proper socialization and positive induction into the role of parent if they are to perform this responsibility adequately. This sets up the possibility that the father-child bond will not be as dependable as the mother-child bond. This certainly seems to be the case in our society.

3. *The human father is a mammal.* Among other things, man is a mammal—and in the entire mammalian series there are only two fathers who assume major responsibility for their offspring. Most male mammals

---

[21] This is an unpublished study of a tavern frequented by blue-collar construction workers.

[22] Reuben Hill, *Families under Stress* (New York: Harper & Bros., 1949).

[23] Kingsley Davis, *Human Society* (New York: Macmillan Co., 1949), p. 400.

[24] Mead, *Male and Female.*

are present for the fertilization and are seldom seen after that. The wolf, oddly enough, is one of the exceptions, often helping to feed the young and baby-sitting with them while the mother is away from the den.[25]

Compared with other mammalian fathers, the human father is a paragon of virtue. But he is still a mammal, and some American fathers appear to function pretty much at that level. These are, however, only a small minority.

4. *The human father is also a primate.* In the literature on the monkeys and the great apes, it appears that the father's role after procreation is to protect the female (or females) and their offspring, but with only one exception does he ever assume any major responsibility for their daily care.[26] Here, again, the average human father makes the other primate fathers look bad.

5. *The father's parental role in the United States is peculiarly tied to the success or failure of the pair-bond between himself and his wife.* In a great many human societies, a father can still be a good father even if his marriage leaves much to be desired: mistresses or women of some category other than wife are made available to him, and he can still reside in his home with his wife and children.[27] This is usually not the case in our society. In modern America men are expected to be faithful to their wives or else leave the home and marry the other woman.

All of this means that if anything happens to the marriage of the American male he may find himself separated from his children and partially cut off from them—and this may happen in spite of his honest desire to be a good father. In other words, it is difficult in our society to be a good father if you are not also a good husband. According to Lewis, this has not been the case in societies such as Mexico.[28]

Other complications result if the marriage fails. Sooner or later the husband will find other feminine companionship, often with a woman who has children of her own, so that the man is now committed to two sets of children: his own offspring and those of his new love. In order to attract and hold a divorced woman or a widow with children, the male has to show a substantial interest in her children and their welfare—and in the process may neglect his own children.[29] Thus, he may actually be

---

[25] See Desmond Morris, *The Naked Ape* (New York: McGraw-Hill Book Co., 1967). On the wolf, see Farley Mowat, *Never Cry Wolf* (Boston: Little, Brown & Co., 1963).

[26] See George B. Schaller, *The Mountain Gorilla* (Chicago: University of Chicago Press, 1963).

[27] George P. Murdock, *Social Structure* (New York: Macmillan Co., 1949). In a survey of 250 human societies, Murdock found that a majority of them permit a man to have more than one mate.

[28] See Oscar Lewis, *Five Families* (New York: Basic Books, 1959).

[29] In the tavern study referred to earlier, the writer interviewed one man who was no longer close to his own children living in Indiana with their mother, but he was

doing a good job as a parent but with only one set of children, not necessarily his own.[30]

If we look at the figures on divorce, desertion, and separation, we can see that marital failure is probably one of the major roadblocks to the American father who sincerely wants to be a good parent.[31] This is not the case with the American mother, who retains custody of the minor children in over 90 percent of the cases known to the courts.[32] As a matter of fact, marital failure may enhance the parental role of the mother: she now has the children more exclusively than before and probably extends the amount of time and effort she spends on them.[33]

The novelist Gold has a sketch in which a man is attempting to explain to a young daughter why he will not be living with her and her mother any more (they are getting a divorce). "I still love you," the father tries to explain, "but I no longer love your mother." He goes on to try to make it clear to the child that he still wants to be a *father* but not her mother's *husband.* This is too complex for the little girl, and after a long silence she says: "I'm getting sick of big words like love."[34]

This dependence of the father role on the marital bond is often forgotten by critics of the American father. We think it needs to be kept in mind.[35]

6. *The American father is poorly prepared for his parental role.* This was commented on to some extent in chapter 4, but a few words need to be added at this point. American boys simply do not receive the socialization that helps prepare girls to become mothers. Girls get dolls and baby buggies for Christmas when the boys get guns and footballs. Later on, in high school and college, courses in home economics and child development are elected primarily by girls. And even later, the women's magazines feature child-rearing material, while the men's magazines feature sports and girls in scanty outfits.

---

helping to care for three children who lived with the divorced woman he was then dating. Later on he married this second woman, and for all practical purposes became the father of her children.

[30] For a good analysis of the millions of stepparents in our society, see Anne W. Simon, *Stepchild in the Family* (New York: Odyssey Press, 1964).

[31] For a review of these data, see Robert R. Bell, *Marriage and Family Interaction,* 3d ed. (Homewood, Ill.: Dorsey Press, 1971), chap. 19.

[32] Ibid., p. 506.

[33] See E. E. LeMasters, "Holy Deadlock: A Study of Unsuccessful Marriages," *Sociological Quarterly* 21 (1959): 86–91; see also Morton M. Hunt, *The World of the Formerly Married* (New York: McGraw-Hill Book Co., 1966). When her marriage fails, one of the common defense mechanisms of the American mother is the devotion of her children.

[34] See Herbert Gold, *The Age of Happy Problems* (New York: Dial Press, 1962), pp. 27–33.

[35] This appears to be one of the findings of a study of 100 divorced men now in process at the School of Social Work, University of Wisconsin, Madison.

As a result of all this, the average American male is quite unprepared to be a father—at least socially.[36] He enjoys the process of fertilization and may even look forward to being a father, but he scarcely knows what he is getting into. To some extent, of course, this is also true of many American girls, but it seems to us that nature and our society prepare mothers for their parental role better than they do fathers.

Some problems of the American father

Many books have detailed the various problems of the woman in American society, including the reports of various government commissions established to assess the status of the female in our society.[37] We know of no similar effort to discover the status and the problems of the male in contemporary America. In fact, there are only a few books about him.[38]

In the pages following, a few of the major problems of the American male will be indicated. All of these, in the opinion of the writer, have relevance for an understanding of the American father.

1. *Economic problems.* Although he is relatively affluent, the American father is under constant economic pressure to support his wife and children on an ever and ever higher plane.[39] This pressure can be verified by reviewing the huge increase in consumer credit in recent decades or by reading the personal bankruptcy notices in the evening paper. Some families have more or less solved this problem by having the mother take a job outside of the home. This undoubtedly takes some of the pressure off of the father but may place considerable stress on the mother. There might also be some loss of maternal supervision of the children, plus the possibility of some strain on the marriage.

The strategy of the mass media in our society is to keep several years ahead of the consumer. Just when you and I have decided that a certain type of home refrigerator is all we need, the advertisers begin pushing a new and bigger model that we are supposed to aim for. This was seen

---

36 Benson (*Fatherhood*, pp. 122–24) has a discussion of this.

37 For the latest federal government study, see Margaret Mead and Frances Kaplan, *American Women* (New York: Charles Scribner's Sons, 1965). This is the report of the President's Commission on the Status of Women. In the writer's state there is an active Governor's Commission on the Status of Women—as there are in many other states. The writer is entirely in favor of such commissions but would like to suggest that the American male could stand some study also.

38 When Kendall (*The Upper Hand*) began to study the American male, she discovered that for every book on men in the New York City Library there were literally hundreds of books on women. For some observations on the American father and his problems, see Brenton, "The Paradox of the Contemporary American Father," *The American Male,* chap. 5.

39 For an interesting discussion of personal bankruptcy cases, see George Sullivan, *The Boom in Going Bust* (New York: Macmillan Co., 1968).

in the 1960s in the tremendous drive to outdate the black and white television receivers and replace them with color sets. One father said to us: "Our black and white set works just fine but the wife and kids have been after me for six months to trade it in on a color set." He finally made the trade at Christmas time and found that his old set was worth only $50 on a trade. The new color set cost approximately $500. This man works in a factory and his take-home pay does not average over $400 a month. He says that he manages to get by only because his wife works also.

For the 20 or 30 percent of fathers on the bottom of the economic system, the financial problems are more stark: they are faced with not being able to provide food, clothing, or housing for their families. They are also faced with the knowledge that in a society in which most people are reasonably well off, they are not. This is the meaning of "relative deprivation"—it is not only what you do not have, it is also what the people around you *do* have.[40] In other words, it is quite different being hungry in India where millions are on the verge of starvation than it is being hungry in the United States where most people overeat.

The writer believes that *most* American fathers suffer from economic problems of one kind or another. We even interviewed a young physician earning $25,000 a year who said that his financial pressures were almost too much for him. Only those who have sweated out economic problems know how they can affect family life: the quality of the husband-wife relationship, the feeling of the children for their parents, and the attitude of the father and mother toward being parents. A man's self-image in our society is deeply affected by this ability to provide for his family. Many times the self-image is not too positive.

2. *Marital problems.* These have already been commented on in the previous section of this chapter and only need to be noted here. For the uninitiated, however, it needs to be emphasized that the divorce rate, which is what most Americans think of when they think about marital failure, does not tell the whole story by any means. We have not only divorce, but also separation, desertion, and "holy deadlock"—marriages which are never terminated but are essentially pathogenic for all involved.[41] It may well be that there are more holy deadlock marriages than there are divorces. We just do not know how many American marriages are of the "shell" or "facade" type.[42]

---

[40] For an excellent analysis of poverty in our society, see the collection of essays, *Poverty: Views from the Left*, edited by Jeremy Larner and Irving Howe (New York: William Morrow & Co., 1968).

[41] In the paper "Holy Deadlock" cited earlier, the writer pointed out that unsuccessful marriages that are never terminated legally are counted as successful marriages because they never show up in any other category.

[42] In their survey of upper-middle-class married couples, Cuber and Harroff concluded that perhaps two thirds of these marriages had become "facade" marriages in the middle and later decades of life (see John Cuber and Peggy Harroff, *The Sig-*

But no matter how one looks at it, the failure of his marriage is a major problem for the American father.

3. *Sex life.* Kinsey and his research group found that the American male finds it difficult to confine his sexual interests to his wife.[43] Other studies have reported that the male does not think his wife is a good sexual partner.[44]

Part of the problem here is that the male adolescent peer group does not socialize for sexual monogamy: it stresses the fact that all women are legitimate sexual objects (except mothers and sisters) and that a man is a fool if he does not take advantage of any sexual opportunity. After living in this world for several years, the man finds it difficult to think of his wife as the only legitimate sexual object. Girls at the office, wives of other men, divorced women—he finds many of these women sexually attractive, and he often finds that they view him in the same light. In an urban society there are many opportunities for straying; the controls have to be internal because the external controls of the rural or village society are not present. A substantial number of married men find this situation somewhat more than they can manage.

In the Victorian world a married man would solve this problem by having an affair with a younger woman or a woman of a lower social class. If he was discreet, as Warren G. Harding was,[45] his wife would overlook the matter. And the man would be protected because marriage to this other woman was usually not possible.

Things are not so simple today. Men and women who become involved sexually in modern America are often from the same social class, and marriage is always a possibility. Thus, what starts out as an affair ends up in divorce and remarriage, with the father becoming separated from his children.

One can debate the morality of all of this endlessly. We are only interested in the father's sex life as it affects his marriage and hence his relationship with his children. It seems clear that (1) if his sex life with his wife is not satisfying his tolerance of his marriage will be lowered, and (2) his tendency to look around for another sexual partner will be enhanced. In either event, his role as father will suffer more or less.

4. *Drinking problem.* Our impression is that a substantial proportion

---

nificant Americans [New York: Appleton-Century, 1965]). This study is marred by the fact that the authors do not bother to cite any of the previous studies of marriage in our society.

[43] Kinsey concluded that perhaps one half of U.S. husbands had committed adultery at least once; see Alfred Kinsey et al., *Sexual Behavior in the Human Male* (Philadelphia: W. B. Saunders Co., 1948), p. 585.

[44] For a review of some of this data see Hunt, *World of the Formerly Married.*

[45] President Harding apparently was married to a sexless woman who knew that he had had at least two affairs with other women; see Francis Russell, *The Shadow of Blooming Grove: Warren G. Harding in His Times* (New York: McGraw-Hill Book Co., 1968).

of "bad" fathers in our society have a drinking problem. Trice reports that various estimates conclude that fathers are three to six times more likely to drink alcohol excessively in our society than are mothers.[46]

If a man drinks too much, there are at least four ways in which this affects his performance as a parent: (a) the drinking becomes a real strain on the family budget, and this is true at almost all economic levels except for the very wealthy; (b) the quality of the marriage suffers; (c) when the father is home he is not able to function normally—he is either too good to the children or he is abusive; (d) the attitude of the children toward him changes from positive to negative.[47]

For persons who have never known alcoholism at close range, the events that take place between alcoholics and their families are unbelievable. Only recently we interviewed a young mother with two children who said that during a drinking bout her husband threatened to kill her and both children. When sober this sort of behavior was never apparent in this husband-father. The wife is now afraid of her husband and has obtained a separation.

This woman has reason to be afraid of her husband. The writer, using news reports, tallied 27 children and 7 wives who were murdered in Wisconsin during 1967 by husband-fathers who were reported by the authorities to have "been drinking."

It is true, of course, that excessive drinking by American mothers is becoming more and more frequent in our society, but in this analysis we are focusing on only the father.

This excessive drinking by the father is by no means confined to any one social class. It may be found at all socioeconomic levels in substantial numbers.

5. *The male peer group.* In his study of blue-collar workers in Boston, Gans found that the men liked to spend much of their spare time with other men, away from their wives and children.[48] This sort of behavior was accepted in the particular ethnic group (Italian) and posed no great problems. But a great many American women these days view marriage and parenthood as a partnership and do not readily accept male-only activities. It is the writer's belief that a vast number of American men prefer to spend their spare time with other males and that this is one of the most difficult adjustments they have to make in modern marriage. A certain proportion of them refuse to make this concession to their wives and children and continue to spend most of their spare time with the boys.

At blue-collar levels there may be a certain amount of tolerance of

---

[46] See Harrison M. Trice, *Alcoholism in America* (New York: McGraw-Hill Book Co., 1966), pp. 19–20.

[47] Ibid., chap. 5.

[48] Herbert J. Gans, *The Urban Villagers* (New York: Free Press, 1962).

"segregated sex roles" (as this behavior is called), but America is becoming increasingly a white-collar world and women seem to be less and less tolerant of staying home with the children.

To resolve this sort of strain, the American male has to be domesticated more than he ever has been in the past. To what extent this has been accomplished, or can be accomplished, we do not know. But some men are difficult to harness, as their wives have discovered. When this is the case, it seems likely that the father's role is diminished or affected negatively in some way.

6. *Resentment of women.* In the last several decades, beginning with World War I, American women have been involved in a vast social revolution, the aim of which has been to give them equality with men.[49] This drastic upheaval has thrown the two sexes into more direct competition and has taken from men some of the special privileges they once had—the exclusive right to vote, control of most work opportunities, the double standard of sexual morality, and others. While most men may recognize that women are entitled to social equality, it is not always clear that they really like the position women have won for themselves. In talking with men informally, the writer has been impressed with the underlying hostility that many American men seem to have toward the modern woman. In a recent election a prominent woman in our community was defeated for the school board—a position she was eminently qualified for. We asked a male friend of ours if he had voted for her. "No, I didn't," he said. "I think women are trying to take this town over. It's about time the men began to assert themselves."

This is the way many white persons now feel toward blacks: they are getting "too equal" and something will have to be done about it. It seems to us that the analogy here between the new position of women and the new position of blacks is very real: intelligent persons recognize the need for sexual equality and also for racial equality, but their emotions need more time to get used to the change.

One husband, in criticizing his wife, said to us: "She wanted to wear the pants, now let her take the consequences." In other words, if women want equality they should shoulder half of the load, whatever it is.

To the extent that modern American men do have hostility toward their wives, the role of father will be complicated by this feeling. In some men this is very evident, but we do not know how typical or atypical these men are.

---

[49] For a scholarly analysis of the efforts of American women to obtain social equality, see William L. O'Neill, *Everyone Was Brave: The Rise and Fall of Feminism in America*, (Chicago: Quadrangle Books, 1969). See also E. E. LeMasters, "The Passing of the Dominant Husband-Father," *Impact of Science on Society* (Paris, 1971), **21**: 21–30.

Some general observations on the American father

1. *Today's father has more leisure.* It is fashionable in our society to romanticize the family system of an earlier historical period and to condemn the family of today. It is our belief that in some ways the contemporary American father is an improvement over his predecessors. A good example would be the amount of leisure time the modern father spends with his children. This will be illustrated with a case study.

We recently had a chance to interview at length a man almost 90 years old concerning his boyhood in rural Pennsylvania in the 1880s. This man's mind was quite alert and clear, even though his body was somewhat the worse for wear.

Growing up on a prosperous farm in eastern Pennsylvania in the latter part of the 19th century, Mr. D. could scarcely recall any "leisure" or "play" with his father. One reason was that leisure or recreation was considered to be bad in those days—character and salvation came from hard work.

This elderly man was quite sure that his father had never played baseball with his sons (there were five boys in this family), gone sledding or ice-skating with them in winter, swum with them in the summer. He could remember doing all of these things, but never with either of his parents. Hunting was an exception: the father did hunt with his sons in the fall.

Mr. D. could recall his father and mother taking all of the children to the county fair in the fall; this was an annual event for the whole family and stood out in this elderly man's memory as the fun day of the year.

Vivid memories of *working* with his father on the farm were retained by this man—plowing and sowing seed in the fall and spring; harvesting the various crops; butchering in the fall; doing the endless daily chores.

Sunday was a day of rest, with only the essential work (feeding and watering the livestock) being done. Two church services were usually attended by the entire family.

In essence, this man from the 1880s has no memory of his father as a pal or companion.

In contrast, fathers today go on camping trips with their children, play golf and other games with them, take annual family vacations as a group, go to drive-in movies in the family car, watch television together, and in general spend a lot of spare time with their wives and children.

It is not being proposed that today's father-child companionship pattern is necessarily superior to the father-child work relationship of the earlier rural America—our point is that the contemporary father *does* spend a lot of time with his children. One reason, of course, is that the time is available; he does not (as a rule) have the long work week that his father and grandfather had.

2. *Today's father is more domesticated.* There is some reason to believe that American men have changed drastically since World War II.[50] They are infinitely more domesticated than their male ancestors: they cook more meals, clean more homes, change more diapers, do more baby-sitting, remodel more rooms, and in general are more geared into family activities. Not everybody is entirely happy about this new American male —not even all of the men themselves—but, like him or pity him, the current American male is a new breed.

In the last analysis, only a "new man" can understand and live success-fully with the contemporary American woman. It is simply not possible to produce a modern 20th-century woman and expect her to settle for a 19th-century man.

3. *The new male model is popular.* If today's American woman is unhappy with the American male she doesn't show it by refusing to marry; the marriage rate in our society is at an all-time high.[51] Even divorced men seem to be readily acceptable as marriage partners.[52] It may be that one of the factors producing the high marriage rate is the acceptability of the new male model.

4. *Social class variations in father performance.* If data were avail-able, it might emerge that American fathers are least adequate at the top and bottom of the social class structure. Although no systematic studies of the upper-class father in our society have ever been made, it seems clear that their outside commitments force them to delegate much of their parental role to other persons, boarding-school teachers, summer-camp counselors, and the like.

At the bottom of the social class system, there is considerable evidence that the lower-class father (the 20 or 30 percent at the poverty level) finds his parental responsibilities overwhelming.[53] Not only does he lack the money required to support his family, he also suffers from inadequate education, poor health (physical as well as mental), slum housing, high rates of marital instability, and a host of other problems.

It might be that the best American fathers are found at the stable blue-collar level and in the vast white-collar middle class.

5. *The effects of military service.* Some 15–20 million American men have served in the armed forces since World War II. Almost all of these men became fathers after returning to civilian life—if they were not al-ready fathers at the time of induction.

We do not profess to know how military service affects a man's capac-

---

[50] See Brenton, *The American Male.*

[51] These statistics are reviewed in Bell, *Marriage and Family Interaction,* pp. 138–39.

[52] Ibid., pp. 496–501.

[53] See chap. 5 for an extensive discussion of social class and parenthood.

ity to be a good father.[54] It might be that the experience helps men to mature, and maturity is certainly an asset in being a parent.

The great variety of humans encountered in the armed forces might also help future fathers understand some of the differences they will discover in their own children.

It is also possible that the destruction one sees in military service may be functional for fathers in helping them appreciate the preciousness of human life and motivate them not only to start families when they return home but also to nourish and protect them. This may actually have been a factor in the high birthrate that followed World War II in the United States.

It is difficult to identify the negative impact of military service on future fathers. There is an obvious "crudity factor" that all men in the armed forces are subjected to—crude and obscene language, crude bedroom stories, sexual promiscuity, excessive drinking, gambling—and it is difficult to see how this sort of life prepares a man to be a good husband or a good father.

The writer confesses that he does not know the net effect of military service on future fathers. It is only suggested that this experience be remembered when critics look at the current generation of American fathers.

6. *Differential impact of American culture.* If one looks at the social deviation rates, such as crime, alcoholism, drug addiction, and desertion,[55] it is possible to conclude that the destructive impact of American society is greater on males than females. One either has to believe this or accept Montagu's claim that women are the stronger sex.[56] It seems plausible that different cultures have a differential impact on the two sexes and that ours hits men harder than women. If this is true, it would help to explain some of the paternal deficiencies noted in this chapter.

The unmarried father in American society

A graphic illustration of paternal status (or lack of status) may be seen in the predicament of the unmarried father in contemporary America. Until recently, very little was known about this shadowy figure; and, in the absence of research data, this man was portrayed as a sinister monster who seduced innocent young females and abandoned them when they found themselves pregnant.

---

[54] The following observations are based on three years service during World War II. We doubt that it has changed much since then.

[55] For a review of this data, see Marshall B. Clinard, *Sociology of Deviant Behavior* (New York: Rinehart & Co., 1968).

[56] Ashley Montagu, *The Natural Superiority of Women* (New York: Macmillan Co., 1968).

Recent studies have yielded quite a different picture of the unmarried father: (1)[57] he is usually about the same age as the unmarried mother; (2) he is normally from the same social class as his girl friend; (3) the pregnancy is very often the result of a "love affair"—not a casual sexual encounter; (4) it is not always clear who seduced whom in these relationships; (5) the expectant father is concerned about the welfare of the expectant mother; (6) the boy (or man) is also concerned about the welfare of the unborn child; (7) in some cases, the male has offered to marry the girl and has been refused; and (8) unmarried fathers, as a group, are willing to participate in research projects when invited.

The legal position of the unmarried father in the United States has been extremely difficult—in most states he has all of the responsibilities of a father and none of the rights.[58] In Wisconsin, for example, the courts have held that an unmarried mother may place the child with strangers for adoption even if the unmarried father offers to rear the child.[59] In most states the unmarried father has no right to visit his child even when he is supporting the child. Furthermore, the unmarried father's legal status does not improve even when he has offered to marry the expectant mother and has been refused.

It seems clear that unmarried fathers in American society are the victims of outmoded laws that express traditional myths about these men. American women are not the only victims of ancient sexist legislation in our society.

Summary and conclusion

In this chapter some of the problems of the American father have been analyzed. Two developments seem to be outstanding: (1) the exclusion of fathers from field studies of parents, and (2) the decline in power and prestige of the father in our family system. On this latter point, Benson has written that "a man wields power in the contemporary household only if he has the personal characteristics to pull it off or because of a unique pattern of domestic relationships, not because society backs him up with strong support."[60] The writer agrees with Benson.

---

[57] These studies are reviewed in Reuben Pannor et al., *The Unmarried Father* (New York: Springer Publishing Co., 1971).

[58] This material is reviewed in a special news report from the *New York Times* and reprinted in the *Wisconsin State Journal*, April 30, 1972.

[59] This decision has since been reversed in the U.S. Supreme Court in the case *Stanley* v. *State of Illinois*.

[60] Benson, *Fatherhood*, pp. 99–100.

chapter
nine

Parents without partners

In thinking about parents, it is easy to assume a model of what might be termed "the biological parent team" of mother and father. In this model two parents act as partners in carrying out the parental functions. Furthermore, both of the parents are biological as well as social parents. It is this parent-team model that is analyzed in most of the chapters in this book.

What is not realized by many observers, especially by parent critics, is the fact that a considerable proportion of contemporary American parents do not operate under these ideal conditions. These parents include "parents without partners" (mostly divorced or separated women, but including some men also); widows and widowers with children; unmarried mothers; adoptive parents; stepparents; and, finally, foster parents.

Some of the groups in the list above are amazingly large—Simon, for example, reports that in the 1960s in the United States there were about *seven million* children living with a stepparent.[1] This means that approximately one out of every nine children in modern America is a stepchild.

---

[1] See Anne W. Simon, *Stepchild in the family* (New York: Odyssey Press, 1964), p. 69.

In this chapter we wish to do two things: (1) summarize the statistics on these parental subgroups, and (2) analyze the role complications these parents are confronted with. Some of these parents may actually have certain advantages over so-called normal parents, and where this seems to be the case we will analyze this also.

Mothers without fathers

One of the by now familiar parental types in our society is the mother rearing her children alone. As of 1960 about one household out of ten in the United States was headed by a woman.[2] In an earlier, more innocent America, this mother without father was seen as a heroic figure—a brave woman whose husband had died who was struggling to rear her brood by scrubbing floors, taking in family laundry, and so on. This was the brave little widow of an earlier day.

After the end of World War I, as the divorce rate began to climb, this picture—and this woman—underwent a radical change. With the rapid improvement of American medicine, marriages in the early and middle decades of life were no longer broken primarily by death; now the great destroyers of marriages came to be social and psychological, not biological.

With this shift, the public's attitude toward the mother with no father by her side changed drastically—it became ambivalent. In some cases she might be viewed with sympathy and understanding, if she happened to be your sister or a close friend, but more often she was perceived as a woman of questionable character—either the gay divorcee of the upper social class levels or the AFDC mother living off the taxpayers at the lower social class levels.[3] In either case the image was a far cry from that of the heroic little widow of the Victorian era.

Statistically, and otherwise, these mothers without fathers fall into five different categories: divorced, separated, deserted, widowed, and never married. All of these categories overlap, so that some mothers might at some point in their lives occupy all five positions in the list.

Our procedure in discussing these mothers in their parental role will be to identify the generic patterns and problems shared by all of these mothers, and then to look at the relatively unique patterns that cluster about any specific position.

---

[2] Alvin Schorr has an analysis of this data in *Poor Kids* (New York: Basic Books, 1966), esp. pp. 16–22. One estimate concludes that over 6 million children in the United States are growing up in fatherless homes; See Elizabeth Herzog and Cecelia Sudia, "Fatherless Homes," *Children* 15 (1968): 177–82.

[3] For an excellent discussion of the changing attitudes toward divorced persons, see William L. O'Neill, *Divorce in the Progressive Era* (New Haven, Conn.: Yale University Press, 1967).

Generic features of mothers without partners

1. *Poverty.* It has been estimated that while households headed by a woman comprise only about 10 percent of all U.S. households, they constitute about 25 percent of the families in the so-called poverty group in American society.[4]

In the best study yet published on divorced women, Goode found financial stress to be a major complaint.[5] At any given time, approximately 40 percent of the divorced husbands in this study were delinquent in their support payments, a pattern that seems to be nationwide.[6]

Poverty is extremely relative, as is deprivation. A divorced woman receiving even $1,000 a month in support payments may have to reduce her standard of living from what it was before her divorce.

The reasons for the financial difficulties of these mothers are not mysterious or difficult to identify. Most American men cannot afford to support two living establishments on a high level. This is one reason why some support payments are delinquent. The man usually gets involved with at least one other woman, and this costs money.[7] Often his new woman is not well off financially, and the man may find himself contributing to her support also.

Since a considerable proportion of divorced women are apparently employed at the time of their divorce,[8] they had what is commonly called a two-income family. The mother may continue to work after the father has left the home, but with two living establishments to maintain, two cars, and so on, the financial situation tends to be tight.

In a study of AFDC mothers in Boston, it was discovered that these women faced financial crises almost monthly.[9] They coped with these difficult situations by accepting aid from members of their family; by pooling their resources with neighbors and women friends in the same plight; and by occasional aid from a boy friend.

In several counseling cases with divorced women, the writer was im-

---

[4] Schorr, "And Children of the Nation Come First," *Poor Kids*, chap. 2.

[5] On the financial problems of divorced women, see William J. Goode, "Postdivorce Economic Activities," *After Divorce* (New York: Free Press, 1956), chap. 16.

[6] Ibid.; see chap. 16 for a discussion of the problem of support payments after divorce.

[7] The financial problems of the divorced man were analyzed in a 1968 study (unpublished) conducted by the writer and several graduate students from the School of Social Work, University of Wisconsin. Eighty divorced men were interviewed at length. Financial problems were one of the constant complaints of these men.

[8] On the employment of wives at the point of divorce, see Goode, *After Divorce*, pp. 71–74.

[9] A discussion of the financial crises of AFDC mothers may be found in Sydney E. Bernard, *Fatherless Families: Their Economic and Social Adjustment* (Waltham, Mass.: Brandeis University, 1964); see also Louis Kriesberg, *Mothers in Poverty* (Chicago: Aldine Publishing Co., 1970).

pressed with the annoying feature of the relative poverty experienced by these women—one woman did not have the money to get her television set repaired and this created tension between herself and her children. Another woman, who lived in an area with inadequate bus service, could not afford an automobile. Any person in our society can understand how frustrating problems of this nature can be.

2. *Role conflicts.* Since these women have added the father role to their parental responsibilities, they tend to be either overloaded or in conflict over their various role commitments. The presence of a husband-father provides more role flexibility than these women now have—if the mother is ill, or has to work late, the husband may be able to be home with the children.

When these mothers are employed outside of the home, as a sizable proportion are,[10] the work hours usually conflict with those of the school system. Children leave for school too late, get home too early, and have far too many vacations for the employed mother. There are also childhood illnesses that must be coped with.

It is true that the termination of the marriage has reduced or eliminated the mother's role as wife, but she is still a woman in the early decades of life and men will be in the picture sooner or later. Thus, she may not be a wife at the moment but she will soon be a girl friend, and the courtship role may be even more demanding than that of wife.

It is the writer's belief, based on numerous interviews with divorced women, that being the head of a household is, for most women, an 18-hour day, seven days a week, and 365 days a year job. It would seem that only the most capable, and the most fortunate, can perform all of the roles involved effectively.

3. *Role shifts.* Since the vast majority of the mothers being discussed here—80–90 percent—will eventually remarry, they face the difficult process of taking over the father role and then relinquishing it.[11] This is not easy for most of us; once we have appropriated a role in a family system, it is often difficult to turn it over to somebody else.

Furthermore, these mothers operate in an unusual family system in that, for an indefinite period, they do not have to worry about what the other parent thinks. They are both mother and father for the time being.

This is not entirely true, of course, in the case of the divorced woman, but it seems to be largely true, even for this group.[12] The departed father

---

[10] For an analysis of the employment of mothers with minor children, see F. Ivan Nye and Lois Wladis Hoffman, *The Employed Mother in America* (Chicago: Rand McNally & Co., 1963), pp. 7–15.

[11] See Reuben Hill, *Families Under Stress* (New York: Harper & Bros., 1949).

[12] Goode (*After Divorce,* chap. 21) discusses some of the postdivorce problems of the father and his children.

starts out with the best intentions of "not forgetting my kids," but a variety of factors tend to reduce his parental influence as time goes on.[13]

One divorced woman talked to the writer about the problem of "shifting gears" in her parental roles: "I found it very difficult," she said. "When my husband and I were first divorced he continued to see the children and participated in some of the decisions about them. Then he moved to another state and we seldom saw him after that—but he did continue to send the support checks.

"At this point," she continued, "I assumed almost all of the parental responsibilities, except for the money sent by my former husband and some advice (of questionable value) that my mother chipped in from time to time.

"And then I met the man I am now married to. At first he stayed out of the children's lives, not being sure how long he and I would be going together. But as we moved toward marriage the children became attached to him and gradually he became a foster father to them. Now he has taken over a considerable amount of parental responsibility and I am back almost to where I was before my divorce—I am just a mother again."[14]

In the study by Hill, he analyzed role shifts in a group of families in which the father had been temporarily pulled out of the home for military service. Hill discovered (a) that some of the wife-mothers could not pick up the added responsibility when the father left the home, and (b) that some of the mothers could not relinquish the father role when the husband returned from the service. One has the impression that some of the mothers being discussed here have these same problems.

Once these women have remarried, there is a sort of built-in strain in that one of the parents (the mother) is a natural parent while the other (the father) is only a stepparent. This syndrome will be analyzed later in this chapter, but it needs to be mentioned here.

4. *Public attitudes.* These mothers are operating in deviant family situations, and for the most part the community tends to regard them and their children as deviants.[15] Except for the widow, all of these mothers are viewed with some ambivalence in our society. They receive some sympathy, some respect, and some help, but they are also viewed as

---

[13] In the 1968 unpublished study of 80 divorced men cited earlier (see n. 7 above), the lack of contact with their children was one of the problems most often referred to by these fathers.

[14] This woman was a professional social worker—hence some of her language is a bit technical.

[15] For a discussion of the concept of "social deviation," see Marshall B. Clinard, *Sociology of Deviant Behavior* (New York: Rinehart & Co., 1968), pp. 3–27.

women who are not "quite right"—they did not sustain their marriage "until death do us part."[16]

The unmarried mother, of course, never had a marriage to sustain, and the public has no ambivalence about her; they simply condemn her and that is that.[17]

If these mothers require support from public welfare, they will find the community's mixed feelings reflected in their monthly check—the community will not permit them and their children to starve, but it will also not allow them to live at a decent level.[18]

5. *The well of loneliness.* Any parent rearing children alone will suffer some degree of emotional deprivation. This syndrome appears repeatedly in interviews with divorced and widowed parents. The love partner has been taken away, and whether this was the result of death or divorce, the psychological impact is similar—one half of the parental team has been lost. Sooner or later all (or most) of these parents will reach out for a new life partner, but in the interim it is a very lonely world.

We have now examined some of the generic problems of the one-parent family system, except for the system in which the one-parent is a father, which will be looked at later. Now let us analyze the specific features of the subsystems in the one-parent family.

Specific features of the subsystems in the one-parent family

1. *The divorced mother.* The divorced mother has several advantages over the deserted mother: she at least has had the help of a domestic relations court in spelling out the financial responsibility of the father, also the legal arrangements for custody. In this sense divorce is a lot less messy than desertion in our society.

The divorced mother is also legally free to associate with other men and to remarry if she finds the right person—advantages the deserted woman does not have.

The divorced father, it seems to us, is not in an enviable position in his role as father. He may be happy not to be married to his children's mother any more, but he often hates to be separated from his children.[19]

---

[16] On the attitudes of people toward the divorced person in our society, see Morton M. Hunt, *The World of the Formerly Married* (New York: McGraw-Hill Book Co., 1966), passim; See also Goode, "Social Adjustment," *After Divorce*, chap. 17.

[17] It is possible, of course, for a woman who was once married to become an unmarried mother at a later date—as a widow or as a divorced woman.

[18] Alvin Schorr explores the inadequacy of the AFDC welfare program in his study, *Explorations in Social Policy* (New York: Basic Books, 1968).

[19] In the 1968 study of divorced men, conducted at the University of Wisconsin, there was frequent concern expressed by the men about the welfare of their children after the divorce, (see n. 7 above).

In a sense he still has the responsibility of a father for his minor children but few of the enjoyments of parenthood. To be with his children he has to interact to some degree with his former wife—a process so painful that he was willing to have the marriage terminated.

In the unpublished study of 80 divorced men one of the most frequent regrets expressed by the men was their frustration and concern about their relationships to their children.[20]

The divorced mother has one parental advantage that she shares with all other parents without partners; she does not have to share the daily parental decisions with a partner who might not agree with her strategy. In the Goode study of divorced women, the mothers seemed to think this was an advantage.[21] The parental partner can be of great help if he can agree with his mate on how their children should be reared, but when this is not the case one parent can probably do a better job going it alone.

2. *The deserted mother.* It has already been indicated that desertions in our society are more messy than divorces.[22] There are two reasons: (1) desertion is more apt to be unilateral, with the decision to pull out being made by one party alone; and (2) there is no court supervision of the desertion process—it is unplanned from society's point of view.

The deserted mother is likely to have more severe financial problems than the divorced mother because support payments have not been agreed upon.

Psychologically, desertion is probably more traumatic than divorce, partly because it is more unilateral but also because it is less planned.[23] To the extent that this is true—and we recognize that the evidence on this point is not conclusive—then the deserted mother is handicapped in her parental role by her emotional upheaval or trauma.

This woman also has other problems; she is not legally free to remarry and in a sense not even free to go out with other men since she is technically still a married woman. These feelings, of course, will tend to reflect the social class and the moral subculture of the particular woman.

3. *The separated mother.* If we assume that most marital separations in modern America have been arrived at by mutual agreement, then this mother has certain advantages over the deserted mother. One disadvan-

---

[20] The 80 detailed interviews from this study are not yet fully analyzed.

[21] See Goode, *After Divorce*, chap. 21, for a discussion of how the divorced women in his sample felt about rearing children after the marriage had been terminated.

[22] One of the better discussions of desertion is the paper by William M. Kephart, "Occupational Level and Marital Disruption," *American Sociological Review* (August 1955). Among other things Kephart believes desertion to be more common than is generally thought. He also found that desertion was by no means limited to the lower socioeconomic levels.

[23] The writer has been unable to find any empirical research that compares the psychological trauma of divorce with that of desertion.

tage is that her courtship status is ambiguous; another is that she is not free to remarry.[24] Psychologically, the separated mother should reflect patterns similar to those of the divorced mother: her marriage has failed but she has done something about it and now has to plan for her future life.

4. *The widowed mother.* The one big advantage of this parent is the favorable attitude of her family, her friends, and the community toward her. This tends to be reflected in her self-image, thus giving her emotional support. Once she emerges from the period of bereavement, however, she has to face about the same problems as the women discussed previously —she probably will have financial problems; she will have to be father as well as mother; she may need to get a job; and eventually she will have to consider whether to remarry.

It is difficult to say whether the widowed woman suffers more or less emotional trauma than the women whose husbands are still alive but whose marriages are dead. Both have experienced "death" in one form or another—either psychological or physical.

It is undoubtedly true that some of the marriages of widowed women had also failed before the husband died, but there is no way to discover how large this group is.

5. *The unmarried mother.* This is not the place to review the status and problems of the unmarried mother in our society—the literature on this woman is quite voluminous.[25] It only needs to be said here that this mother has all of the problems of the women discussed before plus a few of her own. She is more likely to be a member of a racial minority—one of the extra burdens she has to shoulder. She is also more likely to be on public welfare[26]—a major burden in itself in our society. Her chances for marriage are not as gloomy as some people once thought,[27] but her chances for a successful marriage may be more dubious.

The unmarried mother has one dubious advantage over the divorced, the deserted, and the separated mothers. She does not have to juggle the

---

[24] On the courtship and remarriage problems of divorced and separated women, see Jessie Bernard, *Remarriage* (New York: Dryden Press, 1956); also Goode, "Steady Dating, Imminent Marriage, and Remarriage," *After Divorce*, chap. 19. Hunt, *World of the Formerly Married,* also analyzes these problems at length.

[25] On the unmarried mother, see the following: Clark Vincent, *Unmarried Mothers* (New York: Free Press, 1961); Robert W. Roberts, ed., *The Unwed Mother* (New York: Harper & Row, 1966).

[26] Bernard, (*Fatherless Families*) states that women under 35 with no husbands in the household are responsible for more children than are the households headed by men under 35. See also Schorr, *Poor Kids,* p. 21. In chap. 7, "Fatherless Child Insurance," Schorr has an excellent analysis of the economic problems faced by unmarried mothers in our society.

[27] See Rose Bernstein, "Are We Still Stereotyping the Unmarried Mother?" *Social Work* 5 (January 1960): 22–38.

ambivalent feelings of the general public toward her; she knows that they disapprove of her almost unanimously.

We are talking here, of course, of the unmarried mothers who keep their children. Those who give up their children for adoption, and those who terminate their pregnancies via the abortionist, have their own problems which will not be discussed in this book.

It is interesting to note that some women in our society have occupied *all* of the positions discussed so far. They have been unmarried mothers, divorced, deserted, separated, and widowed, although not necessarily in that order. We have interviewed two such women and they both were remarkable persons.

One of these women was an unmarried mother at 16, deserted at 18, divorced at 20, widowed at 23, and remarried at 25. Along the way she had accumulated six children and had been separated any number of times.

What impressed us about this woman was not only her lonely journey through the wars of matrimony but her intense concern for the welfare of her children. The general public would undoubtedly have viewed her as a "bad" mother, but our own judgment was that she did quite well with children—her problems were largely with husbands and boy friends. It is too bad that women like this do not write books, for they could tell all of us much that we need to know.

Father-only families

As of 1972 the U.S. Bureau of the Census estimated that there were 796,000 families in which fathers were rearing one or more children under 18 years of age with no mother present.[28] Of this number, 249,000 of the fathers were reported to be widowers, while the rest had either never been married or had experienced marital failure. The writer has been unable to discover any published studies of these father-only families.

It seems likely that these fathers do not continue indefinitely to rear their children alone, that the majority of them remarry, in which case they would experience the same problems of role shifts discussed earlier for mothers on their own.

It also seems likely that these men experience role conflicts between their jobs, their social life, and their parental responsibility.

It is doubtful that these solo fathers would suffer from poverty to the extent found among solo mothers—but the writer has no data to cite in support of this statement.

The rat race experienced by mothers rearing families without the help

---

[28] U.S. Bureau of the Census, *Characteristics of Families*, Series P-20, no. 242 (Washington, D.C., 1972), p. 25, table 5.

of a father would likely be found among these men also; it simply reflects what might be termed "role overload."

Psychologically, judging from case studies to be presented shortly, these men probably suffer from the same syndrome found among mothers who have lost their husbands—loneliness, sorrow, perhaps bitterness, often a sense of failure, plus a feeling of being overwhelmed by their almost complete responsibility for their children. About the only effective treatment for feelings of this nature is to find a new partner and get married—the solution most adult Americans rely on for whatever ails them. These fathers are no exception to this statement.

It would appear that these men have a few problems that would be less likely to bother mothers: the physical care of preschool children and the tasks of home management, such as shopping for food and clothes, preparing meals, doing the family laundry, and cleaning the house. Some men become quite adept at this work after awhile, but for others a stove or an iron remains a mystery forever.

Case studies of fathers without mothers

1. *Case of desertion.* A man of 45 talked to us at length about his struggle to complete the rearing of his three children after his wife had deserted him.

"I came home one night from work and she was gone. A note said that she no longer wanted to live with me and that she thought the children would be better off with me."

"Later on I had a letter from her from California with no return address."

Fortunately, one of this father's children was of high school age and could help with the younger children.

This man says that he went "through hell" for several months—the blow of being deserted, plus the added responsibility for his children, were almost too much for him.

The final solution in this case was the willingness of a widowed sister, with no children of her own, to move in with this family and take over most of the responsibility for the children. After a one-year trial this arrangement seemed to be working out.

2. *Case of divorce.* A man interviewed by the writer had divorced his wife because of an affair she had with a friend of his. Since he felt quite strongly that his wife was not competent to rear their four children, he applied to the court for custody of the children and his petition was approved.

This man was quite definite that he and the children managed better without the mother than they had ever done when she had been present.

"She was always feuding with either me or one of the children. She was moody and negative about life. And she hated any kind of housework. After she left the kids and I got along fine. I did the cooking, they did the housecleaning, and we hired a woman to do the laundry. It worked out just fine."

This man—a remarkable person—even took his four children on a year's tour of Europe after his divorce. Using a combined passenger car and bus, they camped all over Europe, settling down in one country for several months so the children could attend school and study a foreign language.

This man has now remarried. He still has custody of the four children and reports that "everything is fine."

3. *Case involving the death of a mother.* This man talked freely of his life after the death of his wife. He said that since only one of his three children (a boy of ten) was still at home when his wife died, he had decided to "bach it"—in other words, he did not attempt to employ a housekeeper, nor did he invite any of his grown children to move back into the family home.

He said, "I felt that the boy and I could manage by ourselves and that we would be better off that way."

This was a small town and many relatives were nearby if help was needed.

This man had been very much in love with his wife and had no desire to remarry.

Eight years after his wife's death, when the boy was ready for college or a job, the father did remarry. He feels that the plan worked out well for both him and the boy—but when the son was about to leave home, the father felt the need for companionship and so he got married.

The writer does not present these cases as being typical. They simply illustrate some of the patterns to be found in the father-only family in our society.

Is the one-parent family pathological?

Most of us probably assume that the one-parent family is inherently pathological—at least for the children involved. It seems only logical to assume that two parents are better than one—the old adage that two heads are better than one.

In his text on the American family, Bell summarizes several studies that question the assumption that two parents are better than one—judging by the adjustment of the children.[29] This, however, does not say anything about the impact of solo child rearing on the parent, which is the major concern of this book.

If one wishes to debate the number of adults required to socialize children properly, the question can be raised, Who decided that *two*

---

[29] Robert B. Bell, *Marriage and Family Interaction*, 3d ed. (Homewood, Ill.: Dorsey Press, 1971), pp. 419–20.

parents was the proper number? Biologically this is natural enough, but this does not prove its social rightness.

As a matter of fact, a family sociologist, Farber, has asked the question, "Are two parents enough? . . . in almost every human society *more* than two adults are involved in the socialization of the child."[30]

Farber goes on to point out that in many societies a "third parent," outside of the nuclear family, acts as a sort of "social critic" of the child.[31]

In 1968 Kadushin reviewed a mass of studies in an attempt to determine whether the one-parent family system was inherently dysfunctional or pathological. The basic purpose of this study was to determine whether adoption agencies would be justified in considering single persons for adoptions. Kadushin concluded that "the association between single-parent familyhood and psychosocial pathology is neither strong nor invariable."[32] Kadushin also makes the statement: "The material suggests a greater appreciation of different kinds of contexts in which children can be reared without damage."[33]

In a more recent study, Aldous was not convinced that the case against the one-parent family had been proved. In a study of Head Start children, she did not find significant differences in perception of adult male and female roles between father-present and father-absent children when race and social class variables were controlled.[34]

It is obvious to any clinician that the two-parent system has its own pathology—the two parents may be in serious conflict as to how their parental roles should be performed; one parent may be competent but have his (or her) efforts undermined by the incompetent partner; the children may be caught in a "double bind" or crossfire between the two parents;[35] both parents may be competent but simply unable to work together as an effective team in rearing their children; one parent may be more competent than the other but be inhibited in using this competence by the team pattern inherent in the two-parent system.

---

[30] Bernard Farber, *Family Organization and Interaction* (San Francisco: Chandler Publishing Co., 1964), p. 457.

[31] Ibid.

[32] Alfred Kadushin, "Single Parent Adoptions: An Overview and Some Relevant Research" (New York: Child Welfare League of America, 1968); see also Benjamin Schlesinger, ed., *The One-Parent Family* (Toronto: University of Toronto Press, 1970).

[33] Kadushin, "Single Parent Adoptions," p. 40.

[34] Joan Aldous, "Children's Perceptions of Adult Role Assignment," *Journal of Marriage and the Family* 34 (1972): 55–65.

[35] On the "double bind" and its potential impact on children see Virginia Satir, *Conjoint Family Therapy* (Palo Alto, Calif.: Science & Behavior Books, 1964); also Jay Haley, *Strategies of Psychotherapy* (New York: Grune & Stratton, 1963).

Both Kadushin and Schorr make it quite clear that much of the so-called pathology of the one-parent family in American society results from inadequate institutional planning for such families—such as the lack of adequate day-care programs for preschool children.

Foster parents

A relatively new type of parent in the United States is the "foster parent" utilized by social work agencies to care for children whose biological parents are unable or unwilling to assume parental responsibility. As of 1962 about 176,000 children were living with foster parents in our society. This represented about 70 percent of all American children being cared for by private and public welfare agencies.[36]

Kadushin points out that foster parents have largely replaced the "children's home" in our society: as of 1923 about 65 percent of the homeless children in the United States were living in institutions built for such children, whereas today over two-thirds are living in foster homes.[37]

This is not the place to review the whole foster-home movement, but, in view of the increase in foster parenthood in our society in recent decades, a few observations are in order.[38]

1. *Foster parents have no parental rights.* Although about 75 percent of all foster-home placements turn out to be permanent—the child never returns to his own parents—the foster parents usually have no right to permanent custody of the child.[39] As a rule they cannot adopt the child, nor can they prevent the agency from taking the child away at any time for any reason. The agency is not required to "show cause" when it decides to remove a child from a foster home; there is no appeal to the courts.

About the only clear-cut right the foster parent has is the right to be paid—about 95 percent of them receive compensation for taking care of the child.[40]

2. *The foster-parent role is ambiguous.* Foster parents are supposed to express instant love or affection for the foster child, but at the same time they are not supposed to become so attached to a child that they cannot give the child up at any time.

---

[36] Alfred Kadushin, *Child Welfare Services* (New York: Macmillan Co., 1967), p. 363.

[37] Ibid.

[38] See ibid., chap. 9, for an analysis of foster-parent programs; see also David Fanshel, *Foster Parenthood: A Role Analysis* (Minneapolis: University of Minnesota Press, 1966).

[39] Kadushin, *Child Welfare Services.*

[40] Ibid., p. 425.

Kadushin points out that the foster-parent role is quite complex: "Because foster parenthood is an ambiguously defined role," he writes, "its enactment is likely to occasion difficulty."[41]

The role is ambiguous in that it combines a commercial arrangement with an expectation of affection or a willingness to perform beyond the call of duty. When a child is sick, the workday is 24 hours, with no overtime from the agency.

The foster-parent role is ambiguous in that while the job pays, it does not pay very well—and yet the care of the child is supposed to be first class.

Every natural parent and every adoptive parent knows that nobody could pay enough to properly rear a child—even a million dollars would not cover the heartaches and the anguish experienced by most parents at one time or another.

The foster-parent role is also ambiguous in that what is planned as a temporary placement may turn out to be permanent, while a placement that was intended to be permanent may be terminated in a few days if things do not go well.

It is the writer's belief that the foster-parent role is one of the most complex roles attempted by any parent in our society, and the research seems to support this belief.[42]

Adoptive parents

As of 1963 about 120,000 children were being adopted annually in the United States.[43] Of this number, almost half (47 percent) were adopted by relatives. About two out of every 100 children in our society are reared by adoptive parents.[44]

Unlike the foster parents discussed in the preceding section, adoptive parents have all of the rights that biological parents have once the final adoption papers are signed by the court having jurisdiction. Adoptive parents not only have the same rights as natural parents, but also the same responsibilities.

In a well-known study of adoptive parents, Kirk concluded that they have "very special" problems—intense worry as to how the adoption will "turn out," deep feelings of insecurity and/or inadequacy, apprehension, and so on.[45] Reading this book it seemed to us that the feelings Kirk

---

[41] Ibid., p. 396.

[42] Both Fanshel and Kadushin agree on the difficulty of the foster-parent role.

[43] Kadushin, *Child Welfare Services*, p. 437.

[44] Ibid., chap. 10, "Adoption," presents a thorough review of the literature on adoption.

[45] See H. David Kirk, *Shared Fate* (New York: Free Press, 1964). While this book is useful, we feel that Kirk would have had more perspective on parental problems if he had compared a group of natural parents with a group of adoptive parents.

found in adoptive parents are *universal* reactions to parenthood, not just those experienced by adoptive parents.[46]

Biological parents never really know how their children will turn out; most of them feel inadequate and insecure; and almost all of them are literally frightened when they take their first child home from the hospital and realize the awesome responsibility they have assumed—18–21 years of daily responsibility for another human being.

Actually, as we see it, adoptive parents have several advantages over biological parents.

1. *They get to choose their child.* This may not always be the case, but at least they can reject a child that they consider grossly unsuited for them. Biological parents have to accept and keep what "the Lord sends" —bright, dull, retarded, deformed, beautiful, or otherwise.

2. *Adoptive parents are voluntary parents.* These fathers and mothers do not become parents by accident. The adoption process is such that persons who do not know what they are doing are screened out—they never receive a child. Nobody knows how many children in our society were not actually wanted by their biological parents, but the number must be substantial.

3. *Adoptive parents have a probation period and can return the child if necessary.* In most states there is a probationary period of six months to a year in which the adoptive parents can decide whether they wish to assume permanent responsibility for the child. With biological parents the point of no return comes at the moment of conception—except for those willing to seek an abortion.

For the above reasons it seems to the writer that the role of adoptive parent is less complex and less fraught with difficulty than is generally thought. Kadushin estimates that 75–85 percent of all adoptions in our society are "reasonably successful."[47] Whether as much can be said for biological parents in American society may be debatable.

The role of stepparent

There were about 7 million stepchildren in the United States as of the 1960s—roughly one child out of nine.[48] This is approximately double the number of stepchildren in this country in 1900. The 1960 decade was

46 See E. E. LeMasters, "Parenthood as Crisis," *Marriage and Family Living* 19 (1957): 352–55. In this study of natural parents having their first child, we found about the same apprehension that Kirk found in his adoptive parents. This paper received the Ernest Burgess Award from the National Council on Family Relations.

47 Kadushin, *Child Welfare Services,* pp. 482–83. Kadushin also found that older "problem" children could be adopted successfully; see his *Adopting Older Children* (New York: Columbia University Press, 1970).

48 Simon, "The Child's World Changes," *Stepchild in the Family,* chap. 5, has a detailed review of the statistics on stepparents in our society.

the first time in America in which more stepchildren were created by divorce and remarriage than by death. One can visualize the large number of stepchildren when it is realized that some 15 million Americans have now been divorced at one time or another.[49]

Some of the children in these families do not know how to refer to their stepparents—especially so when the father or mother has been married more than twice. One college student, a young man of 20, said to us: "My mother has been married four times. I don't even try to remember the name of her latest husband any more—I just call them by number." Actually, after the second divorce, this boy moved in with his maternal grandparents, whom he now calls Dad and Mom.

A college girl said to us: "Do you have to love your stepfather? Mine wants to be real 'buddy buddy' but I can't stand him."

A divorced woman of 35, now remarried, is rearing two sets of children—two from her first marriage and two from her husband's first marriage. She finds the role of stepmother difficult and frustrating. "The other day," she told us, "one of my stepsons didn't do what I had asked him to do. When I corrected him about this he said—'You're not my *real* mother.' I got mad and belted him one." She went on to say that she also found it difficult when one of the stepchildren accused her of being partial to her own children. This woman finds her second marriage satisfying, but she regards the role of stepmother as being perhaps the most difficult job she has ever undertaken—and especially so when there are two sets of children.

Actually, the kinds of situations in which stepparents find themselves are almost endless. In the previous case, for example, if this woman has any children by her second husband there will be *three* sets of children. At this point she is not enthused about this prospect.

A stepmother may find herself rearing a group of children from her husband's first marriage; a stepfather may find himself in the same spot; both may have children with them from a previous marriage; one or both may have had children in more than one previous marriage; they may have children in their new marriage and thus start another set of children; and so forth.

Historically, the role of stepmother has been considered the most difficult parental assignment in Western society. It was no accident that the terrible woman in Cinderella was a stepmother.

Probably the stepmother role is so difficult because children in our society are closer to their mother than their father, and this means that it is very unlikely that anybody can follow the mother without experiencing some problems.

The following factors can be identified as complicating the stepparent role in our society.

---

[49] Simon, *Stepchild in the Family*, p. 59.

1. *The stepparent is following a preceding parent.* Stepfathers and stepmothers do not start with the child at birth; they follow a preceding father or mother. If the child's relationship with the first parent was positive, this creates difficulty for the stepparent—he or she has to work his or her way into the charmed circle; but if the preceding relationship was negative this also sets up problems—hostility generated in the earlier relationship may be displaced onto the stepparent.

In many different ways, the child will be continuously measuring the new parent against the former parent.

2. *Stepparents have a tendency to try too hard.* Many college students have referred to this in term papers written for the author in which stepparents were discussed.

It seems that the stepparent is so insecure, so afraid of failure with the child, that the stepfather or stepmother pushes the relationship too fast or too hard.[50] Time is required to heal the wounds left over from the previous parent-child relationship, and many stepparents do not give the child enough time.

3. *Some stepparents try to replace the former parent.* Simon and other writers on the stepparent role emphasize that the new parent should usually not attempt to replace the previous father or mother but should see him- or herself as a supplement, meeting needs of the child not met by the previous parent.[51] This is especially the case in which the child continues to see his biological father or mother.

4. *The complex sets of children to be reared by some stepparents.* This was discussed earlier, but one can see how easy it would be for a stepfather or a stepmother to favor his or her biological offspring over the stepchildren, and even if no favoritism is involved the child may feel there is. Blood ties are very deep in human society, and not all of us can rise above this in complex stepparent situations.

For all of the stated reasons, and more, the stepparent in our society has a difficult role. Simon, who probably has the best book on this subject, takes a positive attitude toward stepparents.[52] She points out that millions of children in modern America would literally have no father or mother to rear them if it were not for stepparents.

Summary and conclusion

It would seem that a sizable proportion of American parents operate in situations that are far from ideal—they do not coincide with the dream that most of us have when we start a family.

---

[50] Simon, *Stepchild in the Family,* discusses the problems of stepparents in various chapters. See also Helen Thomson, *The Successful Stepparent* (New York: Harper & Row, 1966).

[51] Simon, *Stepchild in the Family;* and Thomson, *The Successful Stepparent.*

[52] Simon, *Stepchild in the Family.*

If one fourth of all marriages in the United States end in divorce, this alone would produce a significant proportion of parents who are either rearing their children alone (those who do not remarry) or are involved in the stepparent role (those who do remarry). If we add to this the families in which a father or mother has died, we get an additional group.

And then, to all of these must be added the unmarried mothers, the separated, and the deserted who are not yet (or even) divorced.

It is not correct to just add all of these categories because almost all of them overlap at some point in time.

Actually, there are many additional deviant parent situations that we have not even mentioned: mothers whose husbands are away from home because of military service; fathers whose occupations keep them away from their children most of the time; parents who are temporarily in a mental hospital or other medical treatment facility—a tuberculosis sanitarium, for example.

It would seem, from the above, that the total number of American parents who face difficult situations in carrying out their parental responsibilities is larger than most of us realize.

An attempt was made in this chapter to analyze the problems of parents who function under deviant or abnormal conditions. The two largest groups seem to be mothers rearing children with no father present and stepparents of both sexes.

The assumed pathology of the one-parent family was questioned, and an attempt was made to estimate the total number of American parents operating under abnormal circumstances.

chapter
ten

Parents, mass media, and the youth peer group

In this chapter an attempt will be made to analyze the impact of the mass media and the youth peer group on children. It is the thesis of this chapter that the above forces compete seriously with parents in their attempt to influence the values and behavior of their sons and daughters. It is also our belief that the power of the mass media and the youth peer group over young Americans is much greater today than it was in the 19th century or the early decades of the 20th century. The rest of the chapter will be devoted to an examination of these propositions.

Parents and television

One force that the parents of yesterday did not have to cope with is television. There are approximately 70 million persons in the United States under 18 years of age[1]—and these comprise one of the prime targets of the television industry. It has been discovered that the average American child has spent more hours watching television before he goes to kindergarten than he would spend in the classroom in four years of college.[2] By the time an American youngster gets through high school he will have watched television approximately 22,000 hours compared with

---

[1] See Marvin E. Wolfgang, *The Culture of Youth*, (Washington, D.C.: Department of Health, Education, and Welfare, 1967), p. 7.

[2] These figures were used by a panel of Harvard University pediatricians (reported in the *Milwaukee State Journal*, October 18, 1971).

the 11,000 hours he has spent in the classroom. During this time he will have been exposed to about 350,000 commercials.[3]

What type of program is offered these young viewers? By age 14 the average American child has seen 18,000 human beings killed on television.[4] Of 762 leading characters observed on prime-time television, approximately half committed acts of violence. One study concludes that in spite of parental complaints, violence on children's television programs increased during the years 1967–69, mostly on television programs beamed at young children.[5]

The research as yet is not conclusive as to how all of this affects children, but when the Federal Communications Commission (FCC) invited parents to write their feelings about children's television programs, some 80,000 fathers and mothers took the trouble to send letters asking the FCC to impose some program standards on the television industry.[6]

Values portrayed by the mass media

It is the writer's contention that the mass media in American society do not support parents in their basic values. While television represents only one form of mass media—records, movies, mass magazines, and radio are other types—the following analysis is based primarily on data from television. What are some of the values featured in the mass media?

Sex

Teen-agers are in the process of discovering the world of sex—their bodies and their glands are propelling them toward sexual maturity, even though psychologically and socially most of them are far from being mature.

Now there is nothing wrong with sex—as most Americans will testify—and, given the lack of an adequate sex-education program in the United States, somebody has to help these youngsters get some idea of what sex is all about. American novelists have been mining this field for a long time, but in recent decades television and the drive-in movie have muscled their way into this market with great enthusiasm.

---

[3] Paper presented by Gerald Looney of the University of Arizona at the annual meeting of the American Academy of Pediatrics, Chicago, Illinois, October 1, 1971 (reported by the *Wisconsin State Journal* of that date from an Associated Press release).

[4] Ibid.

[5] These data were presented at hearings in Washington, D.C., to determine federal policy on children's television (reported in the *Chicago Tribune*, April 20, 1972).

[6] See Martin Mayer, *About Television* (New York: Harper & Row, 1972), p. 133.

Unfortunately, as the writer sees it, sex in the movies and on television is usually on a physical level visually and verbally, yet is presented to the audience as love—in other words, the signals or cues are confusing. In one sense we are watching physical and genital attraction between a man and a woman, but in another sense we are expected to believe that these two people are in love.

In a newspaper series, a professional observer of the Hollywood motion picture industry made the following statement: "Pictures that depict—indeed glorify—infidelity, nudity, sexual license and vulgarity are being turned out in profusion. They have achieved box office success for several film companies that had previously been near bankruptcy. . . . actors and actresses who break the established moral codes in their personal behavior find the screen moguls automatically disposed to boost the price of their services."[7]

Almost at random we select a motion-picture advertisement of the following nature: "Slaves to their own strange desires. Playthings of each other's unholy passions!"[8]

Violence

Survey after survey has shown the massive dose of violence presented to young and old alike on television and in motion pictures.[9] America is, of course, a violent society, and the mass-media owners are always eager (a bit too eager) to point out that "we only give the customers what they want." On the same kind of logic, call girls and the distributors of illegal narcotics could plead the same defense. Human beings have many self-destructive tendencies, and all human societies do what they can to hold these to a minimum level. It is difficult to see how modern films and television programs are helping to achieve this end.

The idealization of immaturity

In a study of teen-age subculture,[10] one of the major points developed is that today's teen-ager no longer worships adult heroes—his idols are just as juvenile and immature as he is. In commenting on this in the *Sat-*

---

[7] Martin Abrahamson, United Press Hollywood columnist, *Milwaukee Journal*, September 10, 1968.

[8] *Milwaukee Journal*, September 15, 1968.

[9] For a merciless analysis of violence and sadism in so-called children's programs in the mass media, see Gilbert Seldes, *The Public Arts* (New York: Simon Schuster, 1956); see also Otto N. Larsen, ed., *Violence and the Mass Media* (New York: Harper & Row, 1968).

[10] Grace and Fred Hechinger, *Teen-Age Tyranny* (New York: William Morrow & Co., 1963), pp. 151–52.

urday Review, the education editor, Paul Woodring, put this point in the following words:

The adolescent of an earlier age was eager to grow up, and the heroes he chose to emulate, while not always admirable, were usually adult. Today's teen-ager often chooses a model no older and no more mature than himself—a juvenile who has achieved wealth and fame at an early age with the help of just a little talent or beauty plus a hard-driving publicity agent. It is not difficult to understand why such models are chosen—they provide the basis for elaborate daydreams of what is seemingly possible for any adolescent who "gets a break," without much long waiting or hard work, without going to college or even completing high school. By comparison the prospect of a career emulating that of Abraham Lincoln or Florence Nightingale seems decidedly dull.[11]

In the face of such daydreams, parents often find it difficult to sell their children on the facts of life—that for most Americans hard work and years of training are required to compete in the society.

Materialism

The well-known semanticist Hayakawa is quoted as saying that the antimaterialism of today's youth may be a reaction to television's message that "material possessions are everything, that this headache remedy, this luxurious carpeting, this new model car [will bring happiness]."[12]

American parents are themselves inclined to be materialistic—as is the whole society—but one often has the feeling that parental materialism cannot compare with that portrayed in the mass media.

The writer still has vivid memories of two mass-magazine advertisements of a few years ago that seemed to have hit a new low: in one, a mother, surrounded by her husband and children, is looking at a new car and says: "Our new Plymouth is the greatest thing that ever happened to this family."

In the other advertisement, aimed at the Christmas trade, a father is shown heading for home (at least we hope so) pulling a child's sled on which reposes a case of a famous brand of whisky. The writer likes a drink as well as most Americans, but somehow this picture was revolting.

One of the interesting features of mass-media materialism is the effort made to make it seem free. You just get out the credit cards and off you go to Hawaii, with no cash needed. This is similar to what Woodring was

---

[11] Paul Woodring, *Saturday Review,* March 23, 1963, p. 72.

[12] Paper given by S. I. Hayakawa at annual meeting of the American Psychological Association in San Francisco, 1968 (reported in the *Milwaukee Journal* September 3, 1968).

writing about in the quotation earlier—no real effort is required to enjoy the fruits of the affluent society.

Hedonism

One modern dictionary defines *hedonism* as "the doctrine that pleasure is the principal good and should be the aim of action."[13]

Without debating the merits of this philosophical system, it does seem that the mass-media message in our society is essentially hedonistic. This reflects the fact the the ultimate aim of most mass media is that of entertainment and escape. It is usually assumed by advertisers that Americans see enough reality in their everyday life; when they watch television they want to escape reality and be amused.

To the extent that this is true, teen-agers (as well as most other Americans) are exposed to an unreal world when they turn to the mass media.

It may well be, of course, as Riesman suggests, that the drift of our entire society is in the direction of hedonism.[14] With mechanization and automation, the major problem in the affluent society may well be what people do with their leisure rather than what they do at their place of work.

The writer has the impression, not well documented, that the younger generation is considerably more hedonistic than most of their parents. If this is true, it could simply reflect a deep change in basic values in our society, with the youth subculture reflecting the trend more fully than the adult subculture does. Another possible explanation of the difference —if there is a difference—is that young people do not have to face adult reality, as yet, precisely because they are still not adults. American parents are notorious for their desire to protect young people from the harsh facts of life, and the mass media simply share this purpose.

Commercial nature of the mass media

It needs to be remembered that the mass media in American society are operated for profit. This means that the ultimate test of their effectiveness is not what they do to people but how much money they make. In commenting on this, a television executive writes: "Because television can make so much money doing its worst, it often cannot afford to do its best."[15]

---

13 *Webster's New World Dictionary of the American Language,* college ed. (Cleveland: World Publishing Co., 1956), p. 672.

14 See David Riesman et al., *The Lonely Crowd* (New Haven, Conn.: Yale University Press, 1961), chap. 2.

15 Fred Friendly, *Due to Circumstances Beyond Our Control* (New York: Random House, 1967), p. xii; Friendly is a former director of CBS news.

As Mayer makes clear in his extensive study of the television industry in the United States, the so-called regulation of TV is largely a joke—even in the industry itself.[16]

Paternal values versus mass media values

The writer believes that most American parents do not ·agree with the basic values portrayed in the mass media aimed at young persons. The pages to follow attempt to support this argument.

Parents on violence

Most American parents, regardless of what they may have done in their own lives, hope (and pray) that their children will not attack or kill other human beings. As Mead observed long ago, Americans are "counter punchers"—children are taught not to start a fight but also not to run away from one. They are to fight back if they are attacked by someone else.[17]

This is not the world of television and the movies. It is true, of course, that the bad guys always lose on "Gunsmoke" and "Bonanza," and Hollywood has a code that crime does not pay—but nevertheless the violent, ruthless person, like the Devil in old-fashioned sermons, often emerges as a sort of "inverted hero." He may lose the girl, and even his life, but meanwhile he has captured the audience. The old gangster films made by Jimmy Cagney and Humphrey Bogart illustrate what we are talking about.

We grant that researchers are divided as to the long-range effects of such films on children, but our point is that most American parents would prefer that their children not be subjected to such a heavy dose of aggression and violence.[18]

Suppose somebody did a series of television films showing children how to shoplift from supermarkets and other stores more effectively. Even if *most* children who saw the series never actively engaged in shoplifting as a result of the series, would it be in the public interest to show such films? Actually the series might even *lower* the crime rate for juvenile shoplifters by helping them avoid detection, but one can be sure that merchants would create such an uproar that the series would be banned. Parents often feel the same way about various aspects of the mass media, but they seldom are able to obtain any redress.

---

[16] Mayer, *About Television.*

[17] Margaret Mead, *And Keep Your Powder Dry* (New York: William Morrow & Co., 1965).

[18] One of the better studies of the impact of television on children is that of Wilbur Schramm et al., *Television in the Lives of Our Children* (Palo Alto, Calif.: Stanford University Press, 1961).

Mass media owners have a pat answer to parents who protest: "Don't permit your child to watch our programs—or read our comics—if you do not approve of the content." Any parent who has tried this solution knows how difficult it is.

Sexual restraint

In our opinion most American parents in the 1970s are aware that their children, daughters as well as sons, may have sexual relations before marriage.[19] These parents did not grow up in a prudish society and have little hope that their children will be more chaste than they were. But most parents, regardless of their own sexual histories, do hope that their children will use sex constructively in their lives, and that they will subscribe to some sort of decent sex code. One element of such a code is that sex should be combined with affection and/or love.[20]

It seems to us that television, the movies, and many mass magazines do not portray sex in this way. It is presented as an overwhelming physical attraction between a man and a woman, with the individuals having little or no choice about what they do about the attraction. And the relationships are entered into after such a brief courtship that it seems hardly appropriate to describe the interaction as love.

The girls in these programs are presented as being sexually aggressive —something that frightens the average parent.

It may well be that young Americans can still recognize love when they find it, but one has to question how much help they received from the mass media in this matter.

Lifetime monogamy

Most American parents, for better or worse, are committed to lifetime monogamy. Even if this arrangement did not work out for them, they still hope that it will for their children. And it is still true that most Americans have been married only once—the divorced men and women are still a minority group (although increasing) in our society.

In the mass-media world, however, it is a rare star performer who has not been married more than once—if not several times. Under American law, of course, this is perfectly legal and moral, but it hardly presents a very positive image of lifetime marriage for the audience.

---

[19] For a careful study of sex attitudes among young people as well as parents, see Ira L. Reiss, *The Social Context of Premarital Sexual Permissiveness* (New York: Holt, Rinehart & Winston, 1967).

[20] On sex as love or affection, see Winston Ehrmann, *Premarital Dating Behavior* (New York: Henry Holt & Co., 1959). Many of these ideas are discussed in Edwin M. Schur, ed., *The Family and the Sexual Revolution* (Bloomington: Indiana University Press, 1964).

Planning for the future

Most parents in our society have come to accept the old banker's cliché that "the future belongs to those who prepare for it." Even though the parents may be in debt, they realize that some thought has to be given to the day of reckoning—not only in regard to financial matters, but also in regard to sex, alcohol, education, and so forth.

The mass media present a vague picture of the future consequence of present action. We see beautiful men and women drinking beer every few minutes on television but nobody ever gets fat. We see all the handsome males and females smoking their cigarettes on television but nobody ever gets lung cancer. We see entire families taking off for Hawaii with nothing in their pockets but a credit card, yet nobody ever goes bankrupt.

Positive aspects of the mass media

It is undoubtedly true that children and young adults learn many different things from television, movies, radio, and magazines and that some of this learning is essentially useful and positive in the lives of these persons. Both television and the movies, for example, have been outstanding in recent years in their portrayal of racial problems.

One has to wonder, however, to what extent the basic values of parents are supported by the mass media. At present the writer's vote would have to be negative.

Parents and the youth peer group

In his study of American society, *The Lonely Crowd,* Riesman takes the position that there has been a significant increase in the power of the youth peer group in recent decades. He writes: "There has been an enormous ideological shift favoring submission to the group . . . the peer group becomes the measure of all things; the individual has few defenses the group cannot batter down."[21]

Coleman, after studying social life in ten high schools, was impressed by the extent and power of teen-age society. He writes: "Our adolescents today are cut off, probably more than ever before, from the adult society . . . our society has within its midst a set of small teen-age societies, which focus teen-age interests and attitudes on things far removed from adult responsibilities, and which may develop standards that lead away from those goals established by the larger society."[22] Coleman did not find

---

[21] Riesman, *The Lonely Crowd,* p. 82.

[22] James S. Coleman, *The Adolescent Society* (New York: Free Press, 1961), p. 9.

that these high school students ignore or even reject the values of their parents—his main point is that parents are in constant competition with teen-age society and are never sure when their wishes will prevail with their adolescent children.

One can shrug off this competition with the old bromide: good parents have no trouble with teen-agers—only poor parents do. Within limits this may be correct, but the stiff competition from the teen-age society still poses severe problems for parents who have only tenuous relations with their adolescent children.

We have pointed out elsewhere in this book that some parents try to beat the teen-agers at their own game by joining them.[23] In his text on the American family Bell has a caustic observation on such parents: "It is a devastating picture of parents," he writes, "because it implies that they are still teen-agers."[24]

In another context Coleman makes this statement: "The adolescent lives more and more in a society of his own; he finds the family a less and less satisfying psychological home. As a consequence, the home has less and less ability to mold him."[25]

Minuchin and associates, in an intensive study of low-income families, concluded that older siblings may influence their younger brothers and sisters more than the parents do.[26]

In the laboratory studies of the family life of the rhesus monkey by Harlow and his research team at the University of Wisconsin, it has been discovered that interference with the normal peer group interaction may affect young monkeys as severely as a breakdown in the mother-child relationship.[27]

If the mass media and the adolescent peer group supported the efforts of parents, no particular problem would exist. If a child is properly socialized (prepared for his adult roles in the society), it does not matter much who or what helped the child to mature. As Bell and many others have pointed out, the nuclear family is not the only social arrangement utilized in human society to prepare children for their place in the adult society.[28]

The problem in relation to these nonfamily influences in our society, as the writer sees it, is that often parents are in conflict with these other

23 See chap. 12.

24 Robert R. Bell, *Marriage and Family Interaction* (Homewood, Ill.: Dorsey Press, 1967), p. 431.

25 Coleman, *The Adolescent Society*, p. 312.

26 See Salvador Minuchin et al., *Families of the Slums* (New York: Basic Books, 1967), p. 219.

27 Personal communication.

28 Robert R. Bell, *Marriage and Family Interaction* (Homewood, Ill.: Dorsey Press, 1967), chap. 14.

forces in their efforts to produce responsible adult citizens out of their children.

The youth counterculture

In the chapter to follow, detailed attention will be given to the so-called generation gap in American society, but at this point it is necessary to make a few observations about what amounts to a counterculture evolved by young people in the United States during the 1960s and the early 1970s.[29] To the extent that this counterculture exists, it poses substantial problems for parents.

In its purest form, the counterculture is a revolt against the middle-class way of life—more specifically, against the upper-middle-class way of life.[30]

Rejection of materialism

The youth counterculture takes the position that parents have become slaves to money, material possessions, and the rat race that is usually associated with these. In matter of fact, as Bernard has pointed out,[31] young Americans today are the most affluent and the greatest spenders of their age ever seen in American society, but on the surface they reject the symbols of middle-class life. They may be attending a college that costs their parents $4,000–$5,000 a year, but they dress as if they were in the poverty group.

Drugs

Many of the parental generation were addicted to alcohol, and the youth counterculture is determined to explore drugs other than alcohol. This began as a debate over marijuana but eventually involved drugs that parents had never heard of. Young people have argued, correctly, that alcohol is itself a very dangerous drug, but most parents feel that at least they know the dangers of alcohol, while they do not know the hazards of drugs their children are experimenting with.

---

[29] On counterculture, see Theodore Rosak, *The Making of a Counter Culture* (New York: Doubleday & Co., 1968); Charles A. Reich, *The Greening of America* (New York: Random House, 1970); and Keith Melville, *Communes in the Counter Culture* (New York: William Morrow & Co., 1972). Parents will find the Reich volume especially helpful in understanding the nature of the youth revolt.

[30] A study of approximately 1,000 young persons who took refuge in the Haight-Ashbury section of San Francisco concluded that a majority were from upper-middle-class homes; see David E. Smith and John Luce, *Love Needs Care* (Boston: Little, Brown & Co., 1971).

[31] Jessie Bernard, "Teen-Age Culture: An Overview," *Annals of the American Academy of Political and Social Science* 338 (November 1961): 1–12.

Dress

The counterculture involves almost a complete revolution in dress, compared with the clothes worn by their parents, with blue jeans and various outfits becoming the symbol of revolt and rejection.

This revolution in dress has been accompanied by the "hair" revolution: long hair and beards for the males and very long hair for the females. Some parents have adjusted to the change in hair styles, but it has been a serious issue in many families in regard to sons.

Sex

While the so-called authorities are still debating about whether there has been a second (or third) sexual revolution in American society,[32] the openness of sex in the 1960s and the 1970s, as well as the new pattern of college men and women living together outside of marriage, has shocked hundreds of thousands of parents. The older generation has charged "moral disintegration," which young persons have resented. The counterculture argues, with some logic, that open sex is just as moral as concealed sex.

Politics

Most American parents are committed to one of the two major political parties, whereas their children have been disillusioned with both the Democrats and the Republicans. Robert Kennedy, Eugene McCarthy, and George McGovern attracted large numbers of young persons, but all of these charismatic figures have either been assassinated or overwhelmingly defeated in the political arena. No political parties of the Left or the Right have been able to attract any large numbers of young Americans, which means that those of the counterculture are politically alienated. Many of these have psychologically withdrawn from the world of politics—they have become a type of anarchist: you do your thing and I'll do my thing.[33]

In this disillusionment with politics is buried the massive impact of the war in Vietnam. Thousands of young men and women have sacrificed (sometimes severely) to protest against the war; political leaders have promised to end the war; yet in the early 1970s the war was still going on. Many young Americans in the 1960s grew up in the midst of a war they did not believe in or consider moral. This resulted in charges by parents

---

[32] For a review of this debate, see Robert R. Bell, *Marriage and Family Interaction*, 3d ed. (Homewood, Ill.: Dorsey Press, 1971), chaps. 7 and 8.

[33] This withdrawal pattern is explored at length in the Haight-Ashbury study (Smith and Luce, *Love Needs Care*); see also the discussion in Melville's study (*Communes in the Counter Culture*).

that their children were not "loyal" to their country, that the young people had no patriotism, and so forth. (It needs to be remembered that millions of the fathers of these young persons had fought in World War II or Korea—conflicts that had the support of most Americans.) Young persons charged that their parents did not really care about the war in Vietnam, that their fathers and mothers had "sold out" to the military-industrial complex. One popular poster on college campuses read: "MOM AND DAD: YOUR SILENCE IS KILLING ME!" Beneath the caption the total dead in the Vietnam war was given.

All of the above have left many young persons extremely skeptical about the health of American society. They may not know what they want in a new social order, but they are quite clear about what they do not like in the present system.

Another result of the war and the issues it has raised has been the creation of a massive gulf between millions of parents and their children.

The writer has no quarrel about the rights of the younger generation to revolt against social conditions that it regards as inefficient, unjust, or immoral. Our point is that individual parents should not feel that they are personally responsible for these feelings and this behavior in their children: they should not feel guilty, as most of them do. Perhaps the parents who should feel guilty are those whose children have *not* struggled against the war in Vietnam and the other injustices in American society.

The problem is that parents have been brainwashed into thinking that they are responsible for anything their children do. One reads articles in the newspapers and magazines that "college students who use marijuana come from unhappy homes."[34] This is like saying that girls who neck were not loved by their parents.

Parents need to recognize that American society is in the midst of a social revolution—and probably a social revolution that is long overdue. How the revolt will turn out nobody knows—nobody ever knows how a social revolution will turn out. But it is ridiculous for parents to think that they can stop the revolution or to feel inadequate because their sons and daughters are on the barricades.

Parental strategies for coping with the mass media and the youth peer group

It is the writer's belief that most American parents have not evolved any successful strategies for dealing with the mass media or the youth peer group. Some parents, of course, seem to overcome almost any odds —their children attend colleges rife with drugs and never use anything stronger than aspirin. One does not know whether these fathers and

---

[34] Statement in the *Chicago Tribune,* April 4, 1971.

mothers are just lucky or very skillful in handling young people. In interviewing such parents you get the impression that even they do not know the secret of their success.

Mass-media strategies

When children are young parents often censor the movies they may attend or the television programs they may watch. Some parents even refuse to own a television set. One mother said to the writer: "We didn't buy a TV set for two or three years because we didn't like the programs offered for children. Then we found that the kids were watching television at their friends' house—which meant that we had nothing at all to say about what programs they were seeing. So we finally bought a set and tried to establish some standards as to what shows they could tune in."

Basically, in this strategy parents are trying to isolate a child from what the parents consider an evil or dangerous world. The weakness in this approach is that it does not prepare the child to deal with such matters when he or she finally encounters them—and sooner or later the youngster will be exposed to almost every facet of the society, good or bad.

Peer-group strategies

There apparently was a time in American society when parents could supervise the peer-group society relations of their children. For example, one reads that at some point in our history a young man had to have permission from a girl's father to "court" the daughter—or to become engaged. This would seem quite unusual today. Young people choose their own friends and usually their own marital partners.

A popular strategy today is to move into a "better" neighborhood, on the assumption that as the houses (and the mortgages) get bigger the children (and their parents) get "nicer." Almost any parent can recite the limitations of this strategy: the deepest revolt against parents is in the upper-income suburbs.

Some parents rely on traditional methods—they immerse their children in the church and attempt to internalize the old virtues: honesty, hard work, patriotism, sacrifice, virginity, etc. This may or may not work. One devout Roman Catholic mother said to the writer: "I took my four kids to mass every Sunday, sent them to parochial schools, had them say their prayers every night—and what good did it do? My daughter is on the pill, my sons never go to church, and I'm the only good Catholic in the family."

Parents try the Boy Scouts, Girl Scouts, YMCA, YWCA, private schools, expensive colleges—all with the hope that their children "will stay out of trouble." One physician known to the writer invested $5,000 sending his son to a private college because the father had read such "terrible things" about students at the state university. Within two semesters the son was so hooked on drugs at the private college that he had to be withdrawn. The father now wonders where you send a son so that "he won't get involved with drugs." It's a good question.

Summary and conclusion

In this chapter an attempt was made to look at mass media from the point of view of parents. It seems to the writer that the major conflict between the values of parents and those of the mass media stems from the fact that parents have learned to live cautiously, with one eye (if not both) on the future, whereas the mass media present a world in which the more interesting people live dangerously and largely in the present.

It was admitted that there are both positive and negative effects of mass media on children and that the research on such influences is far from conclusive as yet.

The chapter also discussed the youth peer group, the counterculture, and the impact of these on parents. The basic thesis was that there has been a vast increase in the power of the youth peer group and that relatively few parents have evolved successful strategies for coping with this force.

In the next chapter an extended look will be taken at social change in American society and its significance for parents.

chapter
eleven

Parents and
social change

It is interesting to note that in the paper by Davis on parent-youth conflict, cited so often in this book, he discusses social change first.[1] He writes:

The first important variable is the rate of social change. Extremely rapid change in modern civilization, in contrast to most civilizations, tends to increase parent-youth conflict, for within a fast-changing order the time interval between generations, ordinarily but a mere moment in the life of the social system, becomes historically significant, thereby creating a gap between one generation and the next.[2]

We are assuming that Davis was correct in this observation, but we wish to push the analysis further than he does in an attempt to see *how* rapid social change affects parents in our society. Before proceeding, however, it may be helpful to make a few observations about the concept of social change.[3]

---

[1] Kingsley Davis, "The Sociology of Parent-Youth Conflict," *American Sociological Review* **5** (August 1940): 523–35. For extensive analysis of the process of social change, see Amitai and Eva Etzioni, eds., *Social Change* (New York: Basic Books, 1964).

[2] Davis, "Parent-Youth Conflict," p. 523.

[3] A useful book on the family and social change is John N. Edwards, ed., *The Family and Change* (New York: Alfred A. Knopf, 1969).

The concept of social change

1. *Social change is not synonymous with social progress.* It is important to remember that in social science analysis, social change is not equated with social progress or social deterioration. It can easily be proven, for example, that the divorce rate in America has increased since 1900, but the evaluation of this change is quite a different proposition. Almost all of the changes discussed in this chapter are of this same nature: they have had both positive and negative impact on American parents.

2. *The rate of social change is not constant.* Societies and their way of life (their cultures) do not change at a fixed or steady pace. The United States, for example, has probably changed more from 1900 to 1970 than it did in the previous two or three centuries. In many ways, the rate of change seems to be cumulative—it follows a curve of acceleration.

3. *Social change in a society is not even or symmetrical.* Many years ago Ogburn pointed this out in his concept of "cultural lag."[4] His thesis was, essentially, that some parts or aspects of a culture change more rapidly than others, and that this creates imbalance and stress in the system.

In this chapter we will see that the parental role in modern America has been complicated by uneven social change—an example would be the urban school year. This developed originally for the benefit of farm parents who wished to have their children help with the farm work during the summer months—but the long summer school recess is not functional for either urban parents or their children. And for the employed mother it is almost disastrous.

Another good example of uneven social change in our society might be the deep social revolution that American women have been going through since World War I in contrast with the slower and less pervasive changes American men seem to have experienced in the same period. To the extent that this has actually been the case—and we recognize that it is merely a hypothesis, not a proven fact—then fathers and mothers would have more difficulty in agreeing on how they should rear their children.

The term *differential social change* is useful in referring to uneven change in our society.

4. *Social change is not usually planned.* In most societies major social changes are not actually planned; they simply evolve in response to some need or they occur as the result of some crisis in the system. An example would be the American public welfare system, which is currently being

---

[4] The concept of "cultural lag" or unequal rates of social change within a society was originally developed by W. F. Ogburn in a book called *Social Change* (New York: B. W. Huebsch, 1922).

subjected to severe criticism. Until the economic disaster of the 1930s, the United States had no modern public welfare system. Voluntary or private social work agencies met family emergencies and did most of the family counseling, with local public welfare agencies meeting the minimal economic needs of the chronically indigent. When this system broke down because of mass unemployment in the 1930s, a new system of local-state-federal public welfare services was hastily improvised. Today it is becoming increasingly clear that this system, designed to help the temporarily unemployed of the 1930s, is not adequate for the 1970s. The clients of today are different and their needs are different.[5] The failure of the welfare system to be properly planned and organized has posed great problems for low-income and minority-group parents, as we have seen in earlier chapters.

5. *The total results of social change are not often anticipated.* In social systems, also families, a change in one part of the system forces change in other parts, for the simple reason that the various aspects of the system are interrelated. Prohibition is often cited by American social scientists as a prime example of the unanticipated results of social change: it was not realized in advance that prohibiting the legal sale of alcoholic beverages would channel hundreds of millions of dollars of revenue into the underworld, thus creating a vast empire of syndicate gangs that still pose problems in urban America.[6]

A good example of unanticipated change in the American family would be the impact of the automobile on parents and children. Not only was the budget of the family drastically altered, but supervision of dating couples became literally impossible. Chaperones at dances, for example, became mere symbols once couples could come and go in automobiles.

6. *Social change is often not desired—it is forced on people.* It is doubtful that most American men really wanted to grant equal social status to women at the end of World War I. In a very real sense the change was forced on the men. This means that social changes of this nature always create conflict, and even after the battle is over, pockets of resistance will be found. Some husbands and fathers in the United States today are still convinced that American political life began to deteriorate the day women began to vote.

Only recently the writer heard a so-called educated person make this remark at a public meeting. "Don't you agree with me," he said to a mixed group of men and women, "that the American family began to decline when the women began to wear the pants?" The women present greeted this remark with cold silence, but a few male heads nodded in agreement.

---

[5] See Alvin Schorr, *Explorations in Social Policy* (New York: Basic Books, 1968).

[6] For a good analysis of the impact of prohibition on American society, see Andrew Sinclair, *Prohibition: The Era of Excess* (Boston: Little, Brown & Co., 1962).

Parents are often caught by this ambivalence about social change. Some parents may go along with the change, while others try to resist it. One parent may accept the change while the other is still fighting it. Another possibility is that the children will welcome the change while the parents deplore it. The "going steady" dating system that swept through American high schools after World War II has been popular with young people but not with parents.[7]

7. *Social change is usually not reversible.* It is rare indeed when a social system, or a family, reverts to a previous state of organization. The American divorce rate, for example, never returned to the prewar level after World Wars I or II. Some sort of permanent change had taken place in the American marriage system during these national crises.[8]

This same principle does not seem to hold for parent models, however: there is, at least in the United States, a certain cyclical pattern to child rearing. Lerner, for example, comments that the extreme permissiveness of American parents that developed during the 1920s and the 1930s seems to have tapered off in the 1950s and 1960s.[9]

These fads or fashions in parent models pose certain problems for fathers and mothers—should they go along with the current fashion or stick to older patterns? What if one parent is contemporary while the other is traditional? American parents have been plagued with dilemmas of this sort in recent decades.

With this background let us now turn to an analysis of a massive social change that American parents are still struggling to cope with—urbanization.

The impact of urbanization on American parents

We do not intend to commit the error so common in sociology textbooks—to present the modern city as the den of iniquity. It is true that all of our crime syndicates are to be found in our large cities, but it is also true that all of our great art museums are found in these same cities. Later in this chapter we will present some of the positive aspects of the city as it affects parents, but at this point we wish to analyze some of the problems American parents found themselves facing once they had left the farm and had settled in the city.

---

[7] On changes in the dating system after World War II, see Robert D. Herman, "The Going Steady Complex," *Marriage and Family Living* 17 (1955): pp. 36–40.

[8] The best analysis of the increase in divorce in the United States is probably Paul H. Jacobson, *American Marriage and Divorce* (New York: Rinehart & Co., 1959), especially chap. 7.

[9] Max Lerner, *America as a Civilization* (New York: Simon & Schuster, 1957), p. 569.

1. *Pluralistic nature of the city.*   The city has been the great melting pot in our society. This means that urban fathers and mothers have had to function in close proximity with parents of diverse ethnic, religious, and racial backgrounds. While this is a source of richness and variety in urban life, it is also a potential source of conflict. Sons and daughters form friendships across cultural and racial lines, and parents are not always sure how to react to this. Young people also fall in love across these lines to the consternation of parents.

In such a pluralistic community, children are exposed to all sorts of "competing models"—such as Catholics, Jews, Italians, Negroes, middle class, or lower class. Children exposed to such a variety of people may question why their own parents think and behave as they do, and this may threaten the parents.[10]

It is true, of course, that the urban communities tend to be segregated by social class and by race, but to some extent the pluralistic nature of the metropolitan community has to be faced by all who live there, parents as well as their children.

2. *The increased leisure of urban youth.*   One great advantage of the farm parent has always been that the children could be kept busy. The opposite situation faces urban parents: school adjourns at 3:30 and children roam the streets; during vacations or the long summer period, urban children find themselves with time to spare. In the more affluent neighborhoods or suburbs this problem is easier to cope with, but in the low-income areas solutions are difficult to find. The present school year was never designed for urban parents and conflicts with the work schedules of both fathers and employed mothers. The urban school should offer at least a half-day program during the summer months, plus some evening and weekend programs.[11]

3. *A more powerful youth peer group.*   One of the results of more leisure time and close physical proximity in the city has been the rise to power of the youth peer group.[12] Urban children may spend 30–50 hours a week talking and playing with members of their peer group, and out of this youth society emerge norms of behavior and loyalties that challenge the power and influence of parents. This is a relatively new development of urban America that rural parents did not have to cope with.

4. *The impersonality and anonymity of the city.*   Parents in the urban

---

10 For an excellent discussion of American immigrant parents and their child-rearing problems, see Oscar Handlin, *The Uprooted* (Boston: Little, Brown & Co., 1952), especially chap. 9, "Generations."

11 An excellent analysis of the deficiencies of the urban school may be found in Peter Schrag, *Village School Downtown* (Boston: Beacon Press, 1967).

12 This data was analyzed in the preceding chapter, and the references will be found there.

community often do not really know with whom their children are associating. Not only do they not know their childrens' friends, they also do not know the parents of these other children. Very often all they know about the peer group of their children consists of what the children choose to tell them. This means that in planning their strategy or making decisions concerning the peer group parents are forced to operate with inadequate or biased data. Any business executive today will tell you that the most modern computer is no better than the information fed into it. The same principle applies to parents.

In an interesting passage in his textbook on the family, Farber points out that parents are forced to take a risk in almost every decision they make—they never have complete knowledge or understanding of any particular child, nor do they ever have all of the facts affecting the particular problem facing them.[13] While this observation applies to all parents, it seems especially to be a condition faced by fathers and mothers in the modern urban community. One mother said to the writer: "All I know about the boys my daughter dates is what she tells me. How am I supposed to help her choose her boyfriends when I don't know anything about them?" It is a good question.

5. *The pervasive nature of urban mass media.* It is true that no American today, except a few hermits and some religious minority groups, can escape the massive attack of the mass media—radio, television, newspapers, magazines, and billboards. To some extent, rural parents have to contend with such forces also, but not to the same extent as urban parents. There is something about the physical crowding of people that heightens the communication process.

In a very real sense, urban parents today operate in an atmosphere of the circus or the carnival. Their children are surrounded by hundreds of pitchmen selling some product or some idea. It is only the very skilled father or mother who can prevail against the highly paid men and women from Hollywood and Madison Avenue.

6. *The urban ghetto.* The problems of minority-group parents were analyzed in a separate chapter, but a few words about urban slums and the problems they pose for parents are appropriate here.

As the affluent white families migrate to the suburbs, the central city of the metropolitan community comes to be composed primarily of low-income whites, blacks, Puerto Ricans, Mexican-Americans, and American Indians. This central city is badly financed because the well-to-do taxpayers live out in the suburbs. This means that schools and other public services are not maintained at desirable levels. Housing is almost universally substandard—the *U.S. Riot Commission Report* says that at least

---

[13] Bernard Farber, *Family: Organization and Interaction* (San Francisco: Chandler Publishing Co., 1964), pp. 493–95.

70 percent of the housing occupied by black families does not meet minimum standards.[14]

It is clear that only superior parents could rear children successfully in such an environment. It is not odd that school dropout and juvenile delinquency rates are high in such areas—the amazing thing is that such behavior is not universal.

The positive aspects of urbanization

The city is often portrayed as the center of evil in our society, but in a very real sense it has been the center of hope—for the millions of immigrants from Europe who got here too late for the free land; and more recently for the American black family.

With all of its problems for parents, the urban community actually offers many advantages: better school systems, with special classes for the handicapped child; better social welfare services, both private and public; better medical and public health facilities; more tolerance for racial and religious minorities; and a greater chance for vertical social mobility.[15]

It can be argued, with considerable logic, that the impoverished rural parent in modern America is in an even more difficult position than the urban ghetto parent. There is no place in the rural agricultural economy for most of the low-income farm children; their parents lack the knowledge and experience to help these children make a successful move to the city; and, finally, the rural community lacks the network of health, welfare, and educational services available to low-income urban parents.[16]

It is an interesting fact that the minority group that has achieved the highest socioeconomic position in the United States—the Jews—is almost entirely metropolitan in residence. And contrary to what millions of Americans think, the majority of these Jewish families entered the socioeconomic system at the bottom. It was their utilization of urban services, such as the urban university, that enabled them to attain a comfortable position in our society.[17]

We have been analyzing the impact of urbanization on parents. Because of the massive move to the city since World War I, farm parents

---

[14] For a discussion of housing in the ghetto, see the *U.S. Riot Commission Report* (New York: Bantam Books, 1968), pp. 467–82; also Lee Rainwater, *Behind Ghetto Walls* (New York: Free Press, 1970).

[15] Some of these positive features of urban life are discussed in Herbert J. Gans, *The Urban Villagers* (New York: Free Press, 1962).

[16] Some of the superior features of the urban welfare system are discussed by Schorr, *Explorations in Social Policy*.

[17] A good analysis of some of the problems faced by Jewish parents in America may be found in Nathan Glazer and Daniel Patrick Moynihan, "The Jews," *Beyond the Melting Pot* (Cambridge, Mass.: M.I.T. Press, 1963), chap. 3.

now constitute less than 10 percent of all parents in the United States. In a sense they have become a minority group—not only in a statistical sense but also sociologically.

The special problems of rural parents in modern America

It could well be true that rural parents in our society are in a more difficult position than urban parents. In some ways the rural revolution in the United States in recent decades has been deeper and more widespread than changes taking place in the city. The mechanization of the farm has greatly reduced the demand for farm laborers, and the increased productivity per farm worker has meant that in each of the recent decades the percentage of the American population engaged in agriculture has declined. As of the 1970s, this figure has been somewhere between 6 and 10 percent.[18]

All of this means that a majority of our farm youth today will be forced to resettle in the urban world.

Historically, the farm family in the United States has been romanticized. The image most of us have is that of the prosperous middle-class farm owner—the one usually portrayed on the cover of mass magazines at Thanksgiving. Americans do not like to think about the lower-class farm families—the farm tenants, the sharecroppers, the farm laborers, or the migratory farm workers. These families, on the average, are probably worse off than most low-income urban families.[19]

In the next few pages we wish to focus on some of the special problems faced by farm parents.

1. *The urbanization impact.* Because of mass media, the automobile, the consolidated school, and general population mobility, farm children are increasingly being subjected to urban values and the urban way of life. This means that a considerable amount of social distance is being created between farm parents and their children. To the extent that the parents are attempting to internalize rural values and a rural way of life in their children, the parents are struggling against the stream—the whole drift of the society is in the other direction.

2. *Farm parents are preparing their children for an urban-industrial world.* Farm parents today face many of the problems American im-

---

[18] One of the best accounts of the farm revolution is Lauren Soth's *An Embarrassment of Plenty* (New York: Thomas Y. Crowell Co., 1965). See also the paper by Lee G. Burchinal, "The Rural Family of the Future," in *Our Changing Rural Society,* ed. James H. Copp (Ames: Iowa State University Press, 1964), pp. 159–97.

[19] We find that most college students are unaware of the fact that the poverty rate is higher in rural America than in our cities. They also do not realize that about three fourths of the rural poor are white; see *White Americans in Rural Poverty,* Agricultural Economics Report, no. 124, (Washington, D.C.: Government Printing Office, 1967).

migrant parents used to face; they have to prepare their children for a world they do not understand themselves. On the farm, historically, a man who was willing to do hard physical labor could get by. Formal education was not very essential. The ability to handle animals was more crucial than the ability to handle people.

These conditions do not prevail in urban America, and to a considerable extent they no longer prevail in rural America either. Trade unions, sex equality, racial integration—ideas that have never been too popular in rural America are dominant today in urban America. Farm children will have to understand and adjust to this world of the city, but their parents may not be too much help in the process.

3. *The rural economy.*   There is simply no place for most of the farm children in the farm economy of tomorrow. Only the well-educated, well-financed farm youth can hope to survive in the agricultural world of tomorrow. Farms of today are larger, more expensive, more mechanized, and more scientifically managed than ever before. The poor farmer has no place in such a world unless he plans to earn his living in a nearby city and run a small farm as a sort of hobby or moonlight operation.

4. *The rural social class barrier.*   Because of the farm revolution, the farm boy or farm girl from a low-income family has little chance for vertical social mobility. Migration to the city offers the best hope for most of these children. The more intelligent farm parents know this. The children of the others will have to find it out the hard way—by experience.

Parental defense mechanisms against social change

How do successful parents—those who seem to have relatively few problems in rearing their children—cope with rapid social change? In the opinion of the writer, there are at least four basic strategies utilized by these parents.

1. *Early parenthood.*   Women today are having most of their children by the time they are 30 years old. Many of them can be heard to say: "I want to have them while I am still young enough to enjoy them."

There are, of course, many potential disadvantages in assuming the parental role at an early age, but one of the advantages is that it does reduce the social distance between parent and child.

2. *The buddy system of parenthood.*   In a sense these parents adopt the attitude that "if you can't lick 'em, join 'em." They virtually become teen-agers themselves and seek to bridge the generation gap in this way.

To some extent such parents resemble the social workers assigned to work with street gangs in our larger cities—they mingle with the young people and try to influence the group from within. One college girl described a mother of this type in this way: "My mother is a real pal. You can do almost anything with her—she fits right into the group."

Some parents seem to achieve a certain amount of success with this buddy approach, but others simply make themselves look ridiculous.

3. *Do not try to understand the younger generation—it is hopeless.* One mother told the writer: "I don't even try to understand my children's generation anymore. My only concern is that they understand *me.*"

These parents take the position that basic values do not change in our society and they hammer away at these in rearing their children. "Honesty and decency and cleanliness don't change," one father said to the writer. "As long as you stick to things like that you can't go wrong. And you'll never be out-of-date."

Essentially, these parents hold themselves aloof from the current fashions in child rearing and stick to the "eternal verities." They remind one of a woman who refuses to raise or drop her hemline just because Paris says to wear the skirts short or long. One woman said to us: "What do I care about what Paris says? My knees are big and bumpy and I don't intend to show them if I can help it." Some parents adopt this approach in their roles as fathers and mothers.

4. *The radar system of child rearing.* Riesman argues that most American parents hedge against social change by using the "radar system" of child rearing.[20] Not being sure of what is right or wrong, these parents train their children to "fit in," to "be adjusted." They equip their children with a built-in radar antenna that provides them with a constant flow of signals as to what is happening in their significant reference groups, and all these children need to do to be adjusted is to alter their values and their behavior to fit the current fashion. Almost all of us do this in choosing our clothes, but Riesman says that "fashions" now include values and norms as well as hemlines or shoe styles.

Whyte develops a similar argument in analyzing the "social ethic" of the middle-class suburbanites reported on in his best seller, *The Organization Man.*[21]

Riesman believes that parents in an earlier America really did not care what other parents were teaching their children.[22] These pioneer fathers and mothers, says Riesman, knew what was right and they internalized these values and norms in their sons and daughters. In any new or difficult situation, then, all these children had to do was to look *inward* to find the solution to their dilemma.

This system of child rearing may work well in a deeply religious society in which parents can operate with "revealed truths" that are assumed

---

[20] David Riesman et al., *The Lonely Crowd,* rev. ed. (New Haven, Conn.: Yale University Press, 1961), pp. 45–55.

[21] William H. Whyte, Jr., *The Organization Man* (Garden City, N.Y.: Doubleday & Co., 1957), esp. chap. 29, "Conclusion."

[22] Riesman et al., *The Lonely Crowd,* pp. 40–45.

to be "eternal." But in a society in which the revealed truths come from the secular priests, who seem to change their truths almost every decade, how can parents find any absolutely certain values or norms to internalize? The answer seems to be that they cannot.

Faced with this neat little problem the smart parent falls back on an even more eternal principle—the law of the jungle, which is to *survive*. "Don't be a sucker, or a martyr," the child is told. "Go along with the group and you can't get too far out of line." In a sense this represents the wisdom of the old sergeant (or the old chief petty officer) when he tells the raw recruit: "Keep your nose clean and you won't get into any trouble."

Riesman has an interesting comment on the inner-directed method of child rearing. "Homing pigeons," he writes, "can be taught to fly home, but the inner-directed child must be taught to fly a straight course *away* from home, with destination unknown; naturally many meet the fate of Icarus.[23]

In an earlier discussion in this chapter we said that some parents try to solve the problem of social change by falling back on the values and norms that are not temporal—they are supposed to apply at all times everywhere. When pressed by the writer in parent discussion groups, such parents usually cite words such as "honesty," "decency," "cleanliness," and so forth. But none of these words, it seems to the writer, mean today what they did in the America of 1910 or 1920. Our grandparents, for example, felt themselves to be clean when they bathed once a week— or even once a month in winter. No body deodorants were used by these men—or the women either. The aroma of honest sweat was not considered offensive. On the contrary, its presence proved that a man or a woman was not afraid to work.

Today, children begin in junior high, if not earlier, to use deodorants, and on television it sometimes seems that the worst sin a father can commit is to take the family's deodorant with him on a business trip.

Would a small-town merchant of the 1920s recognize the word *honesty* if he came back and saw how consumer goods are advertised and sold today?

Would a nice girl of 1910 accept the definition of a *nice girl* that seems to be current today?

It is difficult to see where fathers and mothers in contemporary America would find any eternal truths to teach their children. In a Protestant church known to the writer, a careful survey of the membership conducted on an anonymous basis by an outside research organization found that about 60 percent of the members were "not sure they believed in

---

[23] Riesman et al., *The Lonely Crowd*, p. 42. For the non-Greek scholars it might be pointed out that Icarus crashed into the sea and never made it back home.

God."[24] This seems strange since to join this church new members have to stand up in front of the congregation and take an oath that they *do* believe in God.

What should a modern parent teach his children about lifetime monogamy when some of the best people in our society no longer practice it?[25]

What should a Roman Catholic mother teach her daughter about birth control? Recent surveys show that the average American Roman Catholic no longer supports his church's position on contraceptives.[26] What position should parents take?

In view of the "relativity" of modern values and norms, it is understandable that modern parents turn to a radar system of rearing their children. "After all," one mother said to us, "if radar is good enough for the airlines it should be good enough for parents."

Parents who cannot cope with social change

Although the point is difficult to document, it seems likely that parents who cannot cope with social change must face insuperable barriers in rearing children in modern America.

Riesman makes the point that some parents may be preparing their children for a world that no longer exists. He writes: "Parents who try in inner-directed fashion, to compel the internalization of disciplined pursuit of clear goals, run the risk of having their children styled clear out of the personality market. Inhibited from presenting their children with sharply silhouetted images of self and society, parents in our era can only equip the child to do his best, whatever that may turn out to be."[27]

This point might be illustrated in relationship to the sex conditioning of daughters in contemporary America. If a father and mother were able, somehow, to rear their daughter to believe that she should not neck until she was engaged to be married, it seems likely that such a girl would be priced out of the high school or college dating system—unless by some odd chance she found a boy who had internalized the same norms. The writer has actually interviewed one college woman who reported—and we have reason to believe that she was being honest—that she never necked until she was engaged to be married in her senior year of college.

It needs to be noted, however, that this girl reported very few dates in

---

[24] This survey was done in a metropolitan "liberal" Protestant church in the Midwest in 1967.

[25] In recent years divorces have been reported in the public press for the following elite families: Ford, Rockefeller, Kennedy, and Roosevelt.

[26] See *New Catholic Thinking about Family Planning* (New York: Planned Parenthood Federation of America, 1967).

[27] Riesman et al., *The Lonely Crowd*, p. 47.

high school or college until she met her future husband at the beginning of her last year of college, and that this is the *only* college woman ever interviewed by the writer who said she adhered to such a stringent sexual code.

It is true, of course, that parents may teach their children almost any set of values they wish to, but if they deviate too much from the current model they run two types of risk: they may damage their relationship with their child; or their child may be isolated from his (or her) peer group and be considered odd or peculiar. This is not always undesirable, but it does pose special problems for adolescents with their great fear of nonconformity.

Some parents seem to have difficulty coping with social change because one parent is more contemporary than the other. Not all married couples change at the same rate, so that a traditional father may find himself paired with a modern mother—and this can pose problems in a role such as parenthood that demands teamwork. Actually one of the complexities of the parent role is that we usually have to work at it *in pairs*. This is not easy when we have differential social change between parents.

Some studies indicate that mothers in our society may be more contemporary than fathers.[28] If this is true, then a built-in strain between American parents would be expected. The writer does not believe that the current research is adequate to conclude whether this is the case or not.[29]

Of course, if the American father is as "shadowy" in our family system as some observers seem to think, then whether he is modern or traditional would not make much difference. As we stated in an earlier chapter, however, we doubt very much that fathers in our society have ceased to affect the rearing of their children.

Parents and resocialization

In a society dedicated to rapid social change and progress, as the United States is, the dilemma of parents is clear: they themselves grew up in the world of yesterday, a world that is now largely dead, even if not buried, and this is the world they internalized; they rear their children in the world of today, a world they only partially understand and

---

[28] For an interesting discussion of modernity among fathers and mothers in their parental roles, see John R. Seeley et al., "Parent Education," *Crestwood Heights* (New York: Basic Books, 1956), chap. 9.

[29] In one of the more elaborate modern studies of parents, almost half of the mothers reported disagreements with their husbands over discipline problems with children, with the father reported to be "tougher." See Daniel R. Miller and Guy E. Swanson, *The Changing American Parent* (New York: John Wiley & Sons, 1958), p. 225.

184 Parents in modern America

only partially accept; but they are rearing their children for the world of tomorrow, a world that nobody understands as yet. These conditions are some of the reasons why even intelligent and capable parents often feel confused and bewildered in modern America.

In his paper on parent-youth conflict, Davis refers to the phenomenon of "decelerating socialization."[30] By this he means that parents have already passed the peak of their learning curve by the time they become parents. Thus their efforts to keep up with the world of their children are handicapped by their relatively slow rate of learning in their twenties and thirties. At the same time their children are at the peak of their learning curve.

The situation is even more complex than Davis described it, because the learning of adults (parents) actually involves *resocialization*—that is, they have to unlearn what they absorbed earlier in order to take in the new knowledge.[31]

In a famous paper the anthropologist Benedict analyzed this process of resocialization.[32] She used the term *discontinuity* to describe what happens: a girl learns that sex is bad and something to avoid, yet later as a wife she is supposed to think that sex is good and something to be enjoyed. How does she ever make the transition from stage 1 to stage 2?

Parents face this type of situation almost daily:[33] something they were taught as children that would "never change" is suddenly out of style—for example, that college students do not get married until they have completed their undergraduate degree. Another good illustration would be the old saying that "violence never solves anything." Some black parents are finding this old truism harder and harder to sell to their children.

Parents and future shock

In a book that was on the best-seller lists for over a year, Toffler argued that millions of Americans suffer from what he called "future shock."[34] By this, Toffler means that many of us are so appalled by the signs of the future that we find ourselves depressed and unable to make sense of our world. A striking example would be the prediction that 180

---

[30] Davis, "Parent-Youth Conflict," p. 524.

[31] For an analysis of the process of resocialization, see Orville G. Brim, Jr., and Stanton Wheeler, *Socialization after Childhood* (New York: John Wiley & Sons, 1966).

[32] Ruth Benedict, "Continuities and Discontinuities in Cultural Conditioning," *Psychiatry* 1 (May 1938): 161–67.

[33] An interesting paper is that by Kenneth Keniston, "Social Change and Youth in America," in *The Challenge of Youth*, ed. Erik Erikson (New York: Doubleday & Co., 1968), pp. 191–222.

[34] Alvin Toffler, *Future Shock* (New York: Random House, 1970).

million persons would be killed if a nuclear war broke out between the Soviet Union and the United States.

The writer believes that a great many American parents suffer from future shock in trying to comprehend the behavior of some of their children. The following case studies, based on actual incidents related to the writer by parents or children, will illustrate the point.

Cohabitation at the college level

An upper-middle-class couple received a telephone call from the private college their daughter was attending that the girl had not used her dormitory room or the college dining hall for two weeks. The dean of women's office inquired as to whether the daughter might have returned home. The parents replied that to the best of their knowledge the girl was still on campus. Further investigation revealed that the daughter had been attending classes but had moved off campus into an apartment with three male students, one of whom was her "boy friend."

What are parents supposed to think when they find their daughter living with three men? Her story was that she was having an affair with one of the male students but had had no sexual contact with the other two male residents of the apartment. The parents were prepared for the fact that their daughter might be having an affair in college—this was not unheard of in their generation—but for her to move into an apartment with three men was beyond their comprehension.

When the shock had subsided, the parents withdrew the daughter from college and persuaded her to come home until the next fall. She then returned to the same college and was eventually graduated. She is now married but not to the student she was having an affair with. Her relationship with her parents has returned to what could be called "normal."

In addition to the shock of this event, the parents in this situation suffered a substantial financial loss in that the college refused to refund any room or board payment.

Honors students and LSD

A son who had graduated at the top of his suburban high school class and had won national recognition in college-placement tests was discovered to be experimenting with various drugs—marijuana, "speed," and LSD. The parents had become conditioned to the fact that marijuana is relatively common on university campuses, but it had never occurred to them that their son would experiment with LSD, which they understood to be quite dangerous. Their son told them that other honor students from the same high school had been taking LSD with him. All of the students in the group were from so-called nice families of the upper middle class.

When their shock had subsided, these parents persuaded their son to see a university drug counselor, who convinced the son that LSD was nothing to fool around with. The parents now feel that the crisis has passed and that the son and his friends are over the hard-drug phase of their lives. No permanent break has occurred between the son and his parents.

A nice Catholic girl

Parents with an Italian background, both devout Roman Catholics, learned that their daughter at the state university had been living with her boy friend when they had understood that she was sharing an apartment with a girl friend. They also found out that their daughter had had an abortion.

This situation produced what seems to be a permanent break between the daughter and her parents. The father and mother terminated the daughter's allowance and refused to help her complete her degree, even though she was an honor student. The girl is now working and attending the university on a part-time basis.

In this case the social distance between the parents and the daughter was too great for compromise: the parents could not accept the daughter's social world and she could not accept theirs.

Discussion of the generation gap

In an interesting book Feuer argues that every society experiences a generation gap to some extent but that in every society there are historical periods in which the gap is accentuated.[35] Feuer cites the Russian period from about 1880 to 1920 as an example of a time when parents and children in that society tended to be alienated from each other. In many ways the 1960s was such a period in the United States.

When the writer was growing up, one of the big issues was whether "nice" girls could smoke cigarettes. Believe it or not, entire families were split over this conflict.

In the 1930s, with the nation wallowing in despair, many young persons turned to the Left politically and were thus alienated from their parents. In the 1970s political conflicts as such seem to be relatively rare in American families.

---

[35] Lewis S. Feuer, *The Conflict of Generations* (New York: Basic Books, 1969).

When crises arise with older children, parents have to decide whether they are prepared to face a permanent break with their son or daughter. In some situations known to the writer, parents have taken a position from which they eventually have had to back down. This is illustrated in the following situation. A Jewish undergraduate woman came to the state university without any sexual experience. In her freshman year she lived in a dormitory and began having an affair with a "nice Jewish boy." Every week end they would spend together either in his room or her room. They thought they were "in love" but did not know how deep or how permanent the relationship might be.

In her sophomore year this girl decided that she wanted to share an apartment with her boy friend and he felt the same way. "I didn't like the sneaky relationship we had had in the dorms," she said. They found an apartment they could afford and moved in.

Being an extremely honest person, this girl wrote to her parents and told them where and how she was living. She assured them that this boy was the only man she had ever slept with and that they might eventually be married—as yet she was not sure.

Her parents were shocked. They could not understand how a "nice Jewish girl" could do such a thing. They also refused to help her continue at the university.

This girl, an honor student in high school and college, was prepared for her parents' reaction. She obtained a job and continued her education with a reduced load. She had no intention of moving out of the apartment.

When the winter recess came the parents wrote and asked the daughter if she would bring her boy friend home so that the parents could meet him. One stipulation was the couple were not to sleep together during the visit.

The girl and the young man agreed to the above arrangement. The parents were so impressed with the boy friend and the apparent happiness of their daughter that they offered to help her complete her education. She accepted the offer.

This story ends with the girl's mother insisting on a big wedding when the couple decided to get married in their junior year. Both of the young people are now in graduate school and so far the marriage appears to be successful. The relationship with the parents (on both sides) is excellent.

This girl says: "I am not a sex radical. I do not believe in bed hopping but I also don't believe in hypocrisy. Furthermore, I have seen a lot of poor marriages and I wanted to avoid that if possible."

Actually, this girl is a mixture of traditional and modern: she believes in monogamy and sexual fidelity but she also believes in the right of young persons to test their compatibility for marriage. Persons who regard this girl as a radical should be aware that a survey of junior and senior women at Cornell University concluded that 34 percent of the girls had tried living with a male student while in college and that 80 percent of these reported the relationship to have been a "positive experience."[36]

In an interesting discussion of black and white college students who have been deeply involved in the civil rights struggle in the South, Robert Coles argues that some of the old terms, such as "normal" or "mature" or "radical," are no longer helpful in understanding today's generation.[37] Coles cites a young black man who was fully aware that he might lose his life in the racial struggle but had come to the conclusion that he was willing to pay this price if necessary to change the racial situation in America. Coles' point is that this young man is not "immature"—he is *determined.*

In the case of the Jewish girl discussed above, two further points need to be made: (1) In a book called *The Vanishing Adolescent,* Friedenberg points out that young people are doing things in high school and college that their parents did not do until they were much older.[38] If the girl in the above situation had begun living with a man in graduate school, the parents might not have been so shocked. But undergraduates are now doing what graduate students did in earlier decades. (2) The current generation is much more open about its sexual behavior. Parents have taught their children to be honest and are often not prepared for the consequences.

It is a serious error to believe that better communication will resolve the problems created by the generation gap. It is certainly true that improved communication at the verbal level will clarify intergenerational conflicts, but this does not necessarily resolve them. In fact, in some situations more complete communication will reveal that parents and their children are even farther apart than they had thought.

In his discussion of the American family of the future, Toffler makes this statement: "We have it in our power to shape change. We may choose one future over another. We cannot, however, maintain the past. In our family forms, as in our economic, science, technology and social relationships, we shall be forced to deal with the new."[39] This writer agrees.

---

[36] Eleanor Macklin, "Heterosexual Cohabitation among Unmarried College Students," *Family Coordinator* 21 (1972): 463–72.

[37] Robert Coles, *Farewell to the South* (Boston: Little, Brown & Co., 1972), pp. 216–17.

[38] Edgar Z. Friedenberg, *The Vanishing Adolescent* (New York: Dell Publishing Co., 1962).

[39] Toffler, *Future Shock,* p. 220.

Summary and conclusion

In this chapter the process of social change was examined, and this was discussed in terms of its impact on the parental role in American society. Some of the features of the generation gap were explored, also strategies employed by parents to cope with it. The concept of "future shock" was borrowed from Toffler to help understand some of the more disturbing aspects of the generation gap as viewed by parents.

In the next chapter, the concluding one, attention will be focused on counseling systems used in attempts to help parents.

chapter
twelve

Counseling
with parents

In his book, *Games People Play,* Berne makes the following statement: "Raising children is primarily a matter of teaching them what games to play."[1]

In this chapter on counseling with parents, we are adopting a stance somewhat similar to that of Berne: counseling with parents is primarily a matter of helping them see explicitly what parental model they have been using; examining that model with the parents to see how well it fits them and their children; suggesting alternate models that might work better for them; and, finally, teaching the parent (or parents) how to implement the model decided on. The rest of this chapter will attempt to explain how this counseling system works.

The attitude of the counselor

Before proceeding to parental models and their implementation, a few words need to be said about attitudes that social workers, teachers, ministers, judges, psychologists, and psychiatrists tend to have toward parents.

---

[1] Eric Berne, *Games People Play* (New York: Grove Press, 1964), p. 171.

Parents are often assumed to be guilty before they even get a hearing with the counselor.[2] The child has been doing something wrong, therefore the parents have been doing something wrong. The professional counselors forget that parents are *amateurs*—very few of them ever had any training for the parental role. This means that the professional counselor[3] is usually using professional norms to assess the performance of nonprofessionals.

Counselors who have never been parents tend to underestimate the complexity and hazards of being a parent in our society—they are too willing to condemn parents if a child is having difficulty.[4]

Almost all counselors, including this writer, have feelings and attitudes from their own family experience that sometimes intrude on the counseling situation—appropriately or inappropriately. Some of these attitudes and feelings may be conscious, but others are subconscious or unconscious.

Brim makes it clear that most workers in the family-life-education field reflect a built-in middle-class bias.[5] It seems likely that parent counselors have the same bias.

Most American parents seen by counselors are already suffering from a deep feeling of inadequacy. Regardless of how hard they may have tried, the results of their parental efforts have not been satisfactory. Therefore, it does not seem appropriate or desirable for the counselor to add to this crushing weight of failure. It may help the counselor if he remembers that even unsuccessful parents have often tried hard to rear their children properly—their efforts have simply not paid off.

Finally, parent counselors need to watch that they do not become "child worshippers"—people who seem to be willing to do almost anything to parents "if it will help the child." Parents are people too, and they have as much right to consideration as children have.

With this background let us examine various parent models and attempt to see how better knowledge of them might help parents.

Parent models

Whether they realize it or not, all parents adopt one parent model or another. In the rest of this chapter we wish to examine some of these models to see what their essential characteristics are and to discuss how parent counselors can use the models in working with parents.

---

[2] Orville G. Brim, Jr., *Education for Child Rearing* (New York: Russell Sage Foundation, 1959), especially chap. 9, "Aims of Parent Education."

[3] The term *counselor* is being used generically here to denote any member of the helping professions who works with parents.

[4] This observation is based on contacts with graduate students who are not yet parents.

[5] Brim, *Education for Child Rearing*, passim.

The martyr model

Many parents, without realizing it, adopt the martyr model. "Nothing is too good for my children," they will say, or "I would do *anything* for my child."

The following characteristics are usually found in this model.

Parental guilt. For some reason these parents usually exhibit guilt, and the counselor needs to explore this with them.

Overprotection. Guilt is often accompanied by overprotection. The parent is afraid that something will happen to the child and attempts to set up a "super safe" world for the child. This, of course, almost invariably produces problems for all parties concerned—parents as well as children.

It is our impression that divorced parents, or those whose marriage has failed even though it is still intact, are especially subject to the guilt-overprotection syndrome. Parents with handicapped children will often exhibit this pattern also.

It hardly needs to be said that these martyr parents spoil their children. They cannot set realistic goals for their children, or if they do, the goals are not adhered to.

Revolt or meek submission by the child. A healthy reaction by children living under this parental model is that of revolt—they almost instinctively reach out for a normal life and this inevitably brings them into conflict with the parent or parents. At this point the martyred parent assumes the posture—"look what you are doing to me—and after all I have done for you." Berne analyzes this game as it is enacted between marital partners.[6]

A child that does *not* revolt against the martyr model is a sick child —he will be crippled for life if he does not revolt. This might not be true in some societies, but it is certainly true in the open-class, competitive, impersonal society American children will graduate into.

The famous Irish writer, Sean O'Faolain, has this to say about the martyr model: "Like all women who become slaves to their children, my mother not only exhausted her own emotions but ultimately killed the emotions of everybody around her."[7]

Hostility and resentment by the child toward the parent. In the event of revolt this will be open and obvious. In cases of submission it will be covert and repressed. Martyr parents can never understand this reaction by their children: "Look at that attitude after all I have done for them."

It is the writer's belief that the martyr model is perhaps the most destructive one found in American parents. In some ways it is even more

---

[6] Berne, *Games People Play*, pp. 104–7.

[7] Sean O'Faolain, *Vive Moi!* (Boston: Little, Brown & Co., 1964), p. 108.

destructive than the model of parent neglect—the neglected child is at least free and has a chance of finding a substitute parent.

On an ethical level it is simply not right that a parent should serve as a martyr for a child: it denies the parent his right to a life of his own as an adult; furthermore, it places the child in the inevitable role of the ungrateful offspring.

Some of the most difficult counseling situations in working with martyr parents are found when one parent adheres to the martyr model while the other one rejects it. This can be described as a "split model" situation. When this is found the counselor has to be careful not to be seduced by the martyred parent, and to see the split as an asset—it means that conflict is present and out of this conflict change can be generated.

The best strategy in dealing with martyr parents is to be honest and direct: unless they can be made to see what they are doing to themselves as well as their children the prognosis is not pleasant. These parents have thick defenses and the counselor will often need to be provocative and/or aggressive to get any movement.

The buddy or pal model

A certain number of parents in modern America seem to have adopted the buddy or pal model—they apparently feel that this is a solution to the gap between the generations.

Some students of the family have been rather caustic in their comments on this model. Bell, for example, has this to say:

The middle-class belief that a parent should be a "pal" to his children reflects a social value which gives importance to a common world for parents and children. The belief in a common world has developed around notions of democracy between parents and children and implies they are equals socially, psychologically, and intellectually. If this is true, it is a devastating picture of the parents because it implies that they are still teenagers.[8]

Bell goes on to point out that the pal approach to parenthood is not the only area in which the lines between generations have been blurred in our society.[9]

In a sense the parents who adopt the buddy or pal models are following the old saying, "If you can't beat 'em, join 'em." They are trying to infiltrate the youth peer group and work from within. In some ways they resemble the social workers assigned to work with juvenile gangs on the

---

[8] Robert R. Bell, *Marriage and Family Interaction*, 3d ed. (Homewood, Ill.: Dorsey Press, 1971), p. 463.

[9] Bell, *Marriage and Family Interaction*.

streets of our large cities.[10] These social workers have no authority: they simply attempt to influence the gang leadership. This is not only a difficult role but also a dangerous one—and the writer has a hunch it is no easier for parents.

It is possible that the pal or buddy model received its impetus from the rush of early marriages that followed the end of World War II. The writer interviewed a mother of 20 a few years ago who was taking care of her two preschool children. She just laughed when we asked her if she felt mature enough to be rearing a family.

"Nobody is grown up in this house," she said. "My husband is 20 also and he certainly isn't very grown up."

After a pause she looked at her two children and said: *"I guess we're all growing up together."*

It struck us that her generation—at least some of them—do not accept the traditional idea that you have to be grown up to get married. On the contrary, all you need is somebody who wants to grow up with you. The writer does not know how many young parents in America subscribe to this point of view, but for those that do the pal model may be functional: they would only be kidding themselves if they pretended to be mature adults rearing a family.

Another impetus for the pal or buddy model may have come from the rejection of middle age or old age in our society. Americans do not revere the older person, or assume that he has any great store of wisdom to offer young people. If anything, we tend to pity the older person—and by older the society means anybody over 40. Thus, by the time American parents are dealing with adolescents, they are near (or over) the dividing line between youth and old age. Many of them are tempted to conclude that they might as well pretend to be a pal or buddy because there is nothing to gain by acting your age. Millions of women in our society use this strategy (with some success), and some parents apparently use it also.

The writer happens to believe that the pal or buddy model of parenthood is difficult and risky. Its major problems follow.

It is extremely unrealistic. Our society holds that parents are responsible for the rearing and guidance of their minor children. Parents can be imprisoned for neglect or mistreatment of their children. They can also have their parental rights terminated under certain circumstances.

In view of the "generation gap" in our society, it seems unlikely that

---

[10] For an analysis of the problems in working with teen-age gangs (infiltrating the group), see Irving Spergel, *Street Gang Work: Theory and Practice* (Reading, Mass.: Addison-Wesley Publishing Co., 1966). One of Spergel's points is that this work requires *courage*.

any children are going to be fooled by the pal model of parenthood.[11] They know who the enemy is—and their motto seems to be: "Never trust anybody over 30."

As we pointed out earlier, the pal or buddy model may be realistic for some teen-age parents who are still children themselves, but the model hardly fits the vast majority of American parents.

The roles called for in the model are quite complex. Few of us can cross generation lines effectively and convincingly enough to make this model work. One has to penetrate or infiltrate the youth peer group, understand its subculture, and be accepted by the group. Pal parents cannot fall back on parental authority when the going gets tough—they have to sustain the pal role consistently if the model is to work. Very few parents can achieve this level of role performance.

The pal model requires superior parents to make it work. In World War II we had an opportunity to study at close range two types of officers in the U.S. Naval Air Corps.[12] The traditional officer maintained considerable social distance between himself and his enlisted men—a model that the Navy had found to be effective over the years. This traditional model was well defined and made no great demands on the imagination or creativity of the officer. All he had to do was to follow the rules and not much could happen to him. In the bomber air groups, however, with their long missions and close physical proximity, some officers abandoned the traditional model and adopted a pal or buddy model—their enlisted men did not have to salute officers, first names were used, regulation clothing was not insisted on, and so forth.

It was the writer's impression, based on three years of participant-observation, that only the *superior* officers could adopt the buddy model and get away with it. If the officer was average or below average in ability, the flight crew soon deteriorated and order had to be restored by some subordinate, such as a chief petty officer, if the crew was to function properly.

It is our belief that the same conditions hold for parents: only the superior parent can play the buddy game with his or her children without losing their respect and their obedience.

The pal or buddy model involves considerable risk. This was quite clear in the Naval Air Corps in the opinion of the writer. Several tragic plane and crew losses might have been avoided in the writer's air group if crews had been held under more strict discipline.

We have the impression that the pal model is equally risky for parents: if things do not go well, they have to retreat to a more formal, au-

---

[11] For an interesting analysis of the generation gap, see Richard Lorber and Ernest Fladell, *The Gap* (New York: McGraw-Hill Book Co., 1968).

[12] The observations on officer models in the U.S. Naval Air Corps are based on three years service during World War II.

thoritarian parent model—and this retreat or shift in role is extremely difficult to manage without damaging the parent's image in the eyes of his children.

A professor known to us had been using the buddy model with a graduate seminar. Among other things, he told members of the class that they did not have to come to class if they did not want to. One day this professor went to class and found only one student out of 15 present. He was furious and immediately posted a notice that attendance would be compulsory in the future. The class reacted with resentment, and the semester was completed in the atmosphere of an armed truce.

One of the advantages of the traditional authoritarian parent model is that it allows the father or mother to relax the rules occasionally without damaging the relationship with the children—in fact the relationship should be enhanced. This is not the case when the pal model has been adopted.

In their study of marriage, Bach and Wyden make the following statement about parents and children: "It goes almost without saying that true intimacy can exist only between peers who wield more or less equal power, never between parent and child."[13] The writer thinks there is much to be said for this position.

The policeman or drill-sergeant model of parenthood

Some parents seem to conceptualize their role as that of the policeman or drill sergeant. They are alert to punish the child for the most minor offense, making sure that he obeys the rules at all times. These parents seem to believe that this system of parenthood will keep their children from getting into trouble.

In some ways, this policeman model is a foolproof defense system for the parents: if the child does get into difficulty the parents can always say, "We told him not to do it."

In our opinion this model will not work for most parents in the United States for the following reasons.

Americans tend to be "cop haters." Almost any book on police in the United States, or even casual reading of the daily newspaper, will reveal how unenviable the position of the policeman is in our society.[14] Except on television shows, the police are the bad guys. In a recent incident in the Midwest, a group of citizens stood by while a patrolman was beaten

---

[13] George R. Bach and Peter Wyden, *The Intimate Enemy* (New York: William Morrow & Co., 1969), p. 288.

[14] See, for example, Arthur Niederhoffer, *Behind the Shield: The Police in Urban Society* (New York: Doubleday & Co., 1967).

up by several men who had been creating a disturbance. Not one citizen offered to help the police officer.[15]

From the earliest colonial days, Americans have been allergic to authority, and the allergy seems to be increasing, not decreasing.

The adolescent peer group is too powerful. Parents may get away with the policeman model while their children are quite young, but eventually the parents will be confronted by the adolescent peer group—and as we have seen in earlier chapters, this is a formidable opponent in modern America.

In some ways the policeman and drill sergeant have an advantage over parents: the legal structure is usually on their side. Parents are not always sure of a friendly reception in court—most judges and social workers will identify with the "helpless child." As Lerner says, there are no "bad children in our society—only bad parents."[16] In this sort of atmosphere it is difficult, if not impossible, for the extremely strict or harsh parent to win in our society.

A great deal of love is needed to make the policeman model work. If the parent can achieve the image of the "benevolent despot," strict or even harsh discipline will be tolerated by many children. But warmth and love have to be so obvious and plentiful that the child can never doubt that the parent has the child's best interests at heart.

It is our impression that many parents who adopt the policeman or drill-sergeant model simply do not have enough love for the child to make the severe discipline tolerable. Or if they *do* have the love, it does not get communicated to the child.

Parenthetically, it can be said that much of the open hostility of the poor and minority groups in our society toward the police stems from the fact that these people are convinced that the police do not have their best interests at heart—they view the police as their enemy, not their friend.[17] It appears that many American parents who adopt the policeman model are viewed in a similar way by their children.

The pluralistic nature of our society, discussed in earlier chapters, also poses problems for parents using the policeman model—the norms are not that clear or that specific; there are often divergent or competing norms of behavior, and the child may challenge the right of the parent to

---

[15] In a university city in which the writer was teaching, a group of young people watched passively while a patrolman was beaten up by three men he had tried to arrest for creating a disturbance.

[16] Max Lerner, *America as a Civilization* (New York: Simon & Schuster, 1957), pp. 560–70.

[17] One of the major findings of the *U.S. Riot Commission Report* (New York: Bantam Books, 1968), was the feeling of hostility (if not hatred) that the urban racial minorities have toward the police; see chap. 11, "The Police and the Community."

select a particular norm to be enforced. Here, again, the policeman and drill sergeant have an advantage over parents—the laws governing communities and the regulations in the armed forces are more specific than those with which parents operate.

This model is not functional in our society. If the United States is actually an open-class, competitive society, then a premium would be placed on parental models that emphasize such qualities as initiative, aggression, and competitiveness—qualities that appear to be minimized in the policeman or drill-sergeant model. It needs to be remembered that the police and the armed forces are primarily concerned with maintaining order and discipline, hence the model is functional for those systems. But, to the extent that America is still an open-class, competitive society, the model is dysfunctional for parents; it would not meet the basic needs of either the society or the child.

It is possible, however, to view the situation in an entirely different light—that America has become primarily a socioeconomic system of large bureaucratic organizations, both public and private, and that these systems maximize obedience, discipline, reliability, and conformity, qualities that appear to be attainable with the policeman or drill-sergeant model.

Miller and Swanson found that the middle- and lower-class parents in their sample appear to be preparing their children to "fit into" large bureaucratic organizations.[18] When one remembers that the most expansive sector of the U.S. economy in recent decades has been that of public employment, these parents may be preparing their children very realistically for the America of today and tomorrow.

In reading Riesman and Whyte, one gets the same message—American parents are preparing their children to live and work harmoniously in a tightly organized mass society.[19] Whyte does not like what he sees— nor does Riesman—but the picture they report is quite clear: American society today has more room for the conformist than it has for the innovator.

It may well be that the policeman or drill-sergeant parental model is functional for the lower class and most of the middle class in our society, but that it is dysfunctional for other groups. This appears to be the finding of Miller and Swanson.[20]

The writer believes that the policeman or drill-sergeant model has

---

[18] Daniel R. Miller and Guy E. Swanson, "Child Training in Entrepreneurial and Bureaucratic Families," *The Changing American Parent* (New York: John Wiley & Sons, 1958), chap. 4.

[19] On conformity in our society, see David Riesman et al., *The Lonely Crowd* (New Haven, Conn.: Yale University Press, 1961), also William H. Whyte, Jr., *The Organization Man* (New York: Doubleday & Co., 1957), especially pt. 1, "The Ideology of Organization Man."

[20] For a discussion of the functionality of the two systems of child rearing analyzed in their study, see Miller and Swanson, *The Changing American Parent*, pp. 109–18.

limitations that are not necessary. This will be seen later in the chapter when the fifth and last parental model is analyzed. But before that let us look at the fourth model, the teacher-counselor.

The teacher-counselor parent model

This is the developmental model.[21] The child is conceptualized as an extremely plastic organism with almost unlimited potential for growth and development. The limits to this growth and development are seen as the limits of the parent (and other teachers) to tap the rich potential of the child. Parents themselves are regarded as expendable—only "the child" counts. Discipline may be firm but never harsh—and punishment should be psychological, not physical or corporal.

The good teacher-counselor (parent) always puts the need of the child first—within the tolerance limits of the classroom or the school system itself.

This model has deep historical roots in our society—Christ is usually presented as a teacher or counselor; Benjamin Franklin and Abraham Lincoln, both folk heroes in America, reflect some of the teacher-counselor image. The dedicated (and underpaid) schoolteacher is a warm symbol in the United States, and in these days of social work and psychiatry the image of the counselor casts its shadow across the land.

This model reflects the progressive-school era inspired by John Dewey, also the psychiatric viewpoint pioneered by Sigmund Freud. The child is seen as fragile and plastic but capable of infinite growth and development if enough parental love and guidance are applied. The uniqueness of each child is stressed—not his similarity with other children.

At the middle-class level, this model has probably been dominant in the United States in recent decades. While it has many fine features, the writer believes it also poses the following problems.

Parents are not viewed as ends in themselves. In this system the needs of the child are always paramount. Parents are expected to sacrifice themselves gladly for the welfare of "our children." Such a value system, in the opinion of the writer, can have devastating effects on fathers, mothers, marriages, society, and even the child himself. It is a great burden in later life for a son or daughter to be told, "I sacrificed everything for you." This takes us back to the martyr model discussed earlier in this chapter.

This model is often too permissive. American parents are accused of "spoiling" their children.[22] This is easy to do in the teacher-counselor model because of the great stress placed on the uniqueness of each child

---

[21] For a delineation of the child-development parent model, see Evelyn Duvall, "Conceptions of Parenthood," *American Journal of Sociology* 52 (1946): 193–203.

[22] See Lerner, *America as a Civilization*, pp. 562–68, for a discussion of spoiling of children by American parents.

and his needs—relatively little is said about the needs of the parent or the needs of society. Thus, the child may get the impression that he is the center of the universe.

The model tends to produce anxiety and guilt in parents. Middle-class parents in modern America appear to be afflicted with anxiety and guilt. Lerner doubts that *any* human society has ever produced parents as anxious and threatened as those in our society.[23] Some of the reasons for this have been explored in earlier chapters in this book. Brim argues that one of the chief products of the massive parent-education program in the United States has been parental guilt.[24]

The writer believes that most American parents are reasonably conscientious and competent in their parental role and holds the teacher-counselor model partly responsible for these fathers and mothers being made to feel guilty and inadequate.

The model tends to view parents as experts. When parents try to become experts, they are courting trouble—they can never really learn all of the mystique known to the psychiatrist, the psychologist, the home economist, or the social worker, and if anything goes wrong they will be told: "But that's not what we said. You misunderstood us." In a very real sense, a little knowledge is a dangerous thing.

What also happens is that the professionals (the designated experts) begin to judge parents by professional standards—parents should know this or that or something else.

This model does not adequately present the needs of the society. Since the model focuses primarily on the needs and development of the individual, the requirements of the community and the larger society are necessarily downgraded. This has been one of the factors that has produced a generation that displays relatively little respect for parents or other representatives of the social order.

It would seem that, in any society, a balance must be struck between the imperatives of the society and the needs of the individual—and it is our judgment that this parent model fails to pass this test.

The athletic coach model

It seems to the writer that some of the most successful parents in our society employ a model derived from the role of the athletic coach. As we have analyzed this model, it appears to have the following characteristics.[25]

---

[23] Lerner, *America as a Civilization*, pp. 562–63.

[24] On the production of guilt in parents, see Brim, *Education for Child Rearing.*

[25] The athletic coach model used here was derived from several weeks the writer once spent with a group of coaches at Ohio State University. This group included

Physical fitness. The players must be physically fit for the contest. This involves not only vigorous physical activity but also abstention or moderation in smoking, drinking, late hours, and so on.

Mental fitness. The athlete must be psychologically fit—that is, he must have confidence in his ability and a feeling that he can compete successfully.

Knowledge of the game. The player must know the rules of the game and the penalty for violating them. At times he may knowingly and deliberately violate the rules—but only after calculating the chances of getting caught and the potential gain if he is not caught.

Basic skills and techniques must be painfully learned. There are no "born" star athletes—they may be born with potential, but only hard work will permit them to realize that potential. A player who refuses to practice, no matter how gifted, will not be tolerated on the squad.

The player must have stamina. He must not give up or reduce his effort—even when he is tired. As Woody Hayes, coach of the Ohio State football team, once said: "Victory in football means getting up one more time than your opponent does."[26]

Aggressiveness and competitive spirit. The athlete must desire to compete and to win. There are no "happy losers" among first-rate athletes or their coaches.

The player must accept strict discipline. Regardless of his status on the team—star or substitute—each player must submit to strict discipline. Violation of basic regulations usually results in suspension or dismissal from the squad.

Subordination of self to the success of the team. Each player is expected to put the success of the team ahead of his personal glory. Failure to do this not only brings repercussions from the coach but also from the other players.

The coach is expected to have the welfare of his players in mind at all times. In order for the tight-discipline system in this model to work, the coach must never order a player to do anything that might threaten his welfare—an injured player, for example, no matter how essential to the team, must never be ordered to play if his future may be jeopardized. Most coaches would not even permit a boy to play—even though he requested permission—if further injury at this time could result in permanent damage.

The coach cannot play the game—this must be done by the player. The coach's position here is quite analogous to that of parents: once the game has begun, it is up to the players to win or lose it. The coach has

---

two men who later became nationally famous for their winning teams—Paul Brown and Woody Hayes.

[26] Athletic banquet speech reported in the *Milwaukee Journal,* November 14, 1965.

some advantages over parents—he can send in players and he can substitute one player for another. But he faces the same prospect as parents of sitting on the sidelines and watching players make mistakes that may prove disastrous.

Discussion of the athletic coach model

The writer submits that this model has much to recommend it to American parents. The overwhelming popularity of competitive sports in our society seems to indicate general acceptance of the model among large numbers of youth as well as by the general population.

The model seems to contain a nice balance of aggression, competitiveness, and cooperation. The developmental theme is included in the expectation that each player will realize his full potential. The model emphasizes success but the players, as well as the coach, must also learn how to live with defeat.

The model has some limitations, however, due to the fact that the role of parent is not exactly the same as that of an athletic coach. Some of these limitations are as follows: (1) the coach has had professional preparation for his role—most parents have not. (2) The coach can select his players from a pool of talent—parents have to work with the children they have, talent or not. (3) The coach can substitute one player for another. Parents cannot. (4) The athletic contest for which the coach is preparing his team is more specific than "the game of life" for which parents are preparing their children. The athletic contest is less subject to deep social change than is the society for which parents are training their children. The time span is shorter for the coach also. He does not have to wait 20 years to see whether his efforts paid off. (5) The coach can quit if the situation seems hopeless—parents are not supposed to resign their roles as father or mother. Coaches can also be discharged or fired—something that is legally possible for parents but not common. (6) Coaches are expected to like or at least respect their players—but parents are supposed to love their children.

In an interesting passage, Brim says that "if a social role *requires* characteristics such as friendliness or love, it is almost self-defeating."[27] He goes on to say that "certain acts might be required in a role . . . but that love and similar expressions of feeling cannot be deliberate or contrived."[28] In this respect the athletic coach has an advantage over parents.

Even with the above limitations the writer believes that the athletic

---

[27] Brim, *Education for Child Rearing*, p. 98.
[28] Brim, *Education for Child Rearing*, p. 98.

coach model has many features that parents might utilize with positive results.

The use of these models in counseling parents

It would seem that these models can be used by counselors to help parents see what they are doing. The technique is similar to that used in the client-centered counseling system developed by Rogers—the counselor reflects back to the parents the model they are using.[29] At an appropriate time the counselor should point out that several parent models are available in our society and that perhaps this father and/or mother might do better using another model.

It is recognized that this approach assumes that the parents desire to improve their role performance and are willing to consider modification of their behavior. If this proves not to be the case, then the counselor would have to explore other problems that would seem to be blocking the treatment.

Some trends in parent counseling

In recent years communication theory has emerged as a basic approach in working with parents.[30] In this system many of the problems facing parents are considered to be the result of inadequate or distorted communication between parents and their children, or between the parents themselves. The counselor analyzes the communication network in the family and helps various members of the group to improve their communication skills—not only the messages or signals they send but also the interpretation of messages emanating from the other members of the family unit. The improvement of communication does not necessarily solve parent problems, but it at least clarifies them.

Another influential group in parent counseling in the last decade has been the behavior-modification practitioners.[31] In this approach the parent problems are reduced to specific acts that are dysfunctional for the family system. Parents are taught how to encourage and sustain behavior

---

[29] See Carl Rogers, *Client-Centered Therapy* (Boston: Houghton Mifflin Co., 1951). For a good analysis of the Rogerian counseling system, see Calvin S. Hall and Gardner Lindzey, *Theories of Personality* (New York: John Wiley & Sons, 1957), pp. 467–502.

[30] Some of the principles of communication therapy will be found in Virginia Satir, *Conjoint Family Therapy* (Palo Alto, Calif.: Science & Behavior Books, 1964), and Jay Haley, *Strategies of Psychotherapy* (New York: Grune & Stratton, 1963).

[31] See Sheldon D. Rose, "A Behavioral Approach to the Group Treatment of Parents," *Social Work* 14 (1969): 21–29; also Harry Lawrence and Martin Sundel, "Behavior Modification in Adult Groups," *Social Work* 17 (1972): 34–43.

in their children that will produce a better functioning family unit. According to Rose, the parent-counselor role in the behavior-modification system is conceptualized as that of teacher rather than therapist.[32] The parent then assumes the role of pupil or learner.

Epstein has described a system of parent counseling that seems to be eminently practical.[33] Using a limited number of group sessions, and delimiting the goals of the counseling program, parents are viewed as persons whose managerial tactics have not been successful with their children. In this approach marital problems are not treated, since it is assumed that all parents have marital problems. Personality problems are viewed in the same light: all parents have personality problems. This leaves the Epstein group free to focus on parental problems—what the parents are doing in trying to cope with their children, what the results of these efforts have been, and what can be done to change the coping efforts to get better results.

In all of the above approaches, group counseling seems to be preferred to the traditional individual-psychotherapy model. Another emphasis is on the delimitation of counseling goals. The writer believes both of these trends to be in the right direction.

Summary and conclusion

In this chapter the problem of working with parents in difficulty has been explored at some length. The major emphasis was on helping fathers and mothers see the parent model they are using. Some of the recent trends in parent counseling were also discussed briefly.

---

[32] For a detailed explication of behavior-modification concepts and techniques, see Sheldon D. Rose, *Treating Children in Groups* (San Francisco, Calif.: Jossey-Bass, Inc., 1972); also Lawrence and Sundel, "Behavior Modification," p. 34.

[33] Norman Epstein, "Brief Group Therapy in a Child Guidance Clinic," *Social Work* 15 (1970): 33–38.

Index

This book has been set in 10 and 9 point Caledonia, leaded 2 points. Chapter numbers are set in 14 point Craw Modern; chapter titles are set in 18 point Craw Modern. The size of the type page is 27 × 45½ picas.